CW01213541

MEN WHO RULED KENYA

MEN WHO RULED KENYA

The Kenya Administration, 1892–1963

CHARLES CHENEVIX TRENCH

The Radcliffe Press
London · New York

Published in 1993 by
The Radcliffe Press
45 Bloomsbury Square
London WC1A 2HY

175 Fifth Avenue
New York
NY 10010

In the United States of America
and Canada distributed by
St Martin's Press
175 Fifth Avenue
New York
NY 10010

Copyright © 1993 by Charles Chenevix Trench

All rights reserved. Except for brief quotations in a review, this book, or any part thereof, must not be reproduced in any form without permission in writing from the publisher.

A CIP record for this book is available from the British Library

A full CIP record is available from the Library of Congress

ISBN 1-85043-571-5

Phototypeset by The Midlands Book Typesetting Company
Printed and bound in Great Britain by
WBC Ltd, Bridgend, Mid Glamorgan

Contents

Series Foreword		vii
Author's Foreword		xi
Chapter		
1	The Conquistadors	1
2	Which Man's Country?	19
3	The Smack of Firm Government	33
4	The North	48
5	Kenya Colony	68
6	The Sophisticates	77
7	The Unsophisticates	85
8	Gold-diggers, Rustlers and Wizards	99
9	Sloth Belt	109
10	Half-Term	117
11	The Silent North	122
12	Ities, Bandas and Shiftas, 1935–45	142
13	Breakthrough	165
14	No Breakthrough	180
15	Northern Province	188
16	Nairobi's Fair City	198
17	The Heart of the Matter	204
18	Mau Mau	217
19	State of Emergency, I	234
20	State of Emergency, II	253
21	Agrarian Revolution	268
22	The Pastoral Revolution	279
23	Wind of Change	290
	Maps	297
	Administrative Officers mentioned in the text	299
	Sources	303
	Index	311

General Foreword to the Series

A whole generation has passed, nearer two in the case of the Asian sub-continent, since Britain's colonial territories in South-East Asia, Africa and the Caribbean, achieved independence. In the Pacific the transfer of power came about a decade later. There was little interest in recording the official or the personal experience of empire either in the 'inter-war years – viewed by some, often among those personally involved, as the apogee of the British empire – or in the immediate aftermath of empire. And in this latter period attitudes were critical, largely condemnatory and even purposively hostile. This is not surprising: such a reaction is usual at the end of a remarkable period of history.

With the passing of time and with longer historical perspective it was possible to see events in a better and more objective light and the trend was gradually reversed. In due course there came about a more sympathetic interest in the colonial period, both by those in Britain or in the countries of the former empire who were intrigued to know how colonial government operated – in local, everyday practice, as well as at the policy level of the Colonial Office and Government House. Furthermore, those who had themselves been an integral part of the process wanted to record the experience before, in the nature of things, it was too late. Here was a potentially rich vein of knowledge and personal experience for specialist academic historians as well as the general reader.

Leaving aside the extensive academic analysis of the end of empire, the revival of interest in the colonial period in this country may be said to have been stimulated by creative literature. In the late 1960s there were novels, films, radio and TV programmes now and again tinged with a touch of nineteenth-century romance and with just a whiff of nostalgia to soften the sharp realism of the colonial encounter. The focus was primarily on India and the post-1947 imagery of the 'Raj': there were outstanding novels by Paul Scott – surely destined to be one of the greatest twentieth-century novelists – J. G. Farrell and John Masters; epic films like *A Passage to India*, and *Gandhi*, or the charming and moving vignette of *Staying On*, and, for Africa, *Out of Africa* and *Mister Johnson*.

In the second half of the 1970s there emerged a highly successful genre of collective 'colonial' memoirs in the *Tales of ...* format: Charles Allen's splendid trilogy *Plain Tales from the Raj* (1975), *Tales from the Dark Continent* (1979) and *Tales from the South China Seas* (1983), followed by others like *Tales of Paradise: Memories of the British in the South Pacific* (1986) and *Tales of Empire: the British in the Middle East* (1989) – all good history and good reading.

Throughout the period from India's independence until that of the last crown colony there had, of course, been those splendid works which combined both academic history and creative literature: for example, Philip Woodruff's *The Men Who Ruled India: The Founders* (1953) and *The Guardians* (1954); and Jan Morris's *Heaven's Command, Pax Britannica* and *Farewell the Trumpets* (1973–8).

Finally as the 1970s gave way to the 1980s, those voices which had remained largely silent since the end of empire now wanted to be heard. The one-time colonial officials, be they district officers, agriculturists, veterinary, medical or forestry officers, policemen or magistrates, and just as often their wives, began to write about their experiences. They wrote with relish and enthusiasm, with a touch of adventure and few personal regrets. There was a common feeling of a practical and useful task well done, although some thought that more could have been achieved had independence come about more slowly.

These memoirs often began as little more than a private record for the family, children and grandchildren, some of whom had never seen a colonial governor in full fig, shaken hands with an emir or paramount chief, discussed plans with a peasant or local politician, or known at first hand the difference between an *askari* and *alkali*, an *amah* and an *ayah*.

By 1990 the colonial memoir had begun to establish itself as a literary genre in its own right.

General Foreword to the Series

The initiative of the Radcliffe Press in harnessing and promoting this talent, primarily autobiographical but also biographical, promises to be a positive addition to both the historical and literary scenes. Here is a voice from the last Colonial Service generation, relating from personal experience the lives and careers involved in the exercise of latter-day empire. They were part of what was arguably the most influential and far-reaching international event of the second half of the twentieth century, namely the end of empire and the consequent emergence of the independent nations of the Third World. It could perhaps also be argued that this is part of an even greater process – decolonisation 'writ large', a sea-change in world affairs affecting greater and lesser powers into the late twentieth century.

It may well be that by 2066, the centenary of the closing down of the Colonial Office, great-great-grandchildren will find the most telling image of Britain's third and final empire in these authentic memoirs and biographical studies, rather than in the weightier imperial archives at the Public Record Office at Kew or in Rhodes House Library, Oxford.

A.H.M. Kirk-Greene, lecturer in the Modern History of Africa, University of Oxford, and formerly of the Colonial Administration Service, Nigeria.

Author's Foreword

This history has been compiled mainly from the accounts of those who made it, written *at the time* or shortly after. It would, of course, be very wrong to judge their words and deeds by the standards of fifty or a hundred years later. Their accounts have been allowed to stand largely without detailed comment since it is hoped that something of the actual experience and feelings of these men is best conveyed in this way. But judgment of their words and deeds must be for the individual reader, who has the benefit of hindsight in the very different world of the present day.

Its publication has been made possible by a large number of former officers of the Kenya administration and their families who provided money, memoirs, letters, diaries and photographs. To all these I owe thanks, and to many an apology. To make the book viable for publication its original length had to be reduced by about 30 per cent. This meant that many excellent contributions had to be ruthlessly cut or omitted altogether. The officers who appear in it are not necessarily the best, but the most articulate, whose memoirs fit in with the book's plan. Many first-class men are not even mentioned. Their former colleagues will spot immediately those to whom I here refer, and here apologize.

I am especially grateful to Mrs Meg Maxwell who knows the administration well, did most of the research and undertook the laborious task of compiling from incomplete and often contradictory records a list of the officers mentioned with their dates of service, where these can be ascertained. I am also very grateful to the staff of Rhodes House where most of the records are kept.

I much regret that no memoirs of African district commissioners or district officers are included. Several promised to write up their recollections, but none did so . . . probably because they are too busy ruling Kenya today.

1

The Conquistadors

During the 1880s Her Majesty's Government was interested in Kenya ... the country had not yet been invented ... only because it was on the way from Mombasa to Uganda. The Suez Canal route was the lifeline of the Empire; the canal passed through Egypt which depended for its existence on the Nile. Whoever controlled the headwaters of the Nile, in Uganda, controlled Egypt, and the British Government intended to secure it as theirs. So over Uganda, the most prosperous region in East Africa, Britain declared a protectorate maintained by a few hundred Nubian soldiers who had originally been brought from the north by General Gordon. The difficulties of supplying them up the Nile were such that it was far easier by the slavers' overland route from Mombasa. Moreover, the slave trade would thus be discouraged, and suppressing this traffic was the only other consistent British aim in East Africa.

It needed suppressing. In 1907 a British subaltern, R. Meinertzhagen, was shown round a former slave market by a retired slaver who became

> quite excited when he found himself back in his old haunts ... He showed me ... where the girls were kept, where the boys were kept and where they were castrated, and where the men were kept constantly shackled in eights to a heavy log by iron chains. On the way to the coast the castrated boys were best looked after because they were the most valuable but over 50 per cent died; the girls were not shackled but were raped both at night and all through the

day whenever the caravan halted. About 10 per cent of the men died: if a man showed fatigue, he was shot.

It is seldom that the requirements of strategy and philanthropy coincide. Characteristically the British Government tried to do the thing on the cheap, through a chartered company which would organize the traffic to Uganda, bear the costs and the risks, and recoup itself from the untapped riches of the interior. There was therefore set up in 1888 the Imperial British East Africa Company with a head office in London and an Agent in Mombasa. The company established stations at Machakos among the Kamba tribe, and Fort Smith, also known as Kikuyu, five miles northwest of where now stands the centre of Nairobi. The duty of the officers in charge was to collect supplies for caravans and help them through to Naivasha, the nearest outpost of the Uganda Protectorate. This required some tranquillity around the stations, enforced by the company's troops and police.

The scheme was not a success, largely because there were no untapped riches. There was therefore inadequate capital, and no driving force at the head office. In the field, officers who were rough bullied the natives and raided them for supplies to get the caravans through.

To this generalization there were exceptions. One was John Ainsworth who had joined the company's service at the age of 24 after working five years in King Leopold's unsavoury Congo. Happier in the office than in the field, an organizer and a builder, he lacked charm and panache but was diligent, efficient and righteous. Another was Frank Hall, four years older than Ainsworth but junior in the company's service, who had been soldier, teacher, farmer and gold miner in South Africa. Piratically moustachioed, bearded and slouch-hatted (Ainsworth favoured a solar topi), jovial, big game hunter, who never waited on orders or shirked responsibility, in his early days he sometimes swashbuckled, but became a conscientious and caring district commissioner. Almost alone among his colleagues, he was a public school and university product, and very conscious of it.

Of the company's more exotic employees the best was James Martin, alias Antonio Martini, a small, vivacious, Maltese

The Conquistadors

sailmaker who had arrived penniless at Mombasa after being rescued from a shipwreck. He had accompanied exploring expeditions in the 1880s, before being taken on by the company as a caravan master. He could neither read nor write, but could manage men.

From Mombasa to Fort Smith is 345 miles, or 32 days. Transport was by porters of the coastal Swahili* tribe. These had for generations been humping 65lb loads between their own country and the Great Lakes, following slavers, ivory hunters, explorers, missionaries and administrators. In doing so they had spread their own Swahili language (Ki-Swahili), elegant, adaptable and precise, so that by the 1890s it served in a crude form as a lingua franca, understood by a few men of several tribes, and was adopted by the company as the official language needed in a country of about 34 tribal languages.

In 1892 Ainsworth took over Machakos station, the start of his long association with the Kamba tribe. There was a two-roomed mud hut for himself, others for his men, but no stores or tools. Money being unknown in the interior, payment for food and services was in cloth and beads. In every station there was a trade goods store, but in Machakos it was empty. Ainsworth accepted the challenge and built a stone fort, wattle-and-daub offices, stores and barracks, tree-lined roads and a market place.

On arrival at Mombasa in 1893 Hall was ordered to conduct a caravan to Fort Smith and remain there in charge of the station. On the journey everyone suffered from thirst and most from malaria. The authentic note of Victorian exploration is struck by Hall on his recovery from fever: 'my breakfast consisted of a bottle of champagne and a tin of Brand's Extract'. There was always the risk of attack by the Masai, a tribe of pastoral nomads whose young men, the moran, seemed to have no settled occupation. They were, wrote Hall, repeatedly

> sticking up caravans, murdering all hands . . . As the tribe has no fixed territory, it is almost impossible to get at them

*I will eschew the pedantry of writing Wa-Swahili, Wa-Kamba, Wa-Kikuyu etc.

and exterminate the lot, though they get some pretty hot lessons occasionally, for they are always shot like dogs when seen.

The Masai had indeed been the terror of caravans, and were still the bane of their neighbours, especially the Kikuyu. Lest they stop all caravan traffic, the policy of 'shooting like dogs' gave way to one of handling them with kid gloves and employing the blood-thirsty moran as auxiliaries against other tribes. But their lifestyle required neighbours to raid. The protection of the latter by British power was eventually to reduce a proud and predatory people to what some considered a mere tourist attraction.

At Machakos, Hall was welcomed by Ainsworth, his District Commissioner*, who in only a year had made it

> a splendid station. The courtyard in the centre is nicely laid out in flowerbeds; and nasturtiums, mignonettes, sunflowers and heaps of others give it a nice bright look.

At Fort Smith Hall found one of Martin's caravans and seven British officers, some stationed there, some on their way to and from Uganda. Their job was to supply Uganda, a transaction which the Kikuyu saw no reason to assist. Hall, with the language and attitudes of his time, found the Kikuyu

> very treacherous. They attacked and burnt the first station the Coy built near here ... Not many months ago they murdered the mailmen and destroyed the mails, and it is quite a common occurrence for them to cut off a man when he is out to fetch wood or water and kill him just for fun ... Martin's caravan consisted of over 700 men ... so it was decided to give them a good lesson. So next morning

---

*The titles of administrative officers changed frequently in the early years: agent; collector; sub-, deputy-, district and assistant commissioner. For clarity I will commit the anachronism of using the titles which later became standardized – provincial commissioner, district commissioner and district officer (PC, DC, DO).

The Conquistadors

four officers with 200 rifles burnt all the villages* near the offenders' place and destroyed all the crops. I had to stay behind in charge of the fort. The next day Purkiss and I were sent with 150 men to punish the men who had murdered the mailmen and smashed up the boat ... We burnt and destroyed everything. The Kafirs tried to follow up on the chance of regaining some of their cattle; but after a few shots from me at ranges of six to eight hundred yards they soon got sick of it for I think I got two of the brutes right enough. We arrived in camp alright, not a man hurt and we had 196 sheep and goats and 6 head of cattle, so we had done pretty well. We afterwards heard we had killed five men that day, so Purkiss and I were shooting pretty well. While we were away several armed natives appeared on the hills round the camp, so they tried the Maxim though none of them had ever worked it before. However Major Smith fired at a group of five men at 1,500 yards and killed one and wounded two.

This sort of thing went on all the time. Hall records dozens of murders by the Kikuyu alternating with punitive raids. The Kikuyu were spared heavy losses only by the abysmal quality of the company's troops, mainly Swahilis. But even they had no difficulty in defeating men armed with spears and bows. In one of many skirmishes, 'the enemy lost over 90 killed. My men (2 killed and one wounded) were all shot with poisoned arrows'.

But Hall had ideas beyond shooting the Kikuyu and burning their villages. He planted experimental plots and within three years could report great success with wheat, barley and 'cauliflower, lettuces, cabbages etc. which would be well classed at any show in England'.

And he experimented with diplomacy. The nearest thing to a chief among the Masai were Laibons, who were ritual-masters and soothsayers, by virtue of which some had a good deal of influence. A prominent Laibon named Lenana, worsted in civil war, withdrew with his adherents, 'a fine lot and friendly with

*A village consisted of half a dozen huts of poles, mud and thatch.

white men', to the neighbourhood of Hall's *boma*,* in some degree under his protection. There they were cheek by jowl with the Kikuyu, which resulted in stock thefts and tit for tat killings, so when Lenana made overtures, Hall

> called a meeting of all the headmen of the Wakikuyu and it was decided that I was to go with six of the headmen, and see the Masai chief, . . . I took 20 picked men in case of accidents and we had a very jolly walk through forest by-paths for about three hours to the head *kraal*, and here I took my seat under a shady tree and waited. After a time the chief and the general of the elmoran came out. . . Then we got to business. It was a most funny day altogether. Sometimes when I was sitting down one would come up, shake hands and then take off my hat, stroke my hair, pull my beard, pass their hand over my face and then examine my hat, clothes, boots and everything . . . My men simply rolled about with laughter.

Having made peace, he must preserve it. When Kikuyu inveigled some Masai into their village and murdered them, Hall was after them with fifty askaris and a band of moran, coming upon them at dawn and rounding up a thousand goats. They killed six Kikuyu and wounded five, with 600 rounds, 'which was above the average for Swahili shooting'.

A moran's reputation depended on his success as a cattle-rustler and on his prowess at spear-blooding. Nothing would change their habits. They even dared attack Ainsworth's own cattle *boma* at Machakos. Hall wrote:

> He wrote to me to complain officially, thinking the attack was planned by two of my Masai but, as these men had not been away, I knew they had nothing to do with it.

---

*The Swahili word *boma* originally meant a circular hedge of cut thorn branches to keep livestock in and predators out. By association it came to mean the offices, houses and stores within such a ring fence; and eventually, any government station, with or without a fence.

The Conquistadors

After less than two years Hall was already thinking of 'my Masai' and regarding their peccadillos with indulgence. But when one casually blooded his spear on a Kikuyu, Hall (with no legal authority) tried him in an improvised court with two elders from each tribe, and sentenced him to 100 lashes which were administered on the spot 'before all hands'.

It is clear that Hall's sympathies lay with the Masai, who two years earlier had been 'shot like dogs'. But even in the Kikuyu he began to detect signs of grace.

Fancy, the other day I got a deputation to ask if I would hold a meeting with the Kikuyu chiefs and talk over matters . . . It was a long, tedious pow-wow, but at last they all agreed to acknowledge my authority and to refer all disputes to me . . . As they had planned it entirely among themselves, it shows a considerable advance in the right direction.

Hall considered that there could be no progress until the Kikuyu learned to work and trade for money; and it was absurd that loads should have to be carried through their country by porters from the coast.

I called up all the friendly chiefs and told them that unless they took to work like other natives, they would eventually be wiped out and a better people brought into the country, and the general effect has been wonderful. I got 30 of them to carry food loads for Smith for two or three days, and when I called for 100 to go to Machakos to fetch loads for me, over 170 turned up and 105 were written on and brought loads in good time and were delighted with their pay. This is the first time the Kikuyu have ever carried loads, so it is a feather in my cap.

Hall maintained his position by playing off Kikuyu against Masai, and one set of Kikuyu against another. The 'friendlies' were the people living near the *boma*, over whom he appointed as chief a tough called Kinanjui who had proved very useful to sundry caravans. Hall's sphere of influence was gradually extended to a radius of about fifteen miles, within which the Kikuyu were more or less resigned to him bossing them about. He paid well for services, protected them against Masai and other Kikuyu, and punished his own askaris who stole their goats. The Kikuyu never imagined that the 'red strangers' would covet their land.

Often Hall wrote of 'chiefs'; but the main difficulty was that there were no 'chiefs' with whom the British could negotiate. The Masai Laibons had influence but hardly authority. Among the Kikuyu and other Bantu tribes authority was patriarchal, exercised by the elders of the families occupying each ridge. Between Uganda, where real kings held sway, and the coast, administered by Arab governors, a chief was something invented by the white man, like trousers. The Masai Laibon Lenana was invested with the title and brass-headed staff of 'Paramount Chief', but he was nothing of the sort. Kinanjui and other Kikuyu were dubbed 'chief' by virtue of their efficiency and helpfulness, as were some Masai who had been useful as mercenary allies; but many of their own people regarded them merely as creatures of the white men.

It was unusual for any white man to live in East Africa without spending a great deal of time shooting wild animals. It was the excitement of killing lions, leopards, rhinos and buffalos, and profits from the sale of ivory, that drew many men to East Africa.

In December 1894, Hall wounded a rhino

> which saw the smoke and came down on us full steam ahead ... I tried to dodge; but he was too quick and I soon found myself sailing through space. The rhino hardly let me reach ground before he repeated the operation. I came down right on my head and was so dazed I couldn't move, and the old beast stood nosing at me but couldn't get his horn in as I was flat on the ground. So at last he smashed his foot down on my chest which, with about two tons of beef behind it, fairly stove all the breath out of me. Just as I was beginning to think it was all up, he turned and left me.

Back at the fort he found 'a beautiful hole' through the outside of his thigh and terrible bruises. Fortunately there was a doctor

The Conquistadors

there, on his way back from Uganda, and before long Hall was up and limping about.

By 1894 it was clear that East Africa could not be run on a no-cost basis by a chartered company. On 1 July 1895, a British Protectorate over the country between Uganda and the coast was proclaimed by Sir Arthur Hardinge, the Consul-General for Zanzibar, who was later made Commissioner for the Protectorate. It was the responsibility of the Foreign Office, and the more reputable of the company's servants were taken on as government officers.

The caravan arrangements were overhauled. In future transport would be by contract from Mombasa to Fort Smith, then under the military to Eldama Ravine, 130 miles further, where Uganda officers took charge. The District Officer (DO) there, on the Uganda payroll, was the Maltese, James Martin, whom a kindly colleague had taught to sign his name: for more ambitious literary exercises he relied on his Goan clerk. Ainsworth stayed on as District Commissioner (DC) at Machakos, and Hall as DO at Fort Smith on a salary of £250 a year plus £50 Swahili allowance.

Her Majesty's Government decided that Uganda, vital bastion of empire, could no longer depend on long files of laden porters. A railway must be built. The first plate was laid at Mombasa in December 1895, and thereafter all Ainsworth's and Hall's energies were to be concentrated on recruiting labour for clearing the bush, negotiating with the tribes through which the line must pass, and collecting food for thousands of construction coolies imported from India. That the Masai gave no trouble was due mainly to Hall's protégé, Lenana, and to Ainsworth never making impossible demands, and closing his eyes to raiding which he could not stop.

Three months later Hall was the victim of a provoked attack by a wounded leopard, which came at him, low and fast, clawed his body and chewed his knee until killed by his valiant Somali gun-bearer. The wounds turned septic, his knee swelled to an enormous size and for twelve days he thrashed about on his bed in a delirium of pain. His assistant, Edward Russell, sent to Machakos for a prayer book with which to conduct the funeral service. Twenty-two days after the incident the hole made by the rhino in December burst open, allowing a mass of pus to escape from his thigh, but not relieving his knee. Then, providentially, there arrived *en route* to Uganda a surgeon, who operated and saved Hall's life. After nine weeks' convalescence, Hall departed on sick leave to England. He returned in August 1896 to find that Ainsworth had established a new station at Ngong, a couple of miles from Fort Smith, to help with the railway; and as P.C. commuted between this and Machakos. Hall's *locum tenens*, T. G. Gilkison, past his youth and addicted to the bottle, had allowed discipline to become pretty slack, but that would soon be remedied. His garden was in first-rate condition, and he even picked strawberries on the day he arrived. He had horses, and his first crop of oats to feed them. He chose sites for his own house and Ainsworth's half a mile from Ngong fort, an indication of how safe the place had become.

Ngong was humming with Europeans. Besides Hall's two assistants and a military officer, there were representatives of two Mombasa firms, a coffee-planter and three intending farmers including one who was also blacksmith, gunsmith, general handyman and 'a glutton for work, so he should do well'. Early in 1897 the first settler baby was born. Hall wrote that 'James Martin and his wife came for a few days and they had a very jolly time. She is Portuguese but very nice. She plays the organ and sings in several languages.'

Such was the wealth of talent that they had a musical evening, with organ, banjo, whistle and auto-harp.

Hall describes the celebration of the Jubilee in May 1887:

There were two or three thousand natives on the sports-ground, entries were very numerous and competition keen. The Masai won the long-distance races easily; the sack and obstacle-races created immense amusement... The tug-o'-war was splendid, teams of Kikuyu and Masai pulling for nearly five minutes before the Masai won. They then pulled against the troops and after three pulls the troops won amidst intense excitement.

There was a grand parade, a general salute, a *feu de joie*, three cheers for the Queen and a march-past, followed by the distribution of the meat of twelve fat oxen.

The Conquistadors

All the European officers, together with the Goan clerks and two native officers, went to a stupendous lunch, but just as we were going to sit down someone reminded me that I had said the white men would pull the winners of the tug-o'-war. So out we sallied, and started. We had one native officer, which rather spoilt it, but no one cared to object on such an occasion. The soldiers beat us at the first pull, and we beat them at the second. The excitement among the people was quite exhilarating and we all laid down to the third determined to win or die . . . We had an awful pull which nearly finished us, but we managed to get the best of it and returned triumphant to enjoy our lunch.

It seems that the Kikuyu had come to accept Hall's rule, bringing the relief from Masai raids and a measure of law and order with opportunities of trade. (Kikuyu are great traders.) The acreage acquired by the few settlers was negligible. No one gave a thought to the possibility of hundreds of settlers demanding thousands of square miles of land.

But in November 1897, James Martin at Eldama Ravine heard of an Abyssinian army advancing from the north. He issued a robust challenge, written by his clerk.

> Sir, please take note that you are now on British soil. Any act of aggression on your part will be sternly resisted.

He then strengthened the *boma* defences and prepared to sell his life dearly.

The arrival of two travel-worn Europeans, with long hair and shaggy beards, followed by a train of Somalis and laden camels, apprised him that he had over-estimated the emergency which so stirred him. They had trekked a thousand miles from British Somaliland, hunting big game. Their names were Dr Atkinson and Lord Delamere. The latter was to devote all the money he had or could borrow, his courage, keen intelligence and abundant energy, to making the highlands of East Africa a White Man's Country.

On they trekked to Mombasa, via Machakos, where Ainsworth had created an attractive little suburbia with bungalows, offices, an

Indian bazaar, wide tree-lined avenues lined with blue gum trees, vegetable gardens and experimental nurseries. He was just married, to an American mission nurse. He eyed with disgust Delamere's unkempt appearance, 'not a very pleasant object-lesson for the natives'. He reprimanded the peer for leaving his camp-site littered with dead camels. They did not hit it off.

Ainsworth greatly preferred the Kamba to any trophy-hunting lord; he thought they had shortcomings but viewed them with more sympathy.

It is a great mistake to reckon on outwitting the Kamba, for he is not easily duped though he may appear to be so. Nor can he easily be frightened for he will obstinately sit down and await what may come. Nothing makes you more helpless against him than his discovery that your threat is an empty one ... I have always found it best to trust a Kamba, for then he may not fail you; while if he sees mistrust, his curious mind seems to start meditating on what he may hatch ... He will easily make up his mind if he sees that you have made up yours; but once given a choice, his evasions will be endless.

A new station was opened at Kitui, also in Kamba country, sixty-five miles north-east of Machakos and reputed to be a hotbed of slavers. To it was posted Ainsworth's younger brother, James, who ruled with a lighter touch.

An obstacle to opening up the district was the refusal of the Kitui Kamba to act as porters. They considered this to be woman's work, but the Island Race had inhibitions about employing women on it. But James Ainsworth soon solved the problem. The Kamba were great dancers, so when he arrived at Zombe village to find, as usual, that most of the young men had absconded, he announced blandly that actually he had come to see some dancing. In fact he wished to dance himself. But were the local performers good enough? He had heard that those at Makongo were much better.

This produced a riot of protest. 'Not true! No way! Rubbish!'

All right, he would give the Zombe dancers a trial. He even joined them, capering about in pyjamas and gumboots. When

The Conquistadors

they stopped, exhausted, he admitted that they were not bad, but he would have to compare them with their rivals, in open competition. In fact he was going to Makongo next day and they might as well carry his loads. So off they went, a long file of cheerful porters followed by their girl-friends carrying dance regalia.

By these means the district was opened up, without a shot being fired. In Hall's district, too, punitive expeditions were a thing of the past, and he resented soldiers trailing their coats: 'All these military men just come out to get decorations, and if there isn't a row on, they soon make one'. One of his colleagues suggested that every army officer on arrival be issued with a row of medals, from which one would be removed for every campaign in which he took part.

In November 1897, Nubian troops in Uganda mutinied and shot several officers. A call for help came from Naivasha where the commandant was 'in fear of his life, on the watch day and night with the lock of the Maxim gun in his pocket'. With such non-Nubians as he could muster, Hall made forced marches to Naivasha where he found the Nubians on the very brink of mutiny, and replaced them with Swahilis. Then there came a SOS from James Martin at Eldama Ravine, so off he sped again. Paraded in front of Hall's Maxim gun, the Nubians promised to be good – 'I can't tell you how delighted Martin and Wilson were to see us, for they had been in abject fear of their lives for days.'

Hall took leave in 1898 and returned with a wife, Bee, who took to the life and was 'happy as a sand-lark'.

> Bee has made our rooms so jolly pretty and comfortable that old hands can't recognise the old shanty, and our bedroom beats anything of the kind in these parts... We had wonderful luck with all our belongings, even our dinner service arriving without a crack. But the triumph of transport was our piano which reached here without a scratch and in splendid tune, so Bee was very delighted and it gets plenty of exercise every evening.

The approach of the railway was not a matter for unmixed joy. The construction coolies from India were held in low regard by

Hall; he wrote of their camps being crowded with prostitutes and catamites; and being in such numbers, 4,000 to a camp, 'that they raid and steal whenever opportunity offers, and it is almost impossible to bring a charge home to a particular man'.

White traders and transport contractors, buccaneering and heavy-handed, were forever getting embroiled with the natives, and three were killed. An egregious rogue named John Boyes was up to no good among the northern Kikuyu, levying 'taxes' and cheating them out of ivory. (He thought they called him 'King of the Wa-Kikuyu'. Actually they called him 'Eater of beans', a tribute presumably to his flatulence.) It was not until 1902 that the administration was given legal powers, under the Outlying Districts Ordinance, to keep undesirables out of native areas, and to prosecute them if they entered without permission.

For the railway constructors, a ramshackle shanty-town called Nairobi was taking root, partly on a plain which was flooded during the rains and partly on a hill which had no water. Hall wrote of the problems of railway development.

> At present the Protectorate and the railway officials preserve a sort of armed neutrality. Ainsworth has collected all the Protectorate officials (in brass buttons etc.) on one side of the river while the township and all the railway people are on the other, which makes it very awkward for Bee and me, being very good friends of all parties.

However, getting on with everyone was part of a DC's job:

> We gave a great champagne lunch to celebrate the arrival of the railway. Bee ran the whole thing and we had a most sumptuous spread. Salmon and lobster and other salads, beef, beefsteak pie, partridges, hams, tongues, fowls etc., fruit salads, blancmanges, shapes, jellies, tarts, custards and all sorts of luxuries. Thirty sat down, including five ladies.

John Ainsworth, the Provincial Commissioner, was transferred from Machakos to Nairobi to bring order out of chaos. It was a development deplored by Hall who complained that paperwork

The Conquistadors

so proliferated that he could never get out on safari among his Kikuyu.

Ainsworth's idea of administration is to compel all hands to sit at their desks writing despatches. Although living only eight miles off he gave me nineteen despatches in two days. Besides these we have the Treasury Dept. who never seem to understand the simplest entry in the accounts but must write queries; and the Judicial Dept. who want to know, when a man is convicted of sugar-stealing, whether the sugar was white or brown . . . I wish I could see my way to get clear of all this idiotic, snobbish, brass button and uniform business, so-called administration whereas not a single officer has ever been more than 20 miles from his station and we know less about the natives than we knew seven years ago.

Hall and his colleagues had hitherto dispensed a rough justice, sitting sometimes with native assessors, basing their decisions on common sense and tribal custom. But this would not do now. Proper courts were set up in which judges, DCs and DOs, in the role of magistrates, were to dispense justice according to the Indian Penal Code, modified where appropriate by Moslem law and tribal custom. Hall fulminated

This is simply courting disaster by trying to run the show as if it was part of India instead of a country about 2,000 years behind India or any other place. It is hardly one's idea of running a country or protecting natives.

'Or protecting natives' – that is what Hall now regarded as the most important part of his job. The pinchbeckery of the Treasury was exasperating: officers thought themselves disgracefully underpaid (£500 a year for a PC, £400 for a DC and £250 for a DO, with no increments) and in Nairobi were burdened with expensive entertaining. An officer was entitled to three months' leave after eighteen months, with a return passage to the UK, but not to passages for his wife and children. Ainsworth in 1902 could not afford to take the leave due to him. Hall was charged nearly half his year's salary for bringing his wife up from Mombasa.

Marriage before middle age was discouraged. Besides, without private means an officer could not afford a wife. Naturally many officers made other arrangements, keeping native concubines. Officially such goings-on were viewed with disfavour on the grounds that an officer thereby lost the tribe's respect. There was probably not much in this, provided he paid the lady's father the proper bride-price. A more valid objection was that she would involve him in her family's and clan's interests, and even if he did not favour them, he would be assumed to do so. A Foreign Office official recommended a stern prohibition, and lenient treatment of individual offenders. The suggestion of another official that officers be paid enough to enable them to marry was ignored as improvident quixotry.

As more nursing sisters, missionaries, settlers' and officials' daughters arrived in East Africa, these irregular unions became less common, except on the frontier where white women were not allowed. But as late as 1909 a DC was reported for rapes on safari. In Ainsworth's opinion, the offender, Walter Mayes, had 'a character as bad as it can be, yet I can hardly see how we can improve matters by trying to prove these further cases against him'. Ainsworth ended on a rather tame note. 'It is more than unfortunate that the administration contains such men.'

Not even by famine was the Treasury's purse-strings loosened. Hall had

> an awful job with famine and smallpox. I have an average of 370 famine-stricken people to feed daily. Poor beggars, owing to drought their crops failed; *as a matter of fact, the Uganda Relief Expedition* [to suppress the mutiny] *took all their reserve food*, and now they are in a pitiful state. No one could describe the frightful miseries and horrors of the famine. Out of 370 in my camp, 200 are children. We are thousands of rupees over our allowances. We could not send them away starving, though we were advised that funds were expended, so we took it on ourselves and went on feeding them. I started a subscription among the other

The Conquistadors

Kikuyu three days ago and have already got 60 goats, worth 240 rupees, which at least proves that the richer class of natives appreciates our efforts and is willing to help his poorer compatriots.

Smallpox is rampant but thank goodness I have a Medical Officer who vaccinates everybody in sight. We are burying six and eight a day. One can't go for a walk without falling over corpses. Tonight the food supply arrived and I had to go and serve it out, and it is really pretty awful to have to select the living and lay aside the corpses with one's own hand. The natives won't touch a corpse, in fact have to be coerced to bury the dead. I am not squeamish, but this is the worst job I have ever tackled.

With a resentful eye on his PC, Hall wrote of Nairobi:

[In this] tinpot mushroom township they have no less than five different law courts, and it is the most dangerous and lawless spot in Africa. Every night the police bombard indiscriminately with ball-cartridge. The night we arrived there was a regular fusilade. A week before the troops broke out and attacked a Somali camp. Brisk firing went on for over an hour, and the troops not only refused all orders to return but actually broke into the guardroom to obtain fresh supplies of ammunition. Foley, the Captain, was helpless, and Ainsworth and all the others funked the job. The ringleaders were tried by Court Martial and four were sentenced to death. The Government at least had the pluck to enforce the sentence, and the four were shot before an enormous assemblage of natives. This will give you some idea of what they call administration at Provincial Headquarters. Despatches fly around by hundreds, and if paper would do it, this would be the best governed country in the world.

Non-admirers of Ainsworth called Nairobi 'Dead Horse Gulch'. But thank God Hall was to get away from it all, to be DC at a new station some fifty miles north of Nairobi. He and Bee picked the site for the new *boma* on a lovely ridge thirty miles west of Mount

Kenya. They camped in a splendid tent while their mud house was being built.

He held interminable *barazas** with his people, who were friendly and helpful, though deuced noisy neighbours, drumming, singing and dancing all night. They brought him fowls and eggs and eels from the river; and, for a modest payment in beads and cloth, all the thatching grass he needed. He arrested for armed robbery, and sent up for trial in Nairobi, the jovial, disreputable 'Eater of Beans', John Boyes, who had fleeced them right and left.

Frank and Bee Hall looked forward to a busy and interesting time. But in April 1901 he died of dysentery. The new station was named after him, Fort Hall; and sixty years later old men remembered him with respect, even affection.

**Baraza:* a formal assembly or conference.

2

Which Man's Country?

In October 1900, Hardinge was succeeded by Sir Charles Eliot. Cold and reserved, he abhorred exercise and stayed indoors as much as possible, thereby, he claimed, preserving perfect health. He was a curious choice for the rough-and-ready government of a half-savage country.

In December 1901, the first train reached the shore of Lake Victoria Nyanza, at Kisumu. Three months later, in order to bring the whole line under one administration, the eastern part of Uganda, from the lake to Naivasha, was transferred to the East African Protectorate.

Eliot worried about making the railway pay, and the whole Protectorate less of a burden on the British taxpayer. In a private letter to the Foreign Secretary, Lord Lansdowne, in May 1901, he suggested that Africans contribute to the cost of administration by a hut tax; and that settlers be introduced to grow crops which the railway would transport. There was, he pointed out, 'a large area of highland with a cool and invigorating climate, fertile soil and wide pasture-grounds', suitable for European farmers. Lansdowne approved both suggestions.

The hut tax, so-much a hut paid by the head of a family, was simple, requiring no complicated assessment, only diligence and integrity in collection. It was also basically fair, since a man with several huts had several wives, and was therefore affluent. It was seen as a sort of tribute, making the point that the people must contribute something, however little, towards the heavy cost of the administration. As few Africans used money, it was at first often collected in kind. R. W. Hemsted, at Fort Hall, started it in 1902, accepting a sheep instead of cash. By August 746 sheep had been brought in, a baa-ing multitude milling about in the mud round the *boma*. Many turned out to have foot-rot which is infectious, so all had to be returned, embarrassingly and chaotically, to the taxpayers.

Despite such setbacks, hut tax rose from £3,328 (4½ per cent of the total revenue) in 1901–02 to £24,177 (22 per cent) in 1903–04. The taxation of the Masai and the wild nomads of the north was thought to be too risky.

White settlement was a far more contentious matter which bedevilled the country for sixty years, bringing wonderful agricultural development, problems to which there was no solution, tragedy and heartbreak. To most Edwardian Britons the matter seemed crystal-clear. In the East African highlands were a healthy climate and vast areas of land primed with a million years' untapped fertility. No one was cultivating it; no one ever had cultivated it. It was wicked to allow this to be wasted when the world was crying out for what could there be produced. This was a white man's country, and could properly be developed only by the capital, skills and hard work of white men.

Contrary arguments were put by the lobby which included missionaries, political radicals, and many officials in the Protectorate who saw as their first duty the protection of the Africans. This, they maintained, was a black man's country. Given guidance, help and time, blacks could develop it as well as whites; and even if they couldn't, it was still their country.

The Crown Lands Ordinance of 1902, by allowing 99-year leases, gave the go-ahead to large-scale European settlement. In November 1903, Lord Delamere was given a lease of 100,000 acres of potential sheep country, and there was an influx of would-be settlers from South Africa.

Before their arrival in Nairobi, Ainsworth was in his element there as Provincial Commissioner, Kamba, his province comprising Machakos, Kitui, Nairobi and Hall's former Kikuyu district. He set up a headquarters, town-planned, aligned roads and housing estates, pushed the paper around and set an example in social life. The first cricket match was played in 1899, the first race-meeting was held in 1900, the East African Agricultural and Horticultural

Which Man's Country?

Society was founded in 1901. (The Masai Laibon Lenana was one of the cattle judges at its first show.) Nevertheless Eliot on a visit in 1902 was appalled by the rush of settlers for whom no preparations had been made. Some were rough and tough, some were aristocrats impatient of pettifogging bureaucrats, most of them pistol-toting and bent on living the life of the Wild West twenty years after the American West had been tamed. Nairobi was expensive. Week after week they saw their capital draining away and clamoured for immediate leases of the nearest land, which was claimed by the Kikuyu. Ainsworth complained to the Commissioner that settlers took advantage of the lack of a proper map by occupying native clearings and usurping native rights: 'The present ideas for dealing in land are far too liberal when one takes into account the fact that we have to safeguard native interests.'

Eliot replied tartly that the idea was to attract settlers, not to put them off.

On Ainsworth's insistence the boundaries of a Kikuyu Reserve were gazetted. Only land outside this was available for settlement. He was satisfied that all the alienable land was in a neutral zone between Kikuyu and Masai, neither cultivated by one nor grazed by the other. But in fact the boundary, delineated in haste and without full knowledge, did give settlers some land to which the Kikuyu had a good claim. In June 1902, the PC Kenya Province, stationed at Fort Hall, was S. L. Hinde, formerly a doctor in the Congo. Commanding a company of East African Rifles there was Lieutenant Richard Meinertzhagen who quarrelled with Hinde and his methods and formed a low opinion of the Administration in general

> due to the low class of man who is appointed. Few of them have any education, and many do not pretend to be members of the educated class. Sir Clement Hill, who recently visited the colony on behalf of the Foreign Office, remarked that 'so long as Civil Servants are enlisted from the gutter', we could not expect a high standard of administration.

In a punitive expedition launched by Hinde against the Embu

tribe, east of Mount Kenya, Meinertzhagen estimated that 1,500 Africans were slain while government losses were negligible.

With the addition in 1902 of the eastern part of Uganda, the East African Protectorate began to look like modern Kenya. There were five provinces of the original Protectorate – Seyidie or Teita, Tanaland, Jubaland, Ukamba (which included Nairobi and Kikuyu district) and Kenya; and two provinces taken over from Uganda – Naivasha and Kisumu. To the north of these was a blank on the map, recognized by other European powers as a British sphere of influence. The enlarged Protectorate measured 450 miles from east to west, and 600 miles from the German East Africa border to Abyssinia. In 1903 a Secretariat was set up, the Chief Secretary filing papers in his bedroom, the clerks working in a tent.

Officers transferred from the Uganda cadre were considered a cut above their new colleagues. They included F. J. Jackson, renowned as big-game hunter and ornithologist, who became Eliot's Deputy (later, Lieutenant Governor); and C. W. Hobley, PC Kisumu. Both were opposed to European settlement. The PC Naivasha was S. S. Bagge, an old Africa hand who had been in Uganda for fifteen years. He owed his selection for Naivasha to the fact that he was a gentleman, had a way with him and had ranched in Texas, which should have given him an understanding of the settler's point of view, though he did not share it.

Difficulties here came from the Masai who had grazed much of Bagge's province before the depletion of their herds by rinderpest. In July 1903, Jackson took up cudgels with Eliot on the proposal to alienate the pick of the Masai grazing lands. He and Bagge felt so strongly that while on leave they lobbied the Foreign Office. On hearing this, Eliot blew his top. Bagge, he wrote to Lansdowne, was inaccurate even in small matters, and Jackson

> seems to regard all Masai as angels and all . . . Europeans as devils . . . He limits our task to protecting a few natives and preserving a little game . . .
>
> Your Lordship has opened this Protectorate to white immigration and I think it is well that in confidential correspondence at least we should face the undoubted fact, viz. that white mates black in very few moves . . . There can

Which Man's Country?

be no doubt that the Masai and many other tribes must go under. It is a prospect that I view with equanimity and a clear conscience... I have no desire to protect Masaidom. It is a beastly, bloody system, founded on raiding and immorality, and the sooner it disappears the better.

But others did desire to protect Masaidom, and on 4 March 1904 Eliot wired in a huff to the Secretary of State:

> I am the proper person to advise Your Lordship on the internal affairs of this Protectorate. Should Your Lordship prefer to be guided by the advice of my subordinates, such as Messrs Jackson and Bagge, I have the honour to tender my resignation.

It was accepted in May 1904. He was succeeded by Sir Donald Stewart, a simple soldier who liked whisky, abhorred paperwork and seldom read files. To him Lord Lansdowne wrote, 'The primary duty of Great Britain in East Africa is the welfare of the native races.' But this was not announced as policy, nor impressed upon Stewart, whose predilections were indolently pro-settler.

Kisumu was hot, humid, unhealthy and inhabited by a Nilotic agricultural tribe called generally Kavirondo and correctly Jaluo, anglicized to Luo. They were naked, uncircumcized, and considered by some in the Administration to be apt for heavy labour being 'strong in the arm and thick in the head', perfect administratees. The same might be said of the Baluhya north of the Kavirondo Gulf. They had a real chief, a forceful and energetic character named Mumia with whose help an important administrative centre was set up, Mumia's, on the way to Uganda. Thus with hardly any use of force, control was extended from Kisumu.

Hobley, the first DC Kisumu, was a surveyor and geologist by training. According to Meinertzhagen 'Hobley-Bobley' was no gentleman.

> He is always ambiguous in his letters and boasts of it. He prides himself on 'never letting himself in'. His subordinates

find it most difficult to work on his orders, and they have to assume responsibility which he shirks.

Hobley surveyed and laid out the new township of Kisumu on the Kavirondo Gulf, and proceeded to levy hut tax at a notional Rs 3. From those unable to produce cash or a goat, he accepted chickens, and even crocodile eggs, though it is not clear how these were credited to the Treasury or what the Treasury would do with them. To cope with an outbreak of bubonic plague in Kisumu, Hobley

> demanded the services of a large number of small boys, each to bring a stick, and at the same time offered one pice [one farthing] for each dead rat produced. About a hundred young sportsmen assembled; they then attacked each compound, forming a cordon round each house or shop, and the rapidity and efficiency with which they unearthed rats and killed them was a revelation. We had a big fire going all day and the dead rats were impaled, ten on a wooden skewer, paid for on delivery and then burnt. Many thousands were paid for in the first week, and as I was then running short of small change I reduced the price to one pice for two rats. The boys thereupon spontaneously had a meeting, decided that the new price was not adequate, and retired to their villages.

(The Luo in later years took keenly to trade unionism.)

The pastoral Nandi who lived in the highlands east and northeast of Kisumu, were more difficult to deal with: 'one always felt they would be glad to see the back of us'. Regarded as tough and truculent, they resented the British protection being extended to their natural prey, the Kavirondo, but they were not unwilling to see the railway pass through their country, since it provided an inexhaustible supply of telegraph wire to be coiled round the arms and legs of their girl friends. From time to time they casually speared an English trader, a few coolies, an American missionary. After the last outrage Meinertzhagen's company of the 2nd King's African Rifles (formerly the East African Rifles)

Which Man's Country?

was railed down from Nairobi and marched up to the American Mission at Kaimosi. The DC Nandi was Walter Mayes. Meinertzhagen had seldom taken such a dislike to a man at first sight. He started life as a common seaman from Glasgow, was discharged or deserted his ship in Madagascar . . . His ideas are those of an uneducated man. He is frankly out to make what he can from his job.

He kept not merely a Nandi concubine but a Nandi harem; and the numerous cattle which he seized for fines he kept for himself instead of crediting them to the government. The Nandis' behaviour was, in Meinertzhagen's opinion, mainly the fault of their deplorable DC.

The Nandi treated with contempt an ultimatum to behave themselves or take the consequences. By September 1905, they were thought to be completely out of hand and Sir Donald Stewart authorized a punitive expedition of two KAR battalions, ten Maxim guns, 1,000 Masai moran and an armoured train. Meinertzhagen thought this quite unnecessary if the Laibon*, the spiritual head of the Nandi, were taken out first. He was authorized to kill or capture the Laibon and, having arranged for them to meet unarmed to discuss peace, shot the Laibon allegedly in self-defence. Three courts of enquiry exonerated him, but the considered opinion of the Colonial Office was that 'this action has resulted in the reputation of the British Government for fair dealing and honesty being called in question'. Administrative officers were always embarrassed by the affair.

But the death of their Laibon 'knocked the stuffing out of the Nandi', who lost in this war 500 men, 10,000 cattle and 70,000 small stock. Government losses were in single figures. To make them abandon their pastoral habits and take to agriculture (farmers being regarded as cheaper and easier to govern than

---

*A misnomer. Laibon is a Masai term, the Nandi equivalent being Orkoiyot. But as non-Nandi nearly always spoke of Nandi Laibons, so shall I.

nomads) the Nandi were confined to a fertile but smaller reserve, and the plains of Uasin Gishu which they had grazed were opened to European settlement.

H. B. Partington (Marlborough and Cambridge) was appointed their DC, a marked contrast to Mayes. He would, wrote Hobley,

> listen patiently to some long story of native grievance, ask a question or two and then mumble something in a rather whimsical way, and the native would go off quite happily and do as he directed. It was all the more remarkable because he was not a person of striking mien, was generally untidy, grew an unkempt beard, and his voice carried little conviction... But there it was, he had the power of imposing his will on all natives with whom he came into contact.

When the young men refused to act as his porters, which they thought degrading, he put all the loads into mailbags covered with official seals, and they queued up to carry these as a duty of importance and trust. He advised missionaries that they would make no converts unless they introduced innumerable saints' days on which nobody did any work and everybody got drunk, and proselytization proceeded apace. In his eccentric way he handled the Nandi well and they accepted British rule philosophically. Apart from an incurable addiction of their elders to beer and their young men to stock-theft, and occasional unrest stirred up by the Laibon clan, they became a model tribe.

Furthest flung of officers in the province was H. H. Horne, known as 'Long' Horne. He had ranched in Wyoming, served as Vice-Consul in Mexico and fought in the Boer War. He wrote to his mother in March 1904, from Karungu on the Kavirondo Gulf close to the German border,

> Here I am in my little station, no house, am building one, no nothing. Natives uncountable, perhaps 70,000, neighbours German. Special instructions, to use diplomacy, no friction. Germans have a pleasant habit of shooting my [Africans], fearful bullies ... Some of my natives have never seen a white man and are particularly desirous of not seeing one.

Which Man's Country?

What will I do with them? *Quien sabe?* Some are very turbulent, and it is all I can do to avoid a fight. The poor brutes are only armed with spears, thank goodness. They don't use poisoned arrows, or a fight would simply mean shooting down a few and our work redoubled to make friends again ... I have some ripping Nubian police, all wardogs.

1st April. Here I am in a beastly dilemma. I have to arrest and deport a chief who has been killing friendly natives and taking women and cattle, and has 5,000 spears behind him. I am taking 22 police.

2nd April. Arrived at the village and found a fellow-feeling towards the old rascal. He is a brave old chap and is always killing his neighbours. Had him and 600 people to a conference. Most dramatic. I had him handcuffed in front of them all, my noble Nubians with loaded rifles ready to deal death. After a pow-wow I turned him loose and he swears to be good. I am glad it turned out that way. For about 30 seconds things hung by a hair.

In 1904 Stewart authorized the move of the largest Masai clan, the Il Purko, out of the Rift Valley to the Laikipia plateau. This was done to make room for settlers, but the Masai were very willing to migrate to a country of rich grazing where they would be untroubled by white men. Laikipia, they were formally assured by Stewart, would be theirs 'as long as the Masai race shall exist'. Uncharacteristically, Stewart recorded a caveat that no application for white settlement there should be entertained after the Masai had 'grazed down the grass and made it sweet'. To look after them in their new home, a station was opened at Rumuruti, to which was posted 'Long' Horne. Arriving in January 1905, he found Laikipia very cold but reputedly the healthiest part of East Africa.

The rhino are very thick. I am horribly afraid of the old beasts, they are really very dangerous ... My chief is a most drunken old scoundrel named Gilkison. Drunkenness with Sir D. Stewart at the head is a qualification instead of a drawback ... Gilkie is a sweet old thing, but quite useless ...

I have just heard that a DC who is generally drunk has been dismissed. I can't understand it. I wonder if they are really going to make fellows work and behave themselves.

The Masai on Laikipia were not taxed, and had no neighbours to raid; so they were left to their own devices. Horne was far more concerned with his DC.

I am so cross with my drunken old man. Poor old thing, he has been out of whisky lately and his condition is pitiable... Some of these old soaks live forever...
Why do we form a sort of masonic society and swear never to divulge incompetency or worse? I would sack 60 per cent at least.

Horne's younger brother, Ted, known as 'Short' Horne, joined the Administration after lumberjacking and ranching and was posted to Nyeri. It was not an arrangement of which the elder brother approved. 'I don't like his boss, Hinde. He is rather of the Congo Belge type, a bit of a brute to natives.'

Ted, although a 'luxurious young dog', was showing promise as an administrative officer, and in 1906 was sent to open a new station at Embu, on the eastern slopes of Mount Kenya. A bustling, ebullient little man, he gradually extended his safaris round the mountain. He greatly enjoyed himself and did not economize: 'I knew,' wrote his elder brother, 'young Ted would make the cash fly. He is particularly gifted in that direction.' He was not a great letter-writer: 'It is sheer laziness, the little rascal.' But Ted wrote to his mother in 1907:

All this week we have been preparing for a visit by that swine Churchill, and now he is not coming here. Of course we are all very annoyed.
The Under-Secretary for the Colonies turned up after all and proved to be perfectly charming. He has given me orders to go north and open up a new station at a place called Meru. Of course I am absolutely delighted.

Which Man's Country?

Meru was important: geographically, and as a food-producing district, it was the key to the unknown north. Short Horne was to remain there sixteen years and acquire immense prestige, the father (reputedly in more senses than one) of his people. The Meru are related to the Kikuyu but wilder, and Horne ruled them without shooting. He was a great little man.

'Long' Horne was moved to Lamu, an old Arab town on an offshore island, made up of three-storeyed Arab houses with huge, brass-studded doors opening onto streets so narrow that a man leaning out of a window could shake hands across the street with a friend opposite. The purest Swahili, consisting largely of Arabic words, is spoken there; and Horne enjoyed also improving his legal knowledge among a population of pertinacious litigants.

> The people here are vicious, idle, lying swine, but civilized swine, and have to be handled with kid gloves ... Courtly old chaps, but great rotters.
> [There were enough Goan clerks to make up a tennis four, and enough Europeans for a luncheon party.] I got fresh oysters for soup, fresh prawns for curry, a haunch of gazelle, a nice chicken and all my store delicacies such as olives etc. The Old Lady [Veuve Clicquot champagne] was first rate and the Marsala divine. [For the New Year he stayed with the Sultan of Witu], a cheery old soul, and enjoyed myself hugely. He is a frightful despot and rules his people very strictly, but I found all his doings on the square and sent in a good report.

A drawback to Lamu was that the PC Tanaland was also resident on the island. He was K. McDougall, described in a Colonial Office minute as one who 'speaks, lives and to some extent *thinks* like a native'. But coast Africans were notoriously given to intrigues among themselves, into which McDougall entered with zest. Horne thought:

> He is a low bred, uneducated, cunning Scot, who spits at table, and I am doubtful if I can handle him ... If I can catch him tripping, I'll soon twist his tail and will have

him . . . He is an offensive beast but is now inclined to gush
– told me not to call him 'Sir', call him 'Mac'. This in front of
my clerk. I informed him that I expected in the office that the
formalities will always be gone through, otherwise underlings
might fail in respect to me. He is chewing on this . . . He
is a hard drinker. He gets on your nerves so horribly by
pretending that he is a real gent that you want to kick
him . . . His chief aim is to draw Travelling Allowance.

There was a frightful row, and an official enquiry, because
McDougall caused to be flogged three private enemies of one of
his Arab cronies. Horne reported the proceedings:

McDougall has confessed to what amounts to forgery, lying
and other crimes . . . But I expect they will overlook his
fault. They always do, with these old Company men. He
has been assessed to pay £1,200 damages. I don't think he
can pay it. What a fool a man is not to be honest.

McDougall was not sacked. He settled for £850 damages and
was transferred.

In April 1905, responsibility for the Protectorate was transferred
from the Foreign Office to the Colonial Office, and in the following
year the Commissioner was restyled Governor. Stewart had died
of pneumonia in October 1905 and was succeeded by Sir James
Hayes Sadler, a decent old buffer, nicknamed 'Flannelfoot', whose
guiding principle was to agree with everyone. In 1907 there was
established under his benign aegis a Legislative Council and an
Executive Council, all white, all appointed by the Governor. His
most useful achievement was to move the seat of government and
burgeoning secretariat out of the enervating heat of Mombasa to
Nairobi, in contact with the problems of European settlement
and African administration. But he made no progress with these
problems, applying his mind neither to the settlers' case nor to the
counter-arguments put by, for instance, the DC Kikuyu:

If some of the expenditure which has been incurred by the
Agricultural Department on behalf of European settlers had

Which Man's Country?

been spent in the interests of the Kikuyu and Kavirondo, it is likely that a speedy return would have resulted.

The amenities of Kisumu in 1906 were a tennis-court and the Customs boat, a tub in which the more intrepid sailed the tricky, shallow waters of the Kavirondo Gulf, where wild life added to the hazards of sudden storms; and an unfortunate DO, venturing out on a raft, was upset by a hippo and devoured by crocodiles. One who took a chance was C. M. Dobbs, a long, lanky Irish DO married to a lively Dublin girl. She accompanied Dobbs on safari, dressed for the muggy Nyanza climate in black cotton stockings, three-quarter length skirt, high-necked blouses and sensible underwear. She found tax-collecting for hours on end a back-breaking job and hard on her hands – counting hundreds of coins stuck together with hippo-fat, writing receipts and checking the registers. The 'friendly and child-like' Africans had mastered the rudiments of tax-evasion, borrowing receipts from those who had already paid.

Ainsworth arrived in Kisumu as PC in 1907. He judged morale to be at rock-bottom (though this was certainly not true of the Dobbses) with everyone awaiting the onset of malaria, blackwater fever, sleeping sickness or the plague. Three Europeans had committed suicide in a year. 'Kisumu was not the place for a melancholy man.' He approved of the Kavirondo (or Luo) and used their muscle to make Kisumu a healthier place. To the headmen he

> explained that if their people cut a trench to drain the swamp, the land reclaimed would be available for them and would be very rich soil. In about nine months the trench had been made and, as piece by piece the land was cleared of papyrus, various crops took its place. The natives were well satisfied and Kisumu was largely clear of the mosquito plague.

He laid out a golf-course and even became an addict himself. Money began to circulate, and Ainsworth introduced cotton, ground-nuts and maize. He persuaded the Kavirondo of the value of roads for wheeled traffic and, to stimulate their endeavours, gave bicycles to the more energetic headmen. As their appetite for consumer goods developed, some began working for wages, on roads and drainage schemes at home and on European farms. Others took to commercial fishing. 'One way and another, the people were becoming comparatively well-to-do.' He forbade natives to come into Kisumu naked, and they gradually took to clothes.

He tightened up also on the sartorial slackness of his officials, forbidding the wearing of shorts in the *boma*. Dobbs enquired rather cheekily how far outside the *boma*, before and after a safari, could he put on or must he take off the offending garments. Gone were the days of tennis-shirts at dinner; white duck trousers and dinner-jackets were *de rigueur*.

The Kisii in the hills near the German border speared their DO, G. A. S. Northcote, a Luo and two Indians. In the harsh punishment that followed 160 Kisii were killed and 5,636 cattle captured. The only government casualty was one Nandi auxiliary wounded. Mr Winston Churchill minuted indignantly,

> It looks like a butchery. Surely it cannot be necessary to go on killing these defenceless people on so enormous a scale.

The operation was called off, and to the suggestion that the African General Service medal be awarded to those who took part, a Colonial Office official tartly minuted,

> It might with greater justice be awarded to every private who has qualified on the rifle-range in Nairobi.

Thereafter soldiers desirous of winning medals had to look to the northern frontier.

3

The Smack of Firm Government

In 1909 Hayes Sadler was replaced by Sir Percy Girouard, a Canadian, and an officer of the Royal Engineers with much experience of building and running railways in Africa. His was a dynamic personality; he got things done and was respected by settlers and officials who felt that at last there was a lead from the top. He believed both in European settlement and in safeguarding African interests, and tried to reconcile the two. At a dinner in his honour Delamere remarked that the antagonism between official and settler had disappeared. (Actually it hadn't. When the Governor, taking an early morning walk, politely passed the time of day with a young official, he was told, 'Go to hell, you bloody settler.')

Girouard took a short, hard look at the administration and thought little of it. There were fifteen government departments but no overall policy, system or continuity. The PCs, he informed the Colonial Secretary, were 'hopelessly self-satisfied or supine'. Hobley was widely distrusted and inclined to do too many things, none of them well. Hinde was 'lazy and unreliable', Lane was 'self-satisfied, pig-headed and highly unpopular'. Jackson, hankering after the good old pre-settler days, and Hobley who could never work well in a white community, should go to the coast or be transferred to Uganda. John Ainsworth was anathema to Delamere and most settlers. J. W. McClennan and Bagge were the best, the only ones with the right social background to deal with settlers, but they were soon to retire.

Girouard's preoccupation with the social status of administrative officers was due to the elevated rank of many leading settlers.

Men Who Ruled Kenya

Men like Lord Delamere and the Honourable Berkeley Cole were unlikely to take kindly to orders from any DC, a functionary unknown in Cheshire and Fermanagh since Cromwell's Major-Generals, least of all from a 'counter-jumper'. In 1910 social acceptability meant public school and university or a regular commission. Of two hundred men who joined the administration between 1895 and 1914 about half were public school men, one-third were university graduates and one-fifth had held regular commissions in the army or navy*. Most of this élite must have entered the service after 1910, for in that year the Colonial Office set up a selection board recruiting mainly university graduates. It was unfortunate, thought Girouard, that many of the old and bold did not measure up to them. 'We want,' he told Stephen Bagge, not with the most perfect tact, 'no more pioneers and cow-punchers.'

In May 1910, Girouard issued a memorandum for PCs and DCs, 'with the object of promoting continuity in policy and similarity in administrative action'.

It opened with a crack of the whip:

> It is the duty of Provincial Commissioners to carry out loyally the policy of the Governor and not to inaugurate policies on their own.

> Administrative officers should regard themselves as political officers rather than as administrators, governing indirectly through chiefs and headmen.

> I warn those officers who are in favour of direct rule that if we allow the tribal authority to be ignored or broken, we who are a small minority shall be obliged to deal with a rabble, with thousands of persons in a savage or semi-savage state all acting on their own and making themselves a nuisance to society generally. There could be only one end

---

*vide T. H. R. Cashmore, 'A Random Factor in British Imperialism', in Twaddle, M., *Imperialism, the State and the Third World*, London: British Academic Press, 1992.

to such a policy and that would be the destruction of the rabble.

Already there was a problem of detribalized Africans who left the authority of their chiefs to live on farms and in towns.

The elaborate structure of native custom and belief is apt to fall apart at our touch, yet we express surprise at the disorder of our own creation. We hold out inducements to natives to leave their homes to work, yet we are astonished that they will not always return to their reserves.

Moving from general principles to detail Girouard ordered that every officer must be reported on every year, confidentially, by his superior. Continuity of policy must be maintained by regularly kept provincial and district record books, divided into no less than eighteen sections including trade, revenue, medicine men and wizards, stock diseases, verbal arrangements with natives, the education of the sons of chiefs. Quarterly and annual reports – typewritten, on foolscap paper, one side only, quarter-margin, terse and concise, no slang or vernacular words – must be submitted by PCs and DCs to cover innumerable matters including the work of native staffs, chiefs and headmen, judicial statistics, native courts and councils, trade, transport, public works, police, prisons, labour and, of course, taxation.

Every officer must spend at least three months of the year on safaris which should not just be agreeable rambles enlivened by a little shooting. A safari must have a specific purpose and be recorded in a report (as 'pro-forma Appendix A') which must include a description of the route, with sketch-map, of every day's march; notes on weather, campsites, food, water, firewood, chiefs and headmen, attitude of the natives, density of population, cultivation, livestock; a huts count; and an estimate of the number of elders, warriors, women and children in each village and nomad encampment.

The system of tax collection had hitherto varied from one district to another. In remote areas it consisted of little more than the periodic rounding up of sheep and goats which were taken back to the *boma* and consumed as askaris' rations – from the taxpayer's point of view little different from a Masai raid. The system perfected by Ainsworth in Nyanza must be generally used.

There were two taxes, a hut tax levied on all heads of families, and a poll tax levied on young unmarried men, of the warrior age-grade. Every adult male must pay one of these, at Rs 3 a year. The efficiency of collection depended on a hut-count carried out by officers on safari, and an estimate of the warrior age-grade. The latter's traditional duty of raiding and repelling raids having been phased out by Pax Britannica, there was the danger that they would degenerate into bands of idle and dissolute youths defying the authority of their chiefs. Implied though never explicitly stated was the need to tax them in order to make them work. Girouard wrote:

> It is believed that the imposition of a tax on this section will have a good effect on their mode of life; it is not likely to be well received and district officials must proceed cautiously with its collection.

Receipts had to be issued on payment; tax-defaulters had to be listed, reminded and if necessary prosecuted.

By such methods tax collection increased rapidly and in 1911–12 the Protectorate was for the first time solvent, revenue exceeding normal expenditure. Tax collection came to be widely regarded as the rough measure of a DC's efficiency – but not by Girouard himself who wrote that the real measure was 'the ability he had displayed in procuring contentment and satisfaction in his district'.

All departmental officers in a province – but not judges – were subject to the PC's orders. All administrative officers were expected to be properly dressed, in white or khaki field uniforms.

Nevertheless, for all his unremitting labours to improve his administrative officers, their defects continued to vex Girouard. In February 1912, PCs were instructed to

> bear in mind the impossibility of supplying them only with officers possessing the highest qualifications, and the

necessity of finding posts for those whose duties are usually, and perhaps even habitually, carried out in an unsatisfactory manner.

In 1910 C. C. F. Dundas arrived at Kitui on his first posting, having got his job by buttonholing Mr Winston Churchill in a Paris hotel. James Ainsworth was still DC. Dundas and two other DOs were kept pretty busy, they

> made roads and bridges of a sort, built assembly halls, surveyed vast tracts, dispensed medicines and sometimes held post-mortems on beasts, occasionally even on human corpses. We kept accounts, ran the post office, collected taxes, arbitrated in a never-ending stream of disputes both tribal and domestic, and dispensed justice, combining in our single selves the functions of policeman, magistrate, prosecutor, defender and gaoler, sometimes also lunatic keeper. When there was nothing else to do we managed the little township, enforcing rudimentary sanitation on Indian Arab and Swahili traders. We even instituted a school for natives, the first Government school in the country.

Dundas played football with the police, who took to it with zest. A horrified German visitor asked him, 'How can you play with these [Africans]? Suppose one knocks you down, what then?'

Despite all their activity, he and his colleagues did not imagine they were really administering the Kamba, most of whom never set eyes on a white man. They appointed chiefs; but the Kamba recognized as an authority only the head of his family, and paid taxes only to get rid of the tax-collector.

Meanwhile European settlement, promoted by Delamere's enthusiasm, proceeded apace. Most settlers did not expect themselves to do hard, unskilled, repetitive labour. One might build a stone wall, sink a fencepost into rocky ground, set a plough and plough a mile-long straight furrow to show how it should be done, but not as a regular thing. Nor would one do all the hoeing, weeding and herding stock. If the capital, skills, organization and energy were provided by whites, who would do the heavy work?

Traditionally among the Kikuyu most was done by the women, who took pride in it. But Europeans thought this all wrong, and argued that farm work should be done by young men, introducing them to civilization and industrious ways. It was preposterous that they should spend their lives hanging about the reserves, watching the women work and occasionally exerting themselves to steal a cow, while farms languished for lack of labour. Settlers leaned on the administration to supply them with labour, either by direct compulsion or by tightening up tax collection. Girouard wished DCs to 'encourage natives to leave their reserves to work', but with an eye to liberal opinion at home, issued no specific orders; and his wishes were interpreted in accordance with officers' views on European settlement. Thus in Kiambu Charles Dundas allowed Chief Kinanjui, albeit with some misgivings, to fine defaulters two goats. Dundas wrote:

> We were expected to preach the gospel of labour on all occasions. There was a good deal of futile talk of teaching Africans 'the dignity of labour', but it was hardly exemplified in practice.

Next door, in Dagoretti, M. W. H. Beech would have nothing to do with it. It was his first duty, he told the Labour Commissioner,

> to protect the interests of the natives, and to prevent them from being damaged in order to benefit Europeans. Increased taxation was only a means of benefitting the European at the expense of the native.

The settlers' eyes turned towards the sturdy Kavirondo, but in Kisumu was John Ainsworth. Naturally he clashed with Delamere for although

> In his wrong-headed way Mr Ainsworth has the interests of the country at heart ... he has always denied the rights and benefits of the civilization to which he should be a prop

The Smack of Firm Government

and tried to introduce a system which must result in the ultimate demoralisation and degeneration of the native to a drinking loafer.

Ainsworth retorted:

> I have always made it a rule to preach the Gospel of Work amongst all the tribes I have ever had charge of. As regards the Kavirondo, the invariable advice is, 'You must work. Work at production in your own country if you wish, or work outside for wages.' ... The more industrious the natives become in their own areas, the more likely they are to work outside ... An industrious native is always wanting something, his wants extend to luxuries, his standard of living is raised ... I contend, however, that in order to achieve this the people must first learn to become workers in their own country.

Most farmers resorted to the squatter system. Families would be allowed to live on a farm, keep a specified number of their livestock on it and cultivate a specified acreage for themselves provided they did a specified amount of work for the farmer. It seemed a very convenient system. The bush was cleared, the stumps uprooted, the trees converted into charcoal at a very low cost. The Kikuyu liked it. But only the most meticulous farmer could prevent squatters' friends and relations swarming in and their goats ruining the land.

Most settlers were fair employers by the standards of their time, though hardly liberal in race relations. The average farmer was his own doctor, vet, mechanic, surveyor, architect, building foreman, livestock manager, farm planner, arboriculturist, saddler, blacksmith, horse-breaker, draught ox-trainer and accountant. But it was not he who caught the headlines and fixed in the British public's mind the image of the Kenya settler. Settler leaders were men like Delamere, vociferous, articulate, accustomed to command and resenting interference from a middle-class prig wearing a solar topi and starched uniform, speaking impeccable Coast Swahili which no up-country African could understand. (The settlers and their farm labour evolved a sort of pidgin

Swahili, known as Ki-Settler, with a limited vocabulary and no grammar.) There were a few brutes who treated Africans abominably. These were a small and disreputable minority, but when an official appeared over the horizon, all settlers tended to close ranks.

The early settlers had a lot to put up with. Commercial farming at 7,000 feet on the equator was a matter for experiment, hit or miss, and many misses meant bankruptcy. Native cattle were small with a poor milk-yield, native sheep grew coarse hair instead of wool. It therefore seemed sensible to cross them with imported stock. Some imported stock did well, some badly. They died of East Coast fever (the result of heavy infestation by ticks carried by wild animals) while native stock survived. They died of rinderpest brought onto the farm by buffalo or trespassing Masai cattle. When the farmer decided he must fence to keep these out, when he had bought the wire, and obtained permission from the Forestry Department to cut trees for fence-posts *on his own land*, and had put up miles of fencing, it was laid flat in a night by stampeding zebra or elephants. Lions and leopards always seemed to select the most valuable animals – the Hereford bull, the Shorthorn heifer, the Merino ram. The wheat he grew from imported seed contracted rust; the barley, just ready for harvesting, was set alight by sparks from the railway. Coffee-trees wilted, or flourished grossly and were soon exhausted, and no two experts could agree on what was wrong with them. Drought, floods, hail and locusts were fearful hazards.

Another plague was stock-theft. To young men of most tribes, particularly pastoral tribes like the Masai, stealing cattle was a dangerous game, a test of manhood, most prestigious if accomplished by a spear-blooding. Public opinion in these tribes was wholly on the young men's side. Farmers did not see it as a sport. It was maddening to have valuable animals stolen, and a herd-boy speared, just to enhance a moran's prestige. Furiously at a hundred meetings they demanded that the administration *do* something about it. But the administration could do little without sanction of the common law. If a thief was caught he would be prosecuted in court and imprisoned; if the stolen cattle were tracked and recovered, they were returned to the owner less

The Smack of Firm Government

any that the thieves had eaten. But it was very seldom that the thieves were caught, for they were adept at concealing the tracks of stolen animals in those of another herd, and at faking brands. So the settlers complained, *fortissimo*, that the administration was 'soft with natives'.

The only answer to stock-theft was to deal with it in the African way, extracting from the thieves' family or clan, after days of argument with the elders, compensation for the animals stolen. There was then some chance that the thieves' families would discourage their activities. So the settlers and many administrative officers pressed for collective fines to be legalized. Naturally the lawyers and judges and the Colonial Office (fearful of a row in the House of Commons) opposed tooth-and-nail anything so un-British as a fine levied on anyone who had not been found guilty in court. In 1909 the Government passed the law the settlers wanted. But it did not stop stock-theft, which eighty years later is as rife as ever.

All these vicissitudes in the thin, brittle air of the Highlands were not conducive to sweetness of temper; and the easiest way to vent one's fury was on the DC.

Emotional disturbance and irrational behaviour were not confined to settlers. DCs quarrelled bitterly with colleagues over trifles. Some took to the bottle in the belief that whisky cured all ills except DTs. In 1910 Girouard complained of a PC, Lane, 'being drunk in a bar and making use of disloyal utterances'.

Much was made of the differences between official and settler. The local press and some settler politicians blew these up into a bitter feud, as did some officials. Hobley wrote:

> The mass bitterness at times was extremely acute and was deeply felt by the officials, especially as by the rule of the service they had to suffer in silence a continued campaign of abuse.

There were friendships between settlers and officials. As the numbers of each class increased, so did the cross-fertilization as they married one another's sisters and daughters (less frequently, wives). But in general, right up to the 1940s, relations between the two classes was at best wary, at worst bitter. While settlers almost universally denounced officials as being prejudiced against their kith-and-kin, Africans believed that they would always favour their own race.

The vast majority of officials came to East Africa for an adventurous, open air life and to escape a nine-to-five job at home; and governed to the best of their ability in accordance with the principles inculcated at Rugby and Marlborough.

Nearly every DC regarded the law as an obstacle and the judges as his enemies. Even Ainsworth considered that

> To try to apply civilized law among savages is not understood by the savage and is interpreted by him as a sign of weakness.

The judges' point of view was thus expressed:

> While the High Court fully realizes the difficulties experienced by DCs in outlying stations, it cannot lend its sanction to a system which in practice permits the DCs to disregard the laws of procedure.

With his experience of West and South Africa, where hereditary kings and paramount chiefs were a reality, Girouard never really grasped that in East Africa they were not. He urged DCs to rule indirectly through chiefs and headmen, but the difficulty, as Ainsworth observed, was to 'get the natives to recognize any individual of their tribe as a person of authority over them'. Hobley, as PC Kamba, encouraged traditional '*kiamas*', committees of elders of the ruling age-grade who in most tribes were recognized as a sort of court for the settlement of disputes. The Native Tribunals Act of 1911 conferred on *kiamas* modest judicial powers, which they could exercise with due regard to tribal custom. In theory there was a separation of powers. The chiefs collected taxes, recruited labour, maintained roads, arrested malefactors, while the *kiamas* dispensed justice. In practice the distinction was blurred.

It will be recalled that, to make room for more white farmers in the Rift Valley, the Il Purko clan of Masai had been moved in

The Smack of Firm Government

1904, very willingly, to the Laikipia plateau with the assurance that it would be theirs 'as long as the Masai race shall exist'. But, as Stewart had predicted, as soon as the Masai herds had grazed down the grass and made it sweet, settlers began to covet Laikipia. Moreover some Masai, including their paramount chief, Lenana, felt it would be better for the tribe to be all together, in a single enlarged southern reserve than divided by a block of European farms. It was not a straight issue of administration versus settlers. Bagge, the PC Naivasha, who for years had battled for Masai interests, thought that the tribe would be better off on the Loita Plain, south of the Rift Valley, provided there was permanent water for them. Jackson, the Lieutenant-Governor, equally pro-Masai, concurred but with reservations.

> I am, however, glad that I had nothing whatsoever to do with the negotiations which led up to it . . . I would certainly not have interpreted [Chief] Legalishu's 'If you wish us to go, we will go, but we don't want to go' into 'Quite willing' as was cabled home . . . It was a sorry show.

Girouard pressed for the move because Loita 'does not lie in the heart of white settlement as Laikipia does', bringing to farmers the plague of stock-theft and cattle-disease.

At home the liberal conscience was troubled and the Colonial Office, fearful of a 'tornado' in the House of Commons, told Girouard to suspend action pending further instructions. The move, however, had already started, in June 1911.

It was chaotic. Huge herds of Masai cattle trekked slowly across European farms towards the Mau escarpment, where they suffered great losses from the cold and from lack of grass and water. As the leading herds halted, others piled up behind them. One herd had to be quarantined for rinderpest. Eventually they were all herded back to Laikipia to await the next rains.

In the Commons the tornado blew up. The Colonial Secretary, Lord Harcourt, smelled a rat: had Girouard already promised Laikipia to the settlers? Girouard said he hadn't; but Lane, the PC Naivasha, while on leave, told the Colonial Office that promises had been made. The dispute became a semantic wrangle: Girouard denied *promising* land to anyone, but admitted telling two farmers that they would be *considered* for land in Laikipia. On this delicate point he resigned.

Eventually the Il Purko were moved in smaller batches to Loita, but they did not find there the promised water supplies; these had been disallowed by the Treasury as too expensive.

The task of administering the perplexed and sullen Masai in Loita was entrusted from 1912 to 1923 to Hemsted who constantly, and in vain, pressed for the water. He liked the Masai, and learned their language, but was sharply critical.

> They have not the slightest desire to improve themselves, their cattle, their country, the conditions in which they live or anything else. They merely wish to amass large herds of cattle, irrespective of quality, and be left in undisturbed possession of them.

> The elders were nice old gentlemen, rich, apathetic and scared of the moran.

> The section of the community most requiring attention is the moran. The system of a semi-military organization which still exists has a devastating effect on them. They lead useless, idle, vicious lives, and only engage themselves as herdsmen to certain wealthy farmers who only insist on a modicum of work for high remuneration, and carefully refrain from asking them to do anything which they would dislike.*

What did Africans think of their piecemeal conquest and gradually encroaching government by the 'red strangers'?

In the more remote districts they were hardly affected. In Kitui, Dundas wrote with his usual frankness:

> It is in fact far from possible to give any appreciable effect to many laws ... By passive resistance they obtain their own way.

*A side-swipe at Delamere.

The Smack of Firm Government

In smaller, more thickly populated districts Africans did feel the impact of administration. Probably chiefs, interpreters, askaris, farm headmen and traders taking advantage of roads and Pax Britannica thought it was fine, but what did most of the people think? In December 1912, Beech, DO Kiambu, a passionate advocate of African rights, wrote a paper, 'The Kikuyu point of view', based on careful questioning of some fifty chiefs and elders. He believed that they were glad of law and order and the end of Masai raids. They were glad that the *kiamas* were being encouraged. They thought hut tax reasonable, but not poll tax which undermined the authority of heads of families and encouraged young men to go away to work on farms. They deplored the demoralizing effect on the young of missions, and of towns such as Nairobi. They bitterly resented European occupation of land which they regarded as theirs. True, for generations they had not dared to move their cattle out of the forest onto these fine pastures because of the Masai; now the Masai were no danger, but the way was barred by wire fences.

None of the great problems which beset Kenya had begun to be solved in the East African Protectorate. Was this to be a black man's or a white man's country? How could the increasing numbers of detribalized urban Africans be kept out of trouble? What prospects would there be for natives whom the missions and the government were educating? And for the Indians? As for the population explosion consequent on law and order, sanitation and medical services; and soil erosion due to over-grazing, these in 1912 were beyond anyone's imagination.

At the outbreak of war in August 1914, Kisii *boma*, almost on the German border, was evacuated by the British, occupied by the Germans, evacuated by the Germans, looted by the Kisii and re-occupied by the British – all in a few days. The Giryama, on the coast, staged a mini-revolt on local issues which was quelled by one company of KAR. Otherwise the only tribe to give trouble was the Masai; who would not volunteer, and objected to being conscripted into a white man's war.

Kamba, Nandi, Somalis and Kipsigis volunteered in large numbers for the KAR. But the greatest need was for porters.

Men Who Ruled Kenya

The laborious campaign to evict von Lettow's heroic rearguards from German East Africa was bedevilled by appalling difficulties in transport. Horses and mules were wiped out by African horse-sickness, draught oxen by trypanosomiasis caused by the bite of the tsetse fly. The least unsatisfactory form of transport was by porters, conscripted mainly from the Kikuyu and Kavirondo. The administration was under ceaseless pressure to keep up the supply. No war work was more vital and in 1917 Ainsworth was appointed Military Commissioner for Labour with the rank of colonel. It was a job which appalled him. He loved Africans but had to send them south to perish by the thousand of malaria, dysentery, sleeping sickness, exposure. His own estimate was that of 162,000 recruited into the Carrier Corps, 24,000 died: others put the deaths at 40,000.

Ainsworth received the DSO and CBE for work which almost broke his heart. The men he sent to the war had their memorial: the most nauseating of all the nauseating Nairobi slums is still named Kariokor – 'Carrier Corps'.

With a weak Governor, Sir Charles Belfield, settler power increased. Settlers were promised that after the war they would send elected representatives to the legislative council. Self-government, i.e. government by elected whites, seemed almost within reach.

As for the Africans, they had seen white men killing one another, shot and bayonetted by blacks, sometimes running away from blacks. White prestige would never again rise to its pre-war level. The war brought a great flow of money into the reserves from soldiers' and porters' wages and gratuities and from the sale of livestock to feed the army. Results of this included the adoption by the Kamba, Kikuyu and Luo of European-style clothing, and a clamour among these tribes for education.

Post-war developments speeded the migration from the more advanced tribes to the towns, and to 'detribalizing'. Chiefs and Headmen, who by official patronage had acquired authority, began to lose it, particularly among the young and semi-educated. This made the administration's task much harder, and almost all administrative officers greatly preferred 'the man in the blanket' to the man in trousers. Indeed it is a reflection on the British colonial

The Smack of Firm Government

system that it never really came to terms with the product of the civilizing mission.

It was in the Kikuyu tribe, resenting more than others the loss of some of their land,* that these problems were most serious.

---

*The proportion of the White Highlands which the Kikuyu had once cultivated is much debated. It was probably not more than about 5 per cent.

4

The North

The north was another world. Most of the country is scrub-desert, every tree and bush bristling with hooked 'wait-a-bit' thorn which tears at flesh and clothes. One can seldom see more than three hundred yards, often much less. There was then no permanent water except for the Uaso Nyiro, Tana and Juba rivers, the Lorian swamp, and a few clusters of deep wells. It was a country in which small forces were ambushed and cut up, large forces suffered cruelly from hunger and thirst, and both lost their way.

In Jubaland and eastern Borana the dominant race is the Somali, zealous Muslims and said to possess 'the most advanced brain on the East African coast'. The Somali is reputed to be brave, tall, handsome, ready of speech, humorous and intelligent, but rarely truthful or reliable. He has remarkable stamina and endurance of privations. If he feels insulted, he turns sulky and dangerous. He does not consider himself an African, and despises Kenya tribes, 'dirty black fellows with foreskins'.* He rarely condescends to manual labour, but will supervise the labour of others. His life-style is nomadic, based on huge herds of camels, cattle, sheep and goats, on the flesh and milk of which he thrives.

The Somalis were by far the toughest enemy the British encountered in East Africa. Their national hero, Mohamad Abdullah Hassan, was known to the British as 'the Mad Mullah' though he had his wits well about him. For twenty-five years he

---

*Actually, most Kenya tribes circumcise.

The North

evaded, defeated and defied British, French, Italian and Abyssinian forces in the Horn of Africa. In surprise attacks Somalis were formidable, threading their way with wonderful speed through thick thorn-scrub, making their thrusts with lightning celerity and inflicting terrible wounds with spears and broad-bladed knives. They were adept at the tactics of guerrilla war – treachery, surprise, deception, ambuscade; and seldom attacked save at a great advantage in numbers or terrain. In some tribes the fighting men were mounted on hardy ponies and armed with modern rifles.

Three factors facilitated the government of these difficult people. Their tribes and sections were generally quarrelling with one another; some of their hereditary sultans and sheikhs did exercise some authority; and they could not live without their flocks and herds which could be seized as fines for misconduct.

The Somalis' neighbours to the west were the Boran tribe, part-Moslem, part-pagan, of a similar life-style but more stable, less truculent; and some tribes of mixed Somali-Boran blood. There were Arabs along the coast and in trading centres; and the alluvial soil along the Juba river was cultivated by slave-tribes collectively known as Gosha.

By an agreement with the Sultan of Zanzibar in 1891, Kismayu and its immediate interior passed to the company and later to the EAP and British administration gradually extended into the interior of Jubaland. The third Administrator, Todd, was the first Briton murdered by Somalis, stabbed at an argumentative *baraza* in 1893. The Protectorate was proclaimed at Kismayu in 1895.

Peace then ensued for three years during which small outposts were established at Yonte and Mfudu. But in April 1898, Somalis of the Ogaden tribe suddenly stormed Yonte and massacred the garrison. An Ogaden Expeditionary Force then plodded after the elusive enemy, was ambushed, lost twenty-eight men and rifles, and withdrew to Kismayu.

By no means averse to playing off one enemy against another, the Ogaden asked for British protection against Abyssinia, and the PC, Jubaland, A. C. W. Jenner, raised the Union Jack at Afmadu.

Jenner was large and choleric, but liked by Somalis. The liking was mutual: Jenner wrote to Eliot of the Ogaden: 'I have never met natives who show higher qualities.' He was on excellent terms with their fiery, disputatious old Sultan, Ahmed Maghan:

> 'I send you some opening medicine, not very strong, take some whenever you want it and write and tell me how you are,
> Your great friend,
> A. C. W. Jenner.'

But the Ogaden continued to be troublesome, and in July 1900 killed a lot of Gosha. Jenner said they must pay compensation, and Ahmed Maghan prevaricated. Jenner had two Ogaden flogged, for some quite unconnected offence, and the Ogaden bided their time.

In October 1900, Jenner went on safari to Liboi, escorted by thirty-five armed police. One evening in pouring rain, Jenner ordered all the rifles to be stored in his dry tent, and another tent to be pitched for his men. At four in the morning camels were heard stampeding and into the camp charged some 300 men of the Aulihan and Muhamad Zubair sections of Ogaden, screaming and stabbing. Jenner came out of his tent, grappled with one, threw him, and fell on top of him. More Somalis then ran up, stabbed Jenner through and through, castrated him and cut off his head. Nearly all his askaris were served likewise.

A punitive column of battalion strength marched on Afmadu. Ahmed Maghan surrendered and was sent down to Kismayu to stand trial for complicity in Jenner's murder. On 16 February 1901, the column was routed with the loss of a lieutenant-colonel and thirty-eight men. To cap it all, Ahmed Maghan escaped from custody.

A fine of 30,000 cattle was imposed on the Ogaden, who refused to pay. This was reduced to 5,000, a concession which they treated with contempt. However, the last thing the Foreign Office wanted was a war in Jubaland while the army was fighting the Boers and the Mad Mullah. Eliot was:

The North

penetrated with the conviction that it is useless to spend lives and money on subduing the barbarous inhabitants of barren deserts.

The expedition was withdrawn. The Ogaden seemed to have got away with it.

K. MacDougall, PC Jubaland, found this intolerable. He waited until the dry season and then with only 200 men, marched swiftly on the wells at Afmadu where thousands of Ogaden stock were watering. When with much yelling and waving of turbans the herdsmen tried to drive the animals at a gallop into the bush, they were far too thirsty to gallop anywhere. So there was nothing the Ogaden could do but look pleasant while MacDougall returned to Kismayu with 4,000 captured cattle. He had never, he reported, 'seen the Ogaden so loyal and peaceably inclined'.

From the Foreign Office, Sir Clement Hill roundly condemned 'a very provocative action'.

> It is against the Foreign Office policy, against the views of Sir Charles Eliot . . . and against the warnings laid down in previous despatches.

Eliot considered that the country was not worth the money spent on it. It mattered not what the Somalis did in Jubaland so long as they did not do it to their inoffensive neighbours. Besides, the Mullah was on the rampage up north, and this might affect the southern Somalis. Already there had arrived from the north the Marehan tribe, of which three sections collectively known as 'Galti' (Strangers) had been fighting in the Mullah's army. Described as 'Typical, intelligent, fighting Somalis', well mounted and rifle-armed, they were much feared. So the policy in Jubaland was to leave the Somalis alone. The garrisons of Kismayu and Yonte had nothing to do but protect themselves.

Somali pressure along the Tana river was more than the nomad's casual raiding of the peasant. It was part of a migration of Somali tribes out of their barren deserts in the Horn of Africa southwards and westwards towards greener pastures and more plentiful water. If they were not stopped along the Tana, they would soon be grazing below Nairobi. That was their southward thrust. Their westward thrust was towards the wells at Wajir. To stop this was the job of whatever authorities might be set up in Borana.

They had another task which at first seemed more pressing. Very little was known of Borana. It was vaguely, and erroneously, supposed to be rich in ivory, cattle and horses. It was certainly infested with rifle-armed bands of Abyssinian soldiery, indistinguishable from bandits, who descended on the Boran robbing, raping, killing, raiding for slaves, collecting 'taxes', even shooting elephants and altogether behaving in a most reprehensible manner. It seemed desirable to define the British-Abyssinian frontier as a preliminary to ordering them off. This work was done in 1901–02 by a boundary commission headed by Captain Maud, Royal Engineers. The Maud Line was agreed to by the Emperor Menelik, but his local officials professed to know nothing about it. It cut across tribal grazing grounds and separated 'British' tribes from their dry weather wells in Abyssinia; so the tribes on either side were allowed by treaty to have free access to wells on the other side, an arrangement pregnant with squabbling during the dry months when animals are bawling for water and men's tempers are on edge. The Maud Line was supposed to mark the southern limits of Abyssinian rule, but (according to Sir John Harrington, British Minister in Addis Ababa)

> Menelik has every intention of occupying territory which has no visible owner, although he would certainly halt did he find signs of effective opposition on our part.

Naturally His Majesty's Government tried to do the job on the cheap, employing at a salary of £200 a year a travelling 'Frontier Inspector'. The man for the job was Philip Zaphiro, an adventurous Greek who had impressed Harrington by his facility in negotiating with officials in Addis Ababa.

His duty was to represent the British Empire, turn back raiders and halt the tide of Abyssinian expansion along a 400-mile frontier. His forces consisted of about twenty Abyssinian askaris, armed

The North

with old Martini rifles, noisy but inaccurate, which the Somalis disrespectfully termed 'Dusuwen' (big farts).

For his base he chose Moyale, a well-centre about half-way along the Maud Line. Arriving late in 1905 he immediately turned back three Habash *shiftas** whom he found 'putting people in irons, seizing cattle and shooting elephants'. The Boran begged him to protect them but he 'did not see how he could do this with twenty soldiers'.

He was a large, jovial man with a personality which impressed proud and unruly tribesmen. A natural linguist, he soon acquired an essential knowledge of tribal history and a taste for interminable conversations with the natives – a valuable accomplishment. 'As I speak to them in their own language,' he explained modestly, 'they have great confidence in me.' To reinforce that confidence he wore on important occasions an admiral's frock-coat and a scarlet cummerbund.

Ceaselessly he patrolled the Golbo, the low-lying country south of the Maud Line, fighting small *shiftas*, turning back by bluff and portentous diplomatic protest larger incursions of Abyssinian soldiers and officials. Thousands of Boran had fled to British territory to escape the attentions of Menelik's rapacious tax-collectors. This riled the Abyssinians and reduced their fiscal base. Some of Zaphiro's superiors were inclined to appease Menelik by returning the refugees whence they came, but Zaphiro would have none of this.

> If they do not want to stay with the Abyssinians, I do not think we can force them to. No subject of any government can be forcibly detained if the said government is cruel and unjust.

Neither the frontier nor the Golbo was easily patrolled. The former followed roughly the line of the Abyssinian escarpment. It crossed steep stony hills, deep eroded ravines, dry river beds down which rain in the highlands sent roaring torrents. The Golbo was mainly flat with rocky outcrops and lava ridges, which men and horses could cross only with difficulty and much damage to feet

---

*Habash: the usual term for Abyssinians. *Shifta*: a raiding party.

and hooves. It was perfect country for an ambush. One had to move in single file, always on the alert, rifles ready. Every camp had to be planned with an eye to a sudden volley from the bush, a slashing, stabbing rush in the dark.

At the eastern end of his beat the danger was from the Marehan Somalis, particularly the three Galti ('Stranger') sections. In 1906, Zaphiro

> sent word to the Galti that as the country belongs to the British Government they must obey any orders that may arrive. At the same time I have asked two of their chiefs to come up here, but I am not sure they will obey.

They didn't. Zaphiro's reaction was typical.

> If His Majesty's Government should give me permission, I will take some Abyssinians and Boran and disarm these people before it is too late. No expense would occur, as the Abyssinians and Boran would be paid from the raided animals; whilst if the Government were to send a regular expedition it would cost an enormous amount of money. We must do something soon.

His spirited offer was rejected.

Zaphiro realized that the flag follows trade:

> I find that the more a tribe takes to trade, the more friendly does it become towards the other tribes. The trader does not go merely with his personal property, but has animals and goods belonging to other members of his tribe with him; and thus the whole tribe is concerned in his welfare, and treats well strangers from the country to which he has gone. By encouraging trade, I have every hope of allaying the bloodshed which is at present so rife.

An attempt was being made to exploit Borana by a firm with a buccaneering flavour known as the Boma Trading Company,

The North

sponsored by Lord Delamere. It showed great enterprise but little profit, and Zaphiro did not think much of it.

A white man has very little chance of trading successfully in these remote parts. He does not know the habits of each particular tribe, and the natives believe he is an official come to tax them.

One who tried was the irrepressible John Boyes, who turned up in Moyale trading in cattle and horses just when Zaphiro needed some sick leave. It was agreed, with some misgivings, that Boyes take his place for a few weeks. The misgivings proved justified when Boyes for some trivial misdemeanour proceeded to hang his headman. Just in time, the headman was cut down by Zaphiro's people, and it was decided that the 'Eater of Beans' was unsuited to a diplomatic post.

An attempt was made to improve the Maud Line so as to give the 'British' tribes a fair share of the permanent water. The British Boundary Commissioner, Major Gwynn, arrived in Addis Ababa in June 1908, eager to start, only to find that no Abyssinian Commissioner had been appointed, or could be, because the Emperor was ill. After waiting for some months, he was instructed to proceed on his own. Not surprisingly the Abyssinians refused to accept his proposals, preferring those of their own Boundary Commissioner who proceeded independently of Gwynn but assisted by a German officer. So there were for the next forty-five years the Maud and the Gwynn Lines not recognized by the Abyssinians, and a third line not recognized by the British.

Gwynn found Zaphiro useful as guide, political officer, interpreter and adviser; but rather ungraciously suggested that a British DC at Moyale would be more appropriate than 'one accustomed to the moral code of the Levant'. So Zaphiro returned to Addis Ababa where he became Oriental Secretary to the British Legation and a CMG. Of all the *condottieri* who advanced British interests (and not infrequently their own) in Africa, he was among the best.

To facilitate the control of Borana, Marsabit station was opened in October 1909 by Geoffrey Archer, 'a huge lad, mad keen on birds'. Marsabit is a thickly forested mountain, with ample rainfall and a volcanic crater lake, rising 3,500 feet above the most awful desert. It is cool, it is healthy, it is delightful.

On the strength of a few lessons on surveying in Nairobi, Archer set out to map his new domain. His erection of survey beacons was impeded by rhinos.

> Every rocky hill was infested with them ... torpid in their habits and never expecting to be disturbed ... The actual erection of a beacon takes time. A concrete slab is let into the ground below the beacon and on it is marked a cross to denote the central position fixed by plumb-line. Above this is set the plane-table. Having taken the round of angles and after hours of calculation, the most fascinating thing is the turning of the handle of the 'sausage-machine' to see the latitude and longitude roll out – and the mean is accepted as correct.

Captain W. E. H. Barrett, with his Nandi mistress, took over Moyale from Zaphiro, responsible not merely for 300 miles of frontier, but for the wells at Wajir, 158 miles to the south. With fifty or sixty deep wells in use (dug no one knows how or by whom, through a 30-foot limestone crust) it was a key point in the NFD, and the object of ceaseless pressure, wheedling, bullying and deceit by Degodia and Ogaden Somalis whose *modus operandi* resembled that of the cuckoo. Begging for water in a drought, one or two Somali families would gain a toe-hold as *shegats* (guests, protégés) of the Boran, Ajuran and Sakuye who owned the wells. They would then gradually call in their friends and relations, and eventually elbow their hosts out.

In March 1910, Barrett with Captain Aylmer and thirty KAR arrived at Wajir. In the hottest and driest month of the year it was pandemonium with the dust, the flies, the bawling of thirsty cattle and roaring of thirsty camels, as the sweating young tribesmen, perched on footholds in the well-walls, a dozen or fifteen to each well, ceaselessly passed up the full and down the empty leather buckets. Barrett found the place:

The North

practically occupied by Somalis, watering stock day and night, the Boran having been turned out of all wells except four ... [I told the Somalis they must] leave Wajir. Three-day time limit with rocket signal. One day's extension given. Typical Somali procrastination, excuse that rocket was not seen. [At last they departed.] I believe, however, that the Somalis have such a hearty contempt for the powers of Government that they will return.

They did, killing seventeen Boran and looting their stock. Evidently Wajir could not be controlled from Moyale, so early in 1912 S. F. Deck, a bustling little man with the air of a sea-dog and the background of a prep-schoolmaster, was posted as DC, Wajir, with thirty KAR 'to see that the rightful occupants are re-established on the wells'. It was like pushing water uphill. Deck was joined by G. A. S. Mure, a DO from Jubaland, whence most of the interlopers came. It was soon clear that a military operation to eject the Somalis was impossible, not least because the camels needed for a military force could be obtained only by hire from the Somalis who were to be ejected. Colonel Thesiger, Inspector General of the KAR, after a visit to Wajir, was

> very nervous as to the safety of the political officers in Wajir, as I think that the danger of their being compelled to give an order which cannot be enforced increases daily.

Indeed, issuing an order which Somalis could ignore was most inadvisable.

It was decided to disarm the Marehan. (The Ogaden were delighted to provide baggage camels for this purpose.) In January 1914, 350 KAR entered Marehan country, fought a battle with the Galti, and retired to Serenli to await reinforcements. A month later the equivalent of two regular battalions tried again, this time with more success. With the help of a troop of Aulihan scouts, they located the enemy herds watering in the dry weather and seized several thousand head of stock. These were handed back to the Marehan at a rate of ten camels or cattle for every rifle or horse surrendered. Some of the Marehan teeth were drawn.

Men Who Ruled Kenya

Inter-tribal enmities did at least ensure that when war came in August 1914 there was little danger of a general uprising of all the Somali tribes to help their fellow-Muslims, the Turks. The KAR on the frontier was replaced by an armed constabulary, composed of Nubians and Somalis. Barrett reported that they were

> fairly satisfactory. Somali askaris, however, although excellent at running a camel safari, are far too friendly with Somali traders from Kismayu and Nairobi, inclined to interfere with the administrative work of the district, give trouble in the station and are heartily disliked by the other tribes to whom they are overbearing and arrogant.

Every frontier DC was a transport officer, arranging for his own safaris and for forwarding supplies to those further afield. The most cost-effective transport was by donkeys, but they could be used only on routes with plenty of water. Porters were the most reliable, but unobtainable except near Meru. Bullock carts were good as far as Archer's Post, in country with plentiful water and grazing, but useless further north. On the whole, camels were the best, but the problem was, how to obtain them when they were wanted. The least unsatisfactory method was to hire them. Riding camels were scarce and had to be grain-fed. Horses and mules did well in some areas, but in others succumbed to African horse-sickness and trypanosomiasis. So on most safaris officers and men walked, while hired camels carried their baggage.

Already hut tax and poll tax were being collected from traders and Gosha. The more amenable nomads paid tribute of about thirty camels or cattle from each section, but it was not considered advisable as yet to tax Somalis or Gurreh. Trade was increasing: every year hundreds of horses and mules, and thousands of cattle, were trekked to Nairobi and the highlands.

The Kismayu area was far more civilized than the NFD. The anopheles mosquito had, by 1914, been almost eliminated. The half-dozen officers lived in large, cool, airy houses; they could bathe, sail, play tennis and billiards and consort at a club; dining on oysters, prawns, lobsters, sea-fish and delicacies imported from

The North

Aden and Mombasa. Liberal, enlightened colonialism occasionally intruded. In 1911 C. L. S. Reddie, DC Kismayu, 'a regular Keir Hardie' according to 'Long Horne', noted after a visit to Gobwen:

> Native Council in its infancy. Should be encouraged and include representatives of Indians and others to discuss use of Town Rates. The DO should not simply order how the money is to be spent but should in council discuss the best means of doing so ... I do not think it is sufficiently realized by officers that their duties are not confined simply to giving orders on how things are to be done; the education of the people in municipal matters and self-government is also their duty. There can be no doubt on this point.

There was none of that in the NFD where Deck replaced Hope as officer-in-charge Northern Frontier District (NFD) and, in July 1914, J. L. B. Llewellin arrived at Wajir to take over from Deck. Known to his colleagues as Long Lu, and to Somalis as Wellin Dera which means the same, he was to become a frontier legend. He learned to speak perfect Somali and became an expert on tribal genealogies (very important); he even made a study of camel brands so that he could tell at a glance the sub-section, even the family, to which a camel belonged. Under Llewellin's probing questions, it was very difficult for a tribesman up to no good to conceal his identity.

At Wajir Llewellin was not surprised to find that Deck and Mure had 'sleeping dictionaries'. In the NFD no white women were allowed, and many Somali girls were beauties. Later he discovered that the Somali they spoke was the women's language, which caused hilarity among their askaris. However both were 'v. nice fellows, Mure Oxford, Deck Cambridge'.

When they departed Llewellin was on his own. The accounts were kept in trade goods, mainly rolls of cloth, and two currencies, rupees and Maria Theresa dollars, the common currency of the Horn of Africa.

> 3. Sept. '14. Counting over trade goods, reconciling book balances. A hard job if not used to it.

4. Sept. '14. Steady sweat at cash-book. Finally got it right except for Rs. 1 and $5 short.
5. Sept. '14. Again at cash-book. Now the trade goods column. Building the store.
6. Sept. '14. At cash-book still. By evening had got it totally exact with Trade Goods ledger.

His next task was to lower the floor of little Deck's house lest he brain himself on the roof. Then he started on the work which would occupy him until 1917.

Most of the time he moved with the tribes, his long legs keeping tireless pace with theirs, his bedding-roll, water-tanks and chop-boxes carried by tall, swaying, grumbling camels. At every encampment along his route he would stop to drink a bowl of cool, creamy camel's milk and exchange the gossip of the desert – a water-hole dried up in one direction, an unseasonal thunderstorm in another; where had so-and-so moved his cattle? Had the scouts reported good camel browse? For months on end he spoke nothing but Somali. He lived mainly on camel-meat (a barren female was like good beef) and on camel-milk, which had a smokey flavour from the burning sticks which were shaken about in the milk vessels to clean them and kill the insects. He could seldom give an unpopular order because he could not compel obedience. To reserve for their rightful owners some of the Wajir wells, he had to resort to argument and bargaining rather than muscle. But blood-money, fines and compensation for murder and stock-theft were in accordance with the Sharia, the Muslim law code, and tribal custom: the tribes understood these, and the more sensible headmen would co-operate in collecting camels and cattle from the culprits or from their families or sections. Besides all this, he had to keep tabs on the Mullah's agents, and on immigrants from British and Italian Somaliland.

A good example of his methods can be seen with regard to slavery – an institution of which the Somalis approved:

23. Oct. '14. Meru boy brought in who had been sold by one Mohamad Zubair to another for a rifle and a bullock. Had the owner in and told him this was forbidden. He said the

The North

man who sold him the boy had a government permit to sell, and produced a bit of paper. The liars! Told Haji Hassan to put a stop to it among the Mohamad Zubair.

Haji Hassan Yera, a Mohamad Zubair notable, had been banned from all government stations for suspected complicity in Jenner's murder. Llewellin thought the suspicions were unjust, and ignored the ban: 'I knew him extremely well,' he told the author. 'We were friends.'

26 Jan. '15. All the Mohamad Zubair chiefs in. Weighed into them and slanged them about the raid. Stopped all passes to buy *buni** and sheep and said if they did not get everything back in 20 days I'd push their stock back beyond Melka Wayo. A rather large boast seeing that I have only 15 askaris and there must be hundreds of them.

5–7 Aug. '15. Work! You've no idea what it is until you have to do it or perish miserably. Not an instant to spare from morn to eve.

15 Aug. '15. Big Id† dinner at Hajali Egal's. After, Mohamad Goda and Farah Jama sang ballads about fighting with the Mullah.

13 Sept. '15. Big row about the murder of a Wata.‡ Two Fai Degodia accused.

15 Sept. '15. The accused in. Found that a Wata had killed the uncle of one of them in revenge for another Wata killed in a fight between Degodia and Gurreh. The fight cannot count as murder, so the two murders compensate and no blood-money is payable. 24 lashes each to the young men for breaking the peace.

10 Oct. '15. At Melka Wayo [on the Uaso Nyiro river]. Buni with Haji Hassan. A crowd of Mohamad Zubair told me two men had been caught by a hippo and showed me the hippo

---

*Buni: the wild coffee berry, much liked by Somalis.
†*Id-ul-Fitr*: the feast at the end of the month's Ramadhan fast.
‡Wata: outcast Boran hunting tribe.

in a bush. I fired two rounds and he dashed out and nearly caught me as I fell over a bush. Then I did the best 50 yard sprint I ever did, but he did not follow, not liking the open in daylight. I saw one of the men he had injured, not dead but dying, his right arm broken at shoulder and wrist and right leg at ankle ... Succeeded in potting the hippo in the evening. Saw the other man dead under hippo's bush, ribs all smashed.

In October 1915, a new DO arrived in Wajir. He was not a great asset, since he spoke not a word of Swahili, let alone Somali, and had been flung out of the window at Archer's Post for cheating at poker. But Llewellin thought he had had a raw deal from the transport staff at Archer's Post, being provided with bullock carts, but

> No Somali headman. No proper outfit. No spare bullocks so no time to graze. Of four teams of eight bullocks, only 23 are now surviving, including 6 very sick. Can't do more than two miles a day. Inadequate supplies, tools of very poor quality, picks bend if they strike rock. Disgraceful!
> 12 Nov. '15. Persuaded Haji Hassan to come to Wajir with me to look after the Mohamad Zubair. He said he would ask the cattle people, and if they agreed, he would come.

Far more isolated, in the furthest north-east corner of the Protectorate, was the DO with the half-Somali Gurreh, Vincent Glenday, known to the tribes as *Faras Adé*, White Stallion, because he usually rode one as he accompanied his people on their seasonal migrations. On one side were the Marehan, truculent as ever, and on the other, the Abyssinian *shiftas* who had recently killed Captain Aylmer. No company would have insured his life.

150 miles to the south, at Serenli in Jubaland, the DC was Francis Elliott, a tall, thin ex-police officer. He was by way of being a Somali expert, learning the language and lore from an attractive Mohamad Zubair girl. But his mastery of these

The North

matters was incomplete: Llewellin found grievous errors in his tribal genealogies, and on his nocturnal perambulations in disguise round Kismayu, he had been preceded by urchins chanting, 'Here comes the Faranghi who thinks we think he is a Somali.' Like many officers on the frontier, he was infected with 'Somali-itis', being so captivated by their courage, intelligence and panache as to believe in Somali truthfulness and reliability.

His right-hand man in Serenli was the Aulihan Sheikh, Haji Abdurrahman Mursaal, possibly the most trusted and least trustworthy Somali in East Africa. In the past eighteen years he had led war-parties which stormed a British outpost at Yonte and massacred a British column; he had probably plotted Jenner's murder. The Italians warned Elliott, the other chiefs warned Elliott, Llewellin warned Elliott, but Elliott insisted on trusting Abdurrahman Mursaal.

Elliott was supposed to do what could be done to check the raiding and counter-raiding between the Marehan, recent enemies, and the Aulihan, recent allies. He and Abdurrahman Mursaal were friends, but their friendship wore thin under the Somali's exasperated conviction that the Englishman, in his efforts to hold a fair balance, favoured the Marehan.

For most of 1915 the Aulihan caused trouble. In December they raided the Samburu tribe in Meru district, killing men, women and children, capturing slaves and thousands of cattle and chasing off a DO who had the good fortune to be a Cambridge three-miler: 'rather a bad show'. Llewellin waited until the Aulihan had cooled down and then talked the headmen into releasing some Samburu boys who had been taken as slaves.

At the end of January 1916, the northern Aulihan, 300 strong, raided the Marehan, killed nine men and got away with 800 camels. This was the last straw. Formally and publicly Elliott gave Abdurrahman Mursaal three days to pay blood-money and return the stolen stock, failing which Aulihan stock would be seized and he himself imprisoned at Kismayu.

Serenli post was on a small hill overlooking the Juba river. It was surrounded by a thick thorn *boma*, beaten down to knee-high so that attackers could not take cover behind it. The bush was cleared for 200 yards, and there were stone breastworks for riflemen and the Maxim gun. The camels were kept in another *boma* half a mile away. The post, garrisoned by a full company of armed constabulary, should have been secure against any attack which could reasonably be expected. But many of the askaris were allowed to sleep with their families in the nearby bazaar, and Elliott's own house was outside the *boma*. Abdurrahman Mursaal was well informed of all that went on in the post by the Aulihan askaris in the garrison. Two days before issuing his ultimatum Elliott had, with unbelievable over-confidence, accepted Abdurrahman's suggestion that, because the askaris were pestering local women, their rifles should be locked in the armoury at night. 'For', said Elliott, 'we are not at war here.' Somali traders warned Elliott of trouble in the offing, as did the Italian commandant at Bardera, four miles away, but he told them to mind their own business.

Four days after the ultimatum Abdurrahman sent into the camp as a present a black bullock, a black sheep and a black goat. The askaris refused to touch the meat. Elliott's interpreter, Ali Awali, and his warrant officer, Mohamad Egal Effendi, warned him that the gift of black animals was a declaration of war. Said Elliott, 'If you are frightened, you had better go over with your families to the Italian side.' When Mohamad Egal urged that at least the askaris should have their rifles at night, Elliott picked up an egg, dropped it and said, 'Somali plots break up like that. They will do nothing.'

That night Abdurrahman Mursaal assembled 500 men and told them that they were to storm Serenli, 'For by Allah I will not be a slave to the Government.' The outlying piquet were all Aulihan. Their commander, Abdurrahman's brother Abdullahi Mursaal, walked up to the sentry on Elliott's house and asked the time. The sentry turned to look at a clock and Abdullahi shot him through the heart.

At the shot, the Aulihan crouching in the bush rushed for Elliott's house. Holding a hurricane lamp in one hand and a revolver in the other, he peered out of the window, and was hit by a bullet behind the ear. He fell back, but had enough life to shoot the first man who burst through the door. Others dashed in and dispatched him with knives, in the presence of his

The North

mistress who, when it was all over, walked down to Abdurrahman Mursaal's house in the bazaar.*

At the barracks the two sentries on duty were both Aulihan, one being another brother of Abdurrahman, Hussein Mursaal. At the first shot they made for the Maxim gun, shooting the Marehan sergeant who tried to stop them. Mohamad Egal Effendi also tried to reach the gun, but Hussein shot him too. The tribesmen swarmed in, shooting and stabbing the askaris who tried to get to their rifles.

The camel-guard 'marched to the sound of the guns', and courageously engaged overwhelming numbers of enemy in the hideous confusion. They had killed several when Abdurrahman Mursaal grabbed one of them, Dab Asal, and told him to turn the Maxim on them. By one of those displays of heroic loyalty which bewilder all who think they know the Somali, Dab Asal refused until they bent back and broke his little finger. He then fired a short burst, swore the gun had jammed, and proceeded painfully to strip the lock. But the sound of the Maxim in the hands of their enemies persuaded the camel-guard to give up the hopeless fight, and they retreated across the river. That was the end, apart from looting the armoury, cutting the throats of the wounded and mutilating the dead.

The sack of Serenli caused quite a panic. There was the obvious danger that, just when the war in German East Africa was going rather badly, all Somalis in Jubaland and the NFD would join the Mullah in a general rebellion.

Llewellin was with the southern Aulihan, sorting out their raid on the Samburu, when two men on mules, sent by Deck, brought the news.

Deck ordered him to evacuate Wajir, adding,

> Cheero. Best of luck. Don't be particular about carrying away all government property. I should avoid the frequented roads as much as possible.

---

*The Aulihan story is that Elliott killed two men in the doorway and then slammed the door. While they hesitated, no one liking to go in first, a shot was heard from inside. Elliott had committed suicide.

'I'm against evacuation', noted Llewellin in his diary. However, orders are orders, so he made for Wajir as fast as possible.

18 Feb. '16. Haji Hassan has arrived at Wajir, for which I am glad. Quietly told Ali Barreh of the Aulihan trouble.
21 Feb. '16. At Wajir. Haji Hassan in and another long talk. Started sending off the women and the non-milking cattle of the askaris. Showers in the direction of Serenli: 'The Mullah's rain'.

Two days later a letter arrived from Deck. 'Where the hell are you? If you want to keep your job, get back to Wajir and evacuate the place.'

26 Feb. '16. Held two night alarms. Pulled down all the grass huts and built a large thorn zareba outside, enclosing the well. Swore Ali Barreh on Koran to assist the Government with all his power, and to keep out scouts in the direction of the Aulihan.
27 Feb. '16. Swore Iman Mohamad, Habr Suliman, to assist the Government. Aulihan have not enough water-pots for a large force.
6 March '16. Evacuation of Wajir. Handed over the store to Haji Hassan and gave him Rs. 2,000 worth of trade goods to use in assisting the Government and keeping things quiet. Better to do that than destroy them.

Far away to the north-east Glenday received similar orders from Kittermaster, Officer-in-Charge, NFD.

Herewith another wire ordering the evacuation of Wajir. It means you will have to go in too. I would risk the Degodia, but dare not risk the Degodia and Marehan, and I think it quite likely we shall have to face the lot. Try to avoid a *sauve qui peut*. I need not tell you to abandon government stores if you think necessary. You see it is suggested that Llewellin is somewhere near Sankuru. If so, God help little X. [Llewellin's DO].

The North

The expected massacre did not occur. No other tribe joined the Aulihan. Soon enough troops were available to re-occupy Wajir and the Gurreh country.

Llewellin re-entered Wajir with the advanced guard of a military column. 'Haji Hassan opened the gate for me. Occupied my old bedder and office.'

The affair at Serenli was almost the last colonial rebellion in the old style, with the rebels fighting with rifles and spears, and the government forces with much the same weapons as the soldiers of Queen Victoria. Thereafter troops would be supported by planes, armoured cars and motor transport, while 'freedom fighters' were to have at their disposal a far more powerful weapon – liberal opinion in Britain and the United States.

5

Kenya Colony

The East African Protectorate came to an end at midnight on 31 December 1920, and the Colony and Protectorate of Kenya was born.*

The administration was brought up to strength by the direct recruitment of officers from the armed services on twenty-year contracts. Chosen for their war records, some were good, some not so good. These filled the gap before normal recruitment was resumed, under the command of Major Ralph Furse, DSO, Eton and Oxford, who was the Colonial Office talent-spotter for the administrative services of the African colonies, choosing men and putting them through a year's course at Oxford or Cambridge in language, law, administration, surveying, road-making, bridge-building, tropical hygiene and much else. The Colonial Service did not attract the athletic or intellectual cream of the Island Race. Blues were grabbed by the Sudan Political Service (86 out of the 256 recruited between 1901 and 1944). Firsts preferred the Home or Indian Civil Services. C. P. Snow's fictional don said, 'He's thought to stand a chance of the Colonial Service if he can scrape a third.' Actually Furse, who himself achieved a third, was looking for men with good manners, a taste for adventure, who had been prefects at their public schools, had achieved seconds at Oxford, Cambridge, St Andrew's or Trinity College, Dublin, and had run or rowed or played something for their colleges. There were, of course, a handful of firsts, thirds and blues.

*The Protectorate was the ten-mile-wide coastal strip, leased from the Sultan of Zanzibar.

Kenya Colony

It was believed, not least by members of the Kenya administration, that they were of a higher quality than officers of other African colonies because they were kept up to the mark by constant criticism from settlers. Statistics seem to support this view. About thirty officers of the Kenya cadre went on to govern other colonies. The equivalent figure from Nigeria, which had a larger cadre, was nineteen.

The pioneers' cure for African recalcitrance had been, 'Give 'em a good hammering, then let 'em off lightly.' After 1918 a hammering was out of the question, being certain to attract unfavourable attention in Parliament, and fatal to the career prospects of the hammerer. The DC ruled by prestige. Prestige had nothing to do with wearing a dinner jacket or refraining from concubinage with native women. It depended on a general assumption that an order once given could not be disobeyed with impunity. So the first rule for the administrative officer was, 'Your order must be obeyed.' The second was its corollary: 'An order likely to be widely flouted should not be given.'

Indirect rule was honoured more in the training course than in the field. In 1922 DCs were directed to govern through 'native councils of elders' who 'in proportion to their proved worth' would be entrusted with local government responsibility. The Native Authority Amendment Ordinance of 1924 authorized the setting up of Local Native Councils (LNCs), part-elected, part-nominated, which could pass by-laws and levy rates. But twelve years later there were only twenty LNCs in thirty-four native districts. The difficulty was that most elders were ultra-conservative, all for traditional practices such as spear-blooding, stock-theft, female circumcision, twin infanticide and beating witches to death; and stubbornly opposed improvements in agricultural practices. To most DCs indirect rule was all right so long as LNCs did as they were told; but in general it didn't work.

Before the war the DC had used the Kenya Police in his district as his private army, supervising their training, discipline, deployment and patrols. Most of them, being of other tribes, lacked local knowledge; but they were available for escorting him on safari, carrying a message, arresting a malefactor, serving a summons, acting as his personal orderly. After the war this was no longer possible. There was an influx of European inspectors and assistant superintendents who commanded the police. The DC had overall responsibility for law and order; but the police were no longer at his beck and call. By 1930 the Kenya Police had been withdrawn from most native reserves (not from the NFD and Turkana). The DC had at his disposal only a few tribal retainers, armed with spears, but he needed his private army. So from 1929 onwards the tribal retainers were gradually converted into rifle-armed tribal police, composed entirely of local men, some 20–30 in each district, responsible only to the DC. Their forte was local knowledge. They might perhaps have been over-helpful to fellow-clansmen, but they had a wonderful record of loyalty. They regarded the Kenya Police as clumsy, corrupt and locally ignorant; the Kenya Police regarded them as country bumpkins. Every now and then the Commissioner of (Kenya) Police recommended that the tribal police be disbanded, and every PC and DC rallied to its defence.

A tribe would take from a DC they knew what they would never take from a stranger. Yet it was rare for an officer to remain in one district for as much as three years. Those responsible for postings had to take account of suitability for a particular district; leave (6 months after 2½ years); health – no one should be left long in a district riddled with malaria; family commitments – some stations were obviously unsuitable for European women and children. With all these factors to be considered, continuity seemed to have a low priority.

Besides, an officer left too long with one tribe was apt so to identify himself with it as to become not its ruler, but its champion against neighbouring tribes, its spokesman against government policy. He was then said to be suffering from 'Somali-itis' or 'Masai-itis'. There were bitter rows between DCs, each siding with 'his' tribe in disputes over water, grazing, stock-theft, spear-blooding. Many a DC procrastinated in implementing a policy which he thought wrong for his tribe; and some argued the toss. E. R. Shackleton when DO Isiolo became so emotionally involved with the Samburu in their quarrel with the Rendille over watering rights that he challenged the DO Marsabit to a duel, each to be supported by an equal number of moran.

There was a language problem. A cadet arrived with a smattering of the classical Zanzibar Swahili, which hardly anyone inland

Kenya Colony

spoke, but no practice in conversation. There were no language teachers like the Indian *munshi*. For help with his Swahili exams the new arrival must resort to textbooks and a clerk in the office, whose native tongue it was not. Most officers attempted as well a tribal language, but with no textbooks, no proper instruction and too short a time with that tribe. They might pass a simple exam, and be able to converse a little on familiar topics with chiefs and tribal police; but there was hardly one who could, without an interpreter, conduct in a tribal language a *baraza* with its cut-and-thrust of question and answer, petition and complaint, jest, repartee, barracking. He spoke Swahili, they spoke Kikuyu or Nandi or whatever, and the interpreter bridged the gap: the administrator and the administered communicated in a language which was the mother-tongue of neither.

Many officers developed absorbing interests, more or less relevant to the job. Several were keen anthropologists and wrote treatises on tribal customs. R. E. Wainwright was a compulsive builder of low-cost rest-houses, bungalows and courtrooms. H. B. Sharpe was the finest landscape gardener in East Africa, beautifying every *boma* in which he was stationed, and designing public gardens at Nairobi and Entebbe. There were tree-enthusiasts, and dam-enthusiasts.

Some DCs of settled districts adopted European settlers as their tribe, and disputed hotly with their colleagues in African districts over trespass and stock-theft. But most would regard a posting to a settled area as a fate worse than death. Settled districts were increasingly run by farmers and businessmen through elected rural and urban district councils. There was no more need for a DC than there was in Chislehurst. So all he did was provide a target for complaints, hear petty cases of theft by employees and non-payment of wages by employers, and collect tax from farm labourers.

Reading the *East African Standard* officials would find themselves described at settlers' meetings as 'nearly Bolshevik', 'a menace to civilization', 'saturated with democratic and socialistic ideas', 'a menace to the prestige of the white man', 'little autocrats'. There were retorts they could have made, but they might not make them. Nor was the settlers' temper improved by dreadful hardship caused by the collapse of world agricultural prices, successive locust invasions, and the conversion of the currency from rupees to East African shillings. Many were reduced literally to living on maize-meal porridge and such vegetables as they could grow and buck they could shoot.

It was extremely frustrating for settlers to have every facility for criticism but only parish-pump power. From 1920 their elected representatives sat in the Legislative Council but in a minority to the official and nominated members. There were settlers, including Delamere, in the Executive Council (roughly equivalent to a cabinet), but they were appointed, and could be dismissed, by the Governor.

In a formal Declaration by the Colonial Secretary, the Duke of Devonshire, in July 1923, the key and opening sentence read:

> Primarily Kenya is an African territory, and His Majesty's Government think it necessary definitely to record their considered opinion that the interests of the African natives must be paramount and that if, and when, those interests and the interests of the immigrant races should conflict, the former should prevail.

The European, Indian and Arab interests must be safe-guarded, and there would be no drastic reversal of past policies on settlement.

> But in the administration of Kenya His Majesty's Government consider themselves as exercising a trust on behalf of the African population, and they are unable to delegate or share that trust, the object of which may be defined as the protection and advancement of the native races.

In other words, there would be no self-governing white dominion which was the aim of the settler leaders.

Naturally the settlers were furious at what they saw as a betrayal, and by a *Conservative* government. Bloody government! Bloody officials!

After the war, with many farms gone back to bush, the settlers were in desperate need of labour. So there was issued in October 1919 Labour Circular Number 1 which instructed DCs to apply, through chiefs and headmen, every possible persuasion to young men to work on farms. It was issued over the signature of the Chief Native Commissioner, John Ainsworth, and ordered precisely the measures which he, as PC, had refused to take ten years earlier.

It was assailed by the settlers for not authorizing compulsion, by the liberal lobby in the United Kingdom as compelling blacks to work for whites. (Actually the only legal *compulsion* on Africans was under the Native Authority Ordinance of 1912, to work up to six days a quarter on communal labour benefiting the whole tribe in his own reserve.) DCs in 'labour producing districts' were ordered again and again to persuade Africans to work on farms; and again and again the government denied there was any compulsion. Inevitably the distinction between persuasion and compulsion became blurred. The missions on one hand, the settlers on the other, denounced any DC who used too much, or not enough, pressure.

The settler in the early 1920s had, as even the missions admitted, some case for getting Africans to work for him; otherwise the country would never get going. But his case was spoilt by a few psychopaths who hated blacks and gave the Kenya settler a reputation which he did not deserve. Nor was it improved by the antics of the tiny but conspicuous 'Happy Valley Set' – drink and drugs, sodomy and wife-swapping – which still fascinate some of the British media to the exclusion of all else in Kenya.

The DCs or DOs started work soon after dawn with a walk or ride round the *boma* to have a look at the tribal police on parade, see that the station hands and detainees were usefully employed and that the place was reasonably clean. After breakfast there might be accounts to check, a monthly report to write, a case of stock-theft or grievous bodily harm to try; and people to see the DC – a chief with some problem, a settler to complain of stock-theft, a Protestant missionary to complain of the Catholics, or a Catholic of the Protestants. By far the most time-consuming work consisted of *shauris*, a portmanteau term comprising complaints, petitions, reviewing native tribunal cases, hearing appeals against the decision of the Appeal Tribunal. One might spend hours unravelling a dispute about three goats two generations ago.

The DC presided over meetings of the local native council, and in backward districts was probably its secretary and treasurer too.

Committees proliferated: a DC by 1940 might have to preside over a dozen a week on education, agriculture, sports, health. In the evening one played some game, went shooting guinea-fowl for the pot, took a ride or walk to work up a thirst for the evening beer, and perhaps worked on a language.

The monotony of this life was relieved by safari, perhaps four or five days every second week. In the 1920s this was always on foot or on horse- or mule-back, baggage carried by porters, donkeys or camels. In the 1930s safaris by car or lorry became more common, a gain in speed and convenience, an immense loss in contact with the tribesmen. There would be *barazas* called to reprove, to commend, or to explain some government order. There might be road-gangs to visit and pay; a case to be heard on the actual scene of the crime, which gave one an understanding denied to the learned judge. There would certainly be work in connection with tax- and rate-collection, either collecting oneself or seeing that the chiefs did so. Registers had to be checked for tax-defaulters, and claims for exemption heard from cripples, war wounded, geriatrics. Jack Clive was once confronted by a pathetic old man, clothed in a sack, who could barely hobble up to him. With a few words of sympathy he wrote out a permanent tax exemption certificate, whereupon the ancient drew himself up to attention, saluted smartly and marched off like a guardsman. Clive joined in the roar of laughter and let him get away with it.

Bush dispensaries, schools, the premises of licensed hides and skins traders all had to be inspected. In wilder districts the people might ask to be relieved of a rogue buffalo, or a cattle-killing lion.

Every DC was painfully aware that there was no money for many necessary purposes. Many thought that their Africans were getting remarkably little for the taxes they paid. The DC Kitui gave evidence before the East Africa Commission in 1925: 'If we left the district tomorrow, the only permanent evidence of our occupation would be the buildings we have erected for our tax-collecting staff.'

In many districts the only healthy account was the goat bag, so called because it originated from the sale of the skins of ration goats consumed by road gangs and such. The Treasury had not spotted this minor source of revenue, so the DC hung on to it, adding unofficial fines, profits from the *boma* vegetable garden,

Kenya Colony

etc. The money was spent on miscellaneous items for which the government would not pay, such as prizes for school sports, an ox slaughtered for *Id-ul-Fitr* or Christmas. One DC built a medical ward and dispensary from his goat bag. It got a DC Narok out of serious difficulties. A random bullet from a hunting party a mile and a half away killed a Masai woman. Her husband claimed compensation, but the person who fired the bullet could not be identified, and in no way would the government accept responsibility. So compensation was paid from the goat bag. Auditors must have known of the goat bag: everyone else did. But they tactfully pretended ignorance.

Boma life was not all sweetness and light. H. E. Lambert writes:

> Some DCs were certainly high-handed, and some of their wives quite royal, so that other wives not infrequently formed an underground opposition, ventilating grievances at innumerable tea-parties ... Then there was the lady who was reputed to have bought a motor-cycle, wherewith to carry her built-in creature comforts to officers in her husband's district. 'Christmas cheer' she called it, though the season was immaterial. The husband was said to have had his innings terminated by a cricket-ball in his middle stump ... Clashes and frustrations were everyday affairs. DOs suffered the Secretariat, the judges, departmental officers, missionaries, settlers and stray anthropologists. We were a long-suffering service. Some of the conflicts were sickening, even heart-breaking, but on the whole we were a happy lot during those middle years.

Happy, no doubt; and busy too – but peering through the fog of detail one asks, 'What was the administration trying to achieve?' and 'What was the object of the exercise?'

In Hall's day the object had been clear: to suppress the slave-trade and facilitate the passage of supplies by caravan and rail between the coast and Uganda. This required a measure of law and order, achieved by diplomacy and force of arms, which became the DC's chief concern. In the early 1900s the tax collection became a DC's basic duty. Then the influx of white settlers made it necessary for the administration to hold a balance between their interest and those of the Africans, though neither would admit that a balance was being held.

By the 1920s the principle of taxation had been accepted, and its collection was no more than a time-consuming chore. With the end of native risings and tribal wars, the maintenance of law and order was reduced to little more than discouraging stock-theft and spear-blooding. The settler-native balance had still to be held; and 'civilization' promoted in the form of education, medical services and roads to open up the country for trade. A new object, growing in importance, was to educate Africans in running their own affairs on more or less European lines, through LNCs and native tribunals. Throughout, a DC must get to know his district and his people.

'Surely,' asks the puzzled modern student of colonialism, 'some attempt must have been made to improve the African's lifestyle by putting in water supplies, teaching better agriculture and animal husbandry, and by checking the soil erosion which was becoming devastatingly apparent?' The answer is, 'Very little', for such measures require money, and between the wars the world slump and the insistence of His Majesty's Government that every colony be self-supporting ensured that there was no money whatsoever for economic development.

One concludes that between the early pioneer and the post-1945 DC whose main concern, after law and order, was economic development, the administration did little more than keep the country ticking over as quietly and cheaply as possible. (From these generalizations must be excepted the NFD, a place apart.)

The DC's greatest difficulty was increasing rejection by Africans, especially the educated, of the tribal authority through which he was enjoined to practise indirect rule and guide Africans towards citizenship as interpreted by the British upper middle class. This was particularly apparent among the Kikuyu, the most educated tribe which brooded most on its grievances. In the early 1920s the Kikuyu produced an articulate opposition politician, Harry Thuku, who caused so much trouble to the administration that he was deported to Kismayu in 1922 after forming the East African Association, the first of a series of Kikuyu political associations.

6

The Sophisticates

Opposition politicians flexed their muscles in the Mwichuki land case at Fort Hall in 1926. Chief Mwichuki owned a *githaka*, a hereditary holding, of some 120 acres in which several hundred people were living and cultivating without his permission. He wished to evict twenty families. The native tribunal heard the case on 4 February 1926. It being a *cause célèbre*, wrote the DC, every member of the *kiama* was present, 'representing every grade in Kikuyu society from mission-trained natives and teachers to chiefs and elders'. They decided unanimously that the squatters should be evicted and their huts burned if they were not removed. (The poles and thatch of a hut could easily be moved and re-erected elsewhere. If it were burned, the hut could be rebuilt in two or three days at the cost of a few shillings.)

The DC, R. G. Stone, supported the *kiama*. So did the PC. The Chief Native Commissioner (CNC), G. V. Maxwell, a new arrival from the Pacific Islands, ordered Stone to proceed with the eviction. But although given ample time to remove themselves and their belongings to friends and relatives half a mile away, the illegal squatters stayed put. Their ringleader was Douglas Mwangi, considered by the administration to be a regular trouble-maker and an associate of Harry Thuku.

The DO Kangema, Major C. E. V. Buxton, MC, was not a man to defy. A somewhat flamboyant extrovert, tall and imposing, heavily handsome with a long jaw and a florid complexion, a Cambridge rowing blue, son of a baronet and possessed of ample private means, Clarence Buxton had a mind of his own and was never one to shirk responsibility. During his service he figured frequently in the news pages of the *East African Standard*, and after his retirement was seldom absent from its correspondence columns. There was no way in which Buxton, with only half a dozen unarmed tribal retainers, could physically move the trespassers; but they could be made to move themselves by burning down their huts. So acting on Stone's orders, on 10 February, after giving final notice, after Douglas Mwangi, breathing vengeance, had taken his people off to houses and shambas which he owned nearby, and after satisfying himself that the huts were empty, Buxton fired the first hut himself and the tribal retainers fired the remainder.

Promptly Douglas Mwangi hurried down to Nairobi and briefed a smart European lawyer, J. Hopley, who claimed 15,227 shillings on account of damages to his clients 'burned out of their houses by the district officer's illegal action', and threatened to sue Buxton in person for it.

To the dismay of the men on the spot, Maxwell and Northcote (Chief Secretary) would not back them. This was seen as very shocking, for though Maxwell was a blow-in from the Pacific, Northcote had twenty years' experience of Africa.

Stone wrote of his interview with Maxwell:

> I very nearly asked to resign on the spot, but a couple of gins and sodas cooled me down.

Hopley was making great play of his poor, aged clients wanting only a place where they could live in peace. 'What he wants', wrote Stone after meeting him, 'is to make his name as a natives' lawyer' (which could be a gold-mine in Nairobi with the Kikuyu taking to litigation like ducks to water).

Stone was prepared, he told Buxton on 12 June, to

> stand up in Court and be shot at, without much confidence in receiving support from headquarters. Do you not think that if a scapegoat *can* be found, he *will* be found? Not much sympathy will be extended to one who has got the government into a mess.

The Sophisticates

To Stone's and Buxton's indignation, Maxwell formally condemned the hut-burning as 'an ill-considered action which I am not prepared to defend', and Douglas Mwangi was offered compensation. Fortunately he refused the offer, hoping for more, and Hopley dropped the matter. But pro-government Kikuyu were left with the feeling that they had been let down, and that even *githakas* were not safe. 'The Kikuyu', wrote Stone, 'have a right to know whether their most cherished institutions are to remain the academic sport of the Bench and the Bar.'

During the war Jack Clive had joined up under-age, lost an arm and risen to be lieutenant-colonel. He was posted as DO to Fort Hall shortly after this case. Scenically and climatically it was a lovely district. The streams, recently stocked, held enormous rainbow trout. He got on extremely well with Stone:

> I caught much of Rodney's enthusiasm for road-grading with an Abney level and nothing provides a pleasanter memory than wading through head-high bracken, sometimes being confronted by a sheer rock wall and having to retrace one's steps a mile or more to achieve a respectable grade, and then the gangs of Kikuyu working cheerfully on the new alignment and the noisy dance when the task was finished.

Stone had humanitarian objections to women crushing sugarcane in hollow logs to make beer for men, and encouraged the purchase of hand-operated sugar-mills. These proved a sound investment for the discriminating purchaser who did nothing but watch customers turn the handle to crush their own cane, and then collect fees from them. Soon there were more than sixty mills in the district, and drunkenness reached hitherto unknown levels. So Stone's successor, S. H. La Fontaine, got the LNC to ban mills, compensating the owners.

> [Clive] had the unpleasant task of dismantling the mills, not without difficulty as the owners hid the spanners, and in an atmosphere of sulky silence. One large mob was truculent and Chief Muraya said to me, 'What would you do if we killed you for this theft?' I replied, 'Obviously nothing, but you'd have a lot of trouble from the police and KAR!'

An early DC had said of the Kikuyu, 'A noisy and excited crowd is seldom dangerous, but when they are silent and sullen it is well to have a care.'

The Mwichuki land case had been a storm in a tea-cup. The row about female circumcision was not. To be accurate, it is not circumcision, but an operation to the private parts of pubescent girls. Among the Kikuyu, Embu and Meru it consists of the excision of the clitoris, the labia minor and part of the labia major, with neither anaesthetic nor precautions against septicaemia. Performed ceremonially and in public, it is a major event in a girl's life, her initiation into adulthood, and is deeply embedded in Kikuyu tradition.

The Protestant, but not the Catholic, missions were loud in denouncing a practice which was excruciatingly painful and dangerous, increased the perils and pain of childbirth, and was thoroughly un-Christian. They refused Communion to those who practised it, and sacked from mission schools teachers who would not abjure the abomination. As a result, by 1929 they had lost 90 per cent of their converts and excommunicated most of the remainder. A handful of Christian elders supported the missions, but the overwhelming majority of the Kikuyu, Embu and Meru, Christian and pagan, conservative and radical, were united in opposition which was orchestrated by the Kikuyu Central Association (KCA) of which the Secretary General was an up-and-coming politician known variously as Johnson Kamau, John Kenyatta and Jomo Kenyatta.

It was the Kikuyu belief that an uncircumcised girl could not conceive or, if she did, must procure an abortion, since her child would be regarded with horror. Was it not obvious, said the propagandists of the KCA, that the white man's object in attacking a custom which everyone knew to be right was to reduce the Kikuyu birth-rate and population so that he could steal what was left of Kikuyu land?

The missions expected support from the government, and protested vigorously when they did not get it, denouncing DCs as reactionary and incompetent. But most DCs believed that a ban, if not openly flouted, would merely drive the custom underground. Anyway, what business was it of the missions? 'Elders hold as

The Sophisticates

tenaciously as missionaries to many mediaeval beliefs.' Through education and some pressure on LNCs, it should be possible to weaken support for this barbarity. In 1930 a gang of young men forcibly circumcised a middle-aged female missionary, from which she died.

Embu escaped the worst of the trouble. Its DC was H. E. Lambert, known always as 'H.E.', a quiet, staid man, somewhat hypochondriacal, who never indulged in tough foot safaris and was always (by Kenya standards) formally dressed in coat, slacks and tie. He was the last of a series of gifted amateur anthropologists in the administration, and had a rare understanding of Africans.

He saw the Kikuyu point of view. On what grounds could missionaries accept the circumcision of boys but not of girls? Christ was circumcised because it was the Jewish tribal custom: uncircumcised, he could not be a Jew. It was the Kikuyu/Embu/Meru tribal custom that girls be circumcised. Teachers and pupils sacked from mission schools on this issue enjoyed posing as martyrs, and the elders greatly resented ignorant children being incited to defy tribal custom.

All right-thinking persons will regard with horror the mutilation at its worst. But would it not be possible to ameliorate the custom into harmlessness while leaving the tribe intact?

His aim was to persuade the tribe to accept as valid a partial circumcision involving the excision of the clitoris and a small cut on the labia minor, to be carried out before a girl was likely to become pregnant and to be pressurized to have an abortion. Lambert found no difficulty in discussing these matters with the LNC: 'the native appears to be much more familiar with the construction of the parts than does the average European'.

Early in 1933 he was transferred to Meru where the row had made the population sulky and resentful. Witchcraft was rife, and secret societies very powerful. The number of abortions on uncircumcised girls was a scandal. The traditional government of the Meru was by Njuris, councils of self-selected leaders and busy-bodies of all age-grades. There was a grand council, the

Njuri Ncheke, for the whole tribe. Horne and his successors had disapproved of Njuris as secret societies dabbling in necromancy. But Lambert, the anthropologist, saw the Njuri Ncheke as a possible ally against less commendable Meru traditions.

He took his time, occasionally making favourable mention of Njuris in conversation, then at *barazas*. The Meru took note. He consulted individual Njuri members confidentially on tribal custom, secret societies, witchcraft. Finally he raised with the Njuri Ncheke the delicate matter of female circumcision and coaxed them into agreeing to the modifications introduced in Embu. He even got the old ladies who performed the operation to attend refresher courses at the hospital on how to do it hygienically.

The row over female circumcision died down as missions drew back from the brink. But the controversy had two momentous consequences. Hitherto African education had been provided mainly by the missions, possibly as ground-bait for converts, with financial help from the government. But in 1929 teachers leaving or expelled from the mission schools with their pupils formed the Kikuyu Independent Schools Association (KISA), which was to be closely linked to Jomo Kenyatta's Kikuyu Central Association and a hotbed of disaffection. Similarly all-African churches broke away from the missions and set up in rivalry, professing Christianity with polygamy and female circumcision as attractive extras.

Even at the height of the trouble, the Meru were nowhere near a state of rebellion. The Kenya Police having withdrawn from the district, Lambert had only a few unarmed tribal retainers to lend muscle to his wishes. When a mad bull ran berserk through the place, the DO, T. C. Colchester, had great difficulty in procuring a rifle with which to despatch it. Eventually one was found, very old and rusty, at the back of the store, among hoes, axes, wheelbarrows and posts for the high jump at the school sports. In a district supposed to be seething with discontent, the DC's *force de frappe* consisted of Tom Colchester and one rusty rifle.

In Embu and Meru necromancy was ubiquitous; and on this, as on much else, Lambert held unorthodox views, pointing out that it took some sixteen centuries to eliminate a belief in it from our own legal system. It was inappropriate to deal with it through the

The Sophisticates

Witchcraft Ordinance because it was seldom possible to produce evidence which would satisfy the Supreme Court.

But a native curse is an evil thing, a prayer to the powers of darkness to do evil to an enemy. The African recognises it as evil and his own system ordains a method of redress which the perpetrator finds painfully expensive.

So in Meru wizards were generally charged before native tribunals, some two hundred a year; they were fined, and made to pay compensation to their victims. Really serious cases, endangering whole communities, were traditionally punishable with death. One day Colchester saw a group of Njuri elders, carrying wands and with white chalk-marks on their faces, who came

> chanting up to the DC's office and announced that they had brought an unusually evil witchdoctor in for justice. They added that he might by then be dead. They had brought him about ten miles, his relatives laying on the first blows, followed by a mass stoning and beating. Near the boma he collapsed and died . . . The district was very much the DC's preserve, with no rival authorities in the shape of a Resident Magistrate or a Kenya Police station . . . No more was heard of it, not even from missionaries.

Lambert's predecessor in Meru, J. G. Hopkins, was a small, sharp-eyed man who looked as though he was planning to sell you something. His colleagues thought him too clever by half. He was the only DC to educate his children entirely from the profits of elephant-hunting. He hunted both inside his own district on control and outside it on licence. The tusks of elephants shot on control, however large, had to be handed in to the government. The tusks of elephants shot on licence belonged to the shooter. As DC, Meru, Hopkins shot a huge tusker on control in his district. But it was within yards of a cairn marking the district boundary, so he wrote himself a cheque, issued himself with a licence and moved the cairn, thus starting a dispute between Meru and Isiolo districts which was still unresolved thirty years later. He aimed to produce in Meru a polo-team which could compete with the settlers' teams in Nanyuki. Hearing that there was in Embu a young DO called Colchester, who rode at only 11 stone and had captained Cambridge at polo, he shanghaied him to Meru. Actually Colchester's blue was for water-polo, but in Meru he none the less had to play ordinary polo, on a pony sold him on advantageous terms by his DC. The pony won some races, and Hopkins tried to buy it back. No deal. One of his ploys was the manufacture of copper ashtrays with a silver Maria Theresa dollar inset, which he sold to his friends. His problem was to obtain the copper. In the NFD, water on safari was carried in 10-gallon copper baramils, which eventually wore out and had to be returned to store in Nairobi. Hopkins, counting on nobody in the Audit Department knowing exactly what a baramil was, ingeniously wrote one off as 'eaten by a lion'. It sufficed for many ashtrays. Despite his idiosyncracies, he was a good DC of the practical sort – not given to anthropological theorizing, but sound on roads, buildings, taxation, law and order; and respected by the tribesmen who liked a 'character'. As PC Rift Valley Province he got on well with settlers, who on his retirement elected him to the Legislative Council where he generally took a strong anti-government line.

7

The Unsophisticates

For a pleasant, undemanding district one could hardly do better than Baringo in Kerio Province, inhabited mainly by Tugen and Suk, related to the Nandi, with a few Njemps, related to the Masai. The original *boma* had been hot and malarial, but a red-headed Titan of immense energy and resource, E. B. ('John Willie') Hosking, had dismantled the cedar-wood houses and offices and transported everything, even the office safe, on hundreds of donkeys and porters up 3,500 feet to a site called Kabarnet, delightfully cool and healthy, on the roof-ridge of the Kamassia escarpment.

Five years later J. W. E. Wightman was DC. The Tugen regarded the Government as a nuisance about which they could do nothing. They accepted with resignation the increase in hut tax from 5 to 8 rupees, while protesting, 'You're a very greedy young man. Can't you settle for 6?' When he started some experimental plots of maize and sweet potatoes they assumed that in some way all this hustle and bustle was to his advantage.

Then, in 1921, came the currency conversion from rupees to shillings, part of the operation being to call in all the silver rupees in Kenya in exchange for florin (2-shilling) notes. Wightman was apprehensive lest the tribesmen regard it as sharp practice. On the contrary, they were delighted. On the appointed day they came in hundreds, the more affluent burdening their wives with tins full of silver rupees, and departing happily with little pieces of paper. There was quite a carnival atmosphere, and Wightman was gratified by their confidence in his integrity. It was his interpreter who disillusioned him: they saw the whole transaction as a sign that the white men were on their way out, taking with them all the country's silver.

R. T. Lambert's first posting was to Machakos in 1925.

I became very attached to the Kamba who appealed to me for their cheerfulness and sense of humour. I often travelled with porters, on foot, and I enjoyed their marching songs.

The *furor Africanus* could overcome the mildest European, a sudden rage at some gross misdemeanour by an African. It overcame Lambert.

The DC, Fazan, had sent me off to organize a display of Kamba arts and crafts . . . When I arrived at the appointed place there was no one about; so I got hold of a drum which my interpreter proceeded to beat furiously. Eventually the chief arrived, blind-drunk. I was so angry that I got the interpreter to put him down and give him six on the bottom. The result was that his location put on the best show in Machakos the following day. [Fazan got word of this and was naturally rather cross.] I offered to make amends and he suggested £5 as a suitable sop to the chief. I handed him this but he refused it. I might easily have got the sack for beating a gazetted chief, but no more was heard of it.

J. M. Silvester, one of the 1913 intake, was a great man for the Kamba, fluent in their language. On safari the porters with their headloads carried on pads of banana-leaves sang as they marched, one half answering the other half. Silvester and his wife translated hymns into Swahili and Kamba and sang these, while the men beat time on water-tins. Their little daughter travelled on a 'monowheel', a sort of chair running on a single bicycle wheel, with handles fore and aft, by which one porter pulled and the other pushed.

In his diary for 3 August 1927, we read for the first time of development in Ukambani:

The Unsophisticates

Had a long meeting from 9.30 a.m. to noon. Fourteen location headmen attended. We discussed the Estimates for 1928, particularly the use of shs 20,000. The suggestions ranged from boarding fees for their children to attend Machakos School; to dams to catch floodwater in the rains; to the planting of trees to stop erosion on the steep and rocky hills. The land suffers from large herds of cattle and goats, and timber cutting by the women for cooking fires. Promised free boxes of tree seedlings from the Forest Station. The seedlings must be closely watched and protected by cages made of saplings and ropes of tree-bark. Thus we hope to save the young trees from goats and women and locusts, with luck!

Silvester caused 2,500 acres of bare hilltops to be planted with young trees and closed to livestock, to check erosion where it started. The Kamba, like all peasants, regarded trees with aversion, but thirty years later Silvester's hilltops were well forested. In 1930 he drove in a T-model Ford to see the first borehole in the district being sunk, to water both cattle and his trees.

The PC was W. G. Campbell whose trademark was his hat worn a-tilt, whence he was known to Africans as 'Kichwa kombo' which means either 'wrong-headed' or 'head on one side'. He was a hard citizen, standing no opposition from anyone. He was also, some thought, a bit of a bounder. When he left the province he raffled his car, and required DOs to flog tickets to Africans. But in his will 'Kombo' Campbell left £20,000 to the Kitui Local Native Council.

He used to go out on tax safaris, like any DO. Well, perhaps not quite like any DO.

A blanket was spread on the ground and each taxpayer threw his money, usually in coppers, uncounted, onto it. There was only one count, in the evening. If there was any shortfall, the chief made it up. Result – no shortfall.

In contrast to the DC's and DO's busy life in an African reserve was the triviality of his work in a settled area. K. L. Hunter went straight from the South African army in German East Africa to be DO in Eldoret. His DC was a nice old gentleman who greeted him reproachfully, 'You are very young, and not likely to be much of a companion to me as I'm rather fond of my liquor.' That was an understatement. He was pickled in alcohol, but indestructible. Hunter became rather fond of the old boy.

The Eldoret streets were all dust in the dry weather, glutinous mud in the rains, churned up by the Boer farmers' ox-wagons. One wet day Hunter pointed out to his chief that he was wearing only one gum-boot. 'Why, bless my soul! So I am. I must have lost it in the mud. Would you mind finding it for me, my boy?'

Another loss was more serious. After a heavy night at the club, the DC vomited down the pit-latrine and lost his false teeth. 'See what you can do about it, my boy.' So help was summoned, a rope was lowered and the teeth found, and the DC inserted them happily next day.

Ken Hunter's next job was DO in West Suk, stationed at Kacheliba. The district, arid and covered with thorn-scrub, teemed with wild animals. In response to an SOS from a road-gang which was being teased by a leopard, Hunter went out with two police askaris armed with rifles, and two tribal retainers with spears. The leopard was located in long grass.

> My eyes met those of the leopard crouching about 6 yards away. The animal sprang and by some lucky instinct I dropped onto all fours and he landed on my back. During the moment or two he was on me, I felt with one hand the soft fur of his belly. Whilst the leopard was thus poised, both police askaris fired and missed. The leopard then took a good purchase on my shoulder and sprang at the Tribal Retainer who was just behind me. In a flash the Tribal Retainer had the whole of his scalp torn away which hung over his face, and the leopard departed. I returned the scalp as one would a cap and we hastened to the boma. We had no doctor, so I removed the scalp and bathed the skull with copper sulphate until the bleeding ceased, and then returned the scalp and sewed it in place with needle and thread. In less than a month the man was back on duty.

The Unsophisticates

When on a foot safari along the Turkwell river I saw a lot of vultures circling and heard bellowing. On investigating, I found an elephant flat on the ground in labour. I watched for a couple of hours until the calf was born and the mother rose to clean it up, and immediately the vultures descended on the afterbirth. The babe could not stand when I left to set up camp, but on returning in the evening I found that mother and calf had departed.

In 1926 the DO, West Suk, was Gerald Reece, who was older than most cadets. Twice wounded in France, he had toiled five years in a London solicitor's office before joining the administration in 1925. He was six and a half feet high, with a small (but far from empty) head and long shanks which covered ground at an amazing speed. He was to become the archetypal frontiersman, impervious to privation and fatigue; but a stomach-wound compelled him to eat very slowly, and caused him pain on safari. The houses at Kacheliba were built on top of great volcanic rocks, to catch the air, but the rocks were hot as hell. The flies, wind and white ants, which destroyed timber, clothes, shoes, made him 'want to sit down and cry'. So did much else about Kacheliba.

In the whole of Kerio Province there is no doctor, and not one qualified chemist to dispense drugs. Every native pays shs 12 a year in tax. Our allowance for medicines is less than 4 cents per native. I have learned to give an intra-muscular injection of bismuth for yaws, and at present there are 17 yaws patients in hospital. Now we are told that this must cease because the government cannot afford to feed in-patients. If, therefore, a man travels 100 miles to ask the white man to cure his ulcer, his [tax] having been extracted from him, he must be sent back to die, or perish by the roadside. And he will remember while the vultures are pecking out his eyeballs how much the white man, his 'trustee', is bearing his burden.

The Turkana, north of the Suk, are the hardest tribe in East Africa. Emaciated as John the Baptist, naked except for ostrich plumes, ivory balls suspended from the lower lip and other embellishments, they live in barren desert west of Lake Rudolf. To survive, they *had* to raid their neighbours. No one else wanted their country, and if they would leave other people alone, they too would be left alone; but they wouldn't, and they became more aggressive as they acquired rifles. From 1912 onwards a series of small military operations had been directed against them; but when their skin-and-bones cattle, sheep and camels were taken as a punishment for raiding, they raided to get more. Most of their rifles were taken from them; but by disarming them, the British implicitly became responsible for protecting them against the Merille, naked savages with hundreds of rifles who lived just across the Abyssinian border. The British by intervening had upset the balance of tribal power. Until 1925 the Turkana were under military rule, but in that year the civil took over, with Glenday DC at Lodwar, Reece and R. T. Lambert at Kolossia.

Kolossia was a dreadful place, but the heaviest cross Reece had to bear was the Kenya Police detachment. It was regarded as a punishment station, and most of the askaris were bad characters. Three joined in a Turkana raid on the Suk; and Reece on safari was brought an agitated message from the district clerk that a constable had shot dead a corporal in a quarrel over a woman, and disappeared with a rifle and 140 rounds of ammunition. The clerk and a pensioned Nubian sergeant-major who kept a shop in Kolossia had broken open the strong room to get more ammunition, and posted double sentries, but 'could not trust any police askaris since this mischief'.

To restore discipline Reece over-reacted, and was reproved by Glenday.

> Impetuosity never did any good in administration. The iron discipline of the soldier is alright for trained forces, but don't base your administration on it. [As for the flogging Reece had ordered], don't try it on with Somalis whatever you do. And for God's sake don't worry and think that everyone is trying to get at you because you are a junior officer.

Because the transport animals were dying in a drought, the *boma* was moved to the Turkwell valley where tsetse fly decimated them.

The Unsophisticates

Lambert saw his 'poor mule covered with fly like a swarm of bees. She died shortly afterwards.'

Encroachments from Turkana eastward into Samburu could no more be stopped than a flood tide. The Governor, Sir Edward Grigg, held a *baraza* at which he told the Turkana very forcibly that this must stop, and every tribe must remain in its own country. The Turkana spokesman said that this was an excellent idea, and would His Excellency please start with the white tribe?

Lambert's unhappy successor at Kolossia was A. C. Mullins who complained incessantly to his diary of his mud hut with holes in the walls serving for doors and windows, the earth floor, the branch-and-stick roof covered with mud. There were no cupboards, shelves, bookcases. All his possessions had to be kept in suitcases and boxes which were stood on stones because of white ants. There was no butter, eggs, fruit, vegetables, only goat and tinned food. It was impossible to eat, read or write in evenings made miserable by moths and flying beetles and ants in thousands, scorpions, centipedes, anopheles mosquitoes and flies. His office was covered in sand deposited by dust-devils, with paper flying in all directions.

Fifty miles back along the Kitale road was R. Pedraza, the DO, West Suk. 'We hate each other about as thoroughly as our respective tribes.' But his Turkana tribal retainers were 'a wonderful body of men'.

Shackleton, the would-be duellist, while DO in northern Turkana disappeared from Nairobi ken and was eventually found in the Omo delta at the north end of Lake Rudolf where he established a camp across the border to administer the savage Merille. The fact that they lived in Abyssinia did not in the least deter him: their raids were the bane of northern Turkana, and it was obviously sensible to tackle the problem at its root. The Merille rather liked being administered, but he was moved, and confined henceforth to districts where an eye could be kept on him.

At Kapenguria the DC was G. B. Rimington, MC, ex-Royal Canadian Mounted Police and Royal Dragoons, who was a genius at taming wild animals. He acquired a giraffe, an ostrich and a chimpanzee, all of a malleable age and great friends. He taught the ostrich to pull a light buggy in which he went spinning down the road to Kitale. The chimpanzee, Katalina, was extremely intelligent and a great show-off, delighting in her tricks such as riding a tricycle.

His neighbour in Turkana was W. H. Hale. Their tribes being at enmity, they arranged a joint *baraza* at which Katalina showed an unwholesome interest in the magnificent penises of the Turkana and Suk which, while their owners sat on little wooden stool-pillows, hung to the ground. Rimington gave them fair warning, and tribal enmities dissolved in ribald laughter and fear of Katalina's attentions. Up and down the district trekked Willie Hale, plodding along in front of his camels and adding to his collection of game trophies and photographs. One month he would be holding joint *barazas* with DCs in Uganda and Sudan, sorting our claims and counter-claims over stock-theft and spear-blooding; the next, in the deep south. When in Lodwar he used to dig holes in the river-bed and enjoy warm medicinal mud-baths.

The Kenya Police in Turkana were not allowed to bring their families, so a corps of temporary wives was stationed in Lodwar, handed over from one detachment to the next. It was expected of them that they remain faithful to their temporary husbands, and when one strayed from the path of virtue, the chief wife sentenced her to be chastised by her husband for exactly one minute, with the open hand. The punishment was carried out in public, the lady making an awful hullabaloo as her injured spouse cuffed away. When it was over, Hale thought she might need medical attention. He found her sitting on the ground cooking her husband's meal, and she gave him a brilliant smile.

'Are you all right?' he asked anxiously.

'Fine,' she replied.

The Samburu, the Turkana's eastern neighbours, whose country stretched from Isiolo north-west to Lake Rudolf, resembled the Masai in language, appearance, customs and age-grade systems, though they were less Laibon-ridden, and had more bottom. In a time of drought they had been allowed to occupy Leroghi, an empty, well-grassed plateau north of Laikipia, which the settlers thought had been promised to them, and called 'The Promised Land'. Moreover the Laikipia settlers were plagued by Samburu

The Unsophisticates

moran stealing cattle and 'spear-blooding'. The morans' usual victims were Kikuyu employed by Laikipia ranchers. In the early 1930s the Il Kileko age-grade was nearing the end of its moran service and eager to prove itself before putting aside its barbaric finery, shearing its long hair and settling down to marriage and respectability.

Theodore Powys was manager of Il Pinguan, an enormous ranch in northern Laikipia. One morning in October 1931, he rode off alone to look for grazing for a flock of ewes. Four hours later his pony came trotting back without him, not alarmed, the reins still on her neck. Two days later a search party discovered his remains, scattered by vultures. There were indications, plain to good trackers, that the pony had suddenly propped. There was a place where a lion had been lying, and a lion's hair was found in the congealed blood on his shirt. It seemed that he had been eaten by a lion after falling off when his pony propped at seeing or smelling the beast. It was strange that his head was missing; and his trousers, bloody but not torn, the belt and fly-buttons still done up, had been pulled off him. The inside of his trousers was not fouled by the contents of his stomach. But there was no reasonable doubt that a lion was to blame.

Some weeks later a man called Kibirenge, who lived in the Samburu reserve in the manyatta of Chief Lekopen, told a strange story to a rancher named Cunningham. Some weeks earlier six moran, each carrying two spears*, came to Chief Lekopen and said, 'We have killed a white man. Here are his head and testicles as proof.'

Lekopen swore them to secrecy. 'Now show your trophies to the girls, who will bury them. And the bravest of you can have my daughter.' He then caught sight of Kibirenge and exclaimed, 'We are all dead men. This Kibirenge has seen and heard.'

Nearby lived the only practising Samburu Laibon, a powerful wizard with woolly white hair and pale eyes, greatly feared. On his advice Kibirenge was given five cows as hush-money.

Nevertheless at Rumuruti police station he made a statement naming six moran.

*Moran with peaceful intent carry only one.

Men Who Ruled Kenya

I heard one tell Lekopen, 'We came upon the white man while he was riding. He dismounted to look at our kipandes.* Lesotia speared him in the ribs and Lolobiala in the side. Lesoipa also speared him, in the back. The rest of us rubbed our spears in the blood, took our trophies and came on home.

Kibirenge's story explained the absence of the head; the state of the trousers, pulled off by someone unfamiliar with belt and buttons; the pony's calmness (she would have been terrified by a lion); and the reins lying on the pony's neck. A fresh investigation was made, by the C.I.D.

The personalities of the DC, Thomson's Falls, who administered Laikipia, and the DC, Isiolo, in charge of the Samburu, were important factors. 'Daddy' Cornell at Isiolo was a shy man, more at home among primitive tribesmen than with his own race. He greatly preferred the Samburu to any settler. Trafford at Thomson's Falls was a rare bird, a DC who disliked Africans, and accused Cornell of inciting the Samburu. At a meeting of the Morris-Carter Land Commission they had actually come to blows about their boundary, and had to be separated by Sir William Morris, who said that of all the sights he saw in Africa, this was the most remarkable. Between these two little cooperation could be expected.

The only result of the CID investigation was the discovery, three weeks after his death, of Powys's skull, a thousand yards from his remains. A lion which carries away, and deposits almost intact, his victim's skull is an unusual animal. But Kibirenge failed to pick out some of the alleged murderers at an identification parade. An inquest found that Powys had died from a broken neck caused by falling off when his pony shied at a lion. Kibirenge pleaded guilty to a charge of giving false evidence and was imprisoned for five months. When he came out, he disappeared and was never seen again.

In November 1933, two years after Powys died, the question was raised again by Gilbert Colville, an old-established settler who employed many Samburu and spoke their language. In

*Kipande: an identity card.

The Unsophisticates

official circles he had the reputation of being rude, but too often right.

He said, loud and often, that every Samburu knew that Powys had been murdered by moran of the Lorogishu clan. They had revived the old 'Barangoi' dance, used in the past to celebrate some notable feat of spear-blooding, and were singing a new song, 'The vultures of Il Pinguan are dropping on the beloved of Nairobi'. In this dancing and singing the Lorogishu moran and girls became excited and hysterical.

Colville was allowed to interview in prison a moran, Lekada, held on an unrelated charge. He confirmed Colville's story of the Barangoi dance and song. When he was released because of lack of evidence, Cornell had him brought to Isiolo to be given, without trial, a sound thrashing for causing trouble. One could not get away with that sort of thing in the 1930s, and Cornell was rusticated to Moyale.

Yet another investigation was held. The Laibon was deported and Chief Lekopen came clean, confirming Kibirenge's story. Five Lorogishu moran were charged with the murder, of whom one turned King's Evidence, adding one new piece to the jigsaw: it was on the Laibon's instructions that they had taken Powys's head back to Il Pinguan, lest it be found in the Samburu reserve.

The five were brought to trial in Nakuru. Two more moran turned King's Evidence. Four girls, lovers of the accused, admitted with giggles that they had joined in the Barangoi dance and the Song of the Vultures. Nevertheless there were, three years after the event, discrepancies in the evidence which the learned judge concluded had 'fallen just short of that degree of certainty which would warrant a conviction'.

So the five moran went free, and the Laikipia ranchers raged at a cover-up. Spear-blooding increased to over fifty cases in four years. The Samburu were transferred from the NFD to the Rift Valley Province, to be more closely administered by a DC at Rumuruti, a DO stationed on Leroghi and a punitive police levy force living at free quarters among them.

The first DC of the new dispensation was George Brown, 'Hammer of the Samburu'. His régime was very tough and was intended to be. The morans' spears were confiscated. Any found wearing long red hair, a symbol of moranhood, was forcibly shaved; moran uppishness was corrected by the kiboko. Hundreds of cattle were taken in fines and to feed the levy force. There was no more spear-blooding; but although hundreds of Samburu must have known who had blooded their spears, none were convicted. Eventually, however, the wicked Il Kileko age-grade ceased to be moran and became respectable married men. The Samburu became a tribe approved by almost everyone, except neighbours whose cattle they continued to steal.

Brown was succeeded by a more emollient DC, Sharpe. He was a genius at landscape gardening, and a fairly discreet homosexual. His DO at Maralal was C. F. Atkins, described as 'a BNC rowing tough'. At Rumuruti, with irrigation furrows from a rippling trout-stream and unlimited labour provided by jailed stock-thieves, 'Sharpie' created one of his most beautiful gardens. In Maralal he made another garden round the DO's mud-and-wattle house, with the cedar-forest above and behind, and the great Leroghi plains rolling away in front and below. He brought up a gipsy caravan as his guest-house, and had dug at the bottom of the garden a 'deep drop' from which the occupant could gaze down on the backs of elephants and buffalo. Generally he lived in Rumuruti, but from time to time he and Atkins would change places. Atkins liked the change, girls and tennis and dances. But there was a reckoning, for Sharpie at Maralal used to invite for long and luxurious safaris his friends of the Happy Valley set – Lord Errol who was exuberantly heterosexual, Fabian Wallace who wasn't, Lady Idina Whatever-her-latest-name-might-be, and others of that coterie. They would have the whale of a time with plant-collecting, gin, fun and games, and Sharpie would hold an occasional *baraza* to justify his safari, make notes on shauris that needed settling and hand them over to Atkins to settle. He charged the heavy cost of these jaunts to the Maralal travelling account, so there was no money left for the DO to hire traders' lorries. Atkins would have to walk for a week, thinking unkind thoughts about his chief, to settle some minor dispute, where in a lorry he could have done the return journey in a day. One of Sharpie's respectable safaris was with Elspeth Huxley, plant-collecting in the Matthews Range. Her special attendant was

The Unsophisticates

a strikingly handsome, helpful, friendly TP. 'That,' said Sharpie, 'is one of the moran charged with the Powys murder.' As for Chief Lekopen, his career prospered. When I knew him twenty years later, he was President of the Samburu District Court, and owed a massive cirrhosis of the liver to his genial habit of refreshing himself after his judicial labours with a daily bottle of sweet sherry for his luncheon.

It was a district of extraordinary contrasts. The heavily forested mountains rose to 10,000 feet above sea level, the shores of Lake Rudolf were at 1,200 feet, an inferno of dark brown lava. But this glorious pastoral country was being ruined by over-grazing. When K. M. Cowley was DO there in 1938 it was estimated that the cattle population was 300,000, plus uncountable millions of 'shoats'* far more than the land should carry.

In the NFD there were no cattle inoculations. The administration banned them because natural wastage was the best way of keeping down stock numbers, and with a nomadic population and a 700-mile frontier, an inoculation campaign would be ineffective.

Looking down from Meru over the empty wastes to the north, H. E. Lambert agreed with the NFD policy:

> Destocking is clearly necessary, but were we wise to let science destroy that very healthful thing, disease? The majority of the stock are not actually owned in the individual sense by the man who is ordered to produce it for sale. [He is a sort of trustee for the real owners] He cannot dispose of them in any way whatever, and it is his duty to prevent their seizure. To take them by force is tantamount to the commandeering of entailed estates. As destocking is necessary, it has to be done by some outside agency – rinderpest, or a policeman. If it is done by rinderpest, that is the will of God, and the return of the hides, horns and tail will settle the matter. But if it is done by a policeman, it is an act of war (not mitigated by the payment of money). And it is we who stop the rinderpest and send the policeman.

*Shoats. A convenient term for mixed flocks of sheep and goats.

But in Kenya proper the policy was to eliminate rinderpest, by inoculation; so when Samburu was transferred to the enlightened Rift Valley Province, a livestock officer was soon at work with needle and syringe. It was decided to hold a cattle-count, to see how overstocked Samburu really was, and whether a compulsory cull would be necessary.

Every animal had to be roped, thrown and branded as it was counted. Cowley spent seven months on the job, living in a tent, growing a magnificent red beard, mane and moustachios: *Cavalleria Rusticana*. He personally branded, on the cheek so as not to spoil the hide, over 100,000 cattle, a skill in which Sir Ralph Furse had omitted to instruct him. He, the livestock officer and their team of Turkana labourers became extremely agile at dodging when the outraged steers were released. Cowley went on leave when the cattle count topped 450,000, and was nowhere near finished. A start was made on culling 8 per cent of the 54,000 cattle on Leroghi. But the opposition to the cull became so obstinate and potentially violent that the government called it off.

The order to cull might have been one of those which should never have been given. But yielding to opposition ensured that when a cull was next attempted, in the 1950s, the erosion was much worse and the opposition much harder to overcome – the classic consequence of loss of prestige.

8

Gold-diggers, Rustlers and Wizards

Charles Atkins' first post, in 1930, was as DO Kakamega, in the district of North Kavirondo in Nyanza Province. It was an 'advanced' district, thickly populated by the tribe known then to Europeans as Bantu Kavirondo, to themselves as Baluhya. The climate was equable with just enough rain to keep the country green; the soil was fertile. There were innumerable missions, competing in unchristian rivalry. The DC was a wooden-legged war veteran, Lieutenant Colonel E. L. B. Anderson.

One morning there came into Atkins's office, waiting to see the DC, a tall gangling American who plonked onto the table a quinine bottle full of sparkling sand and told Atkins that it was gold which he had panned from a local river. This was the start of the Kakamega Gold Rush.

It came at an opportune time. Kenya's economy and the settlers' morale were battered by drought, locusts, the collapse of commodity prices. Settlers piled into battered pick-ups with wives and children, tent and kitchen equipment, sacks of flour, potatoes, sugar, posho, picks and shovels and iron basins, with a couple of farm hands perched on top, and set off to peg claims. Few made much money, but they weren't making any money by farming.

Most miners panned for alluvial gold, choosing places where it might be held up by a rock bar across the river; or drilled with an auger a hole about twelve feet deep, extracting samples which were crushed with pestle and mortar. If the result looked promising, a trench was dug and the sand or gravel put through improvised sluice-boxes to separate the particles of gold.

Anderson presided over the unfamiliar scene with calm and urbanity. Kakamega boomed with shops, two banks and four hotels, all surrounded by a mushroom township of tents and huts. There was nothing of the Wild West in it. Bachelors might enliven the Corkscrew Inn on Saturday nights, but the knowledge that Noel Kennaway, DO and magistrate, was a Black Belt judo expert put a damper on the roughest parties. In the firefly-lit evenings a tune on a gramophone, the click of Mah-Jong pieces, the quiet bidding of a bridge four, gave the diggings a domesticated, suburban character. There was even – epitome of suburbia – a wife-swapping set.

In 1929 the Native Lands Trust Ordinance had set aside a reserve for the sole benefit of the Baluhya, 'forever'. Miners, therefore, had to lease the land required for their diggings, on terms laid down by Anderson, a compromise between the miners who thought they should pay only compensation for the loss of crops, and the Baluhya who thought that mining constituted criminal damage to their land. The appointment of a DO as Mines Warden, with responsibility for sorting out disputes, eased the tension. But until they saw that when the gold was exhausted they actually got their *shambas* back, the natives suspected that it was all a trick to steal their land.

The gold rush brought a spin-off in leases, wages, buyers for fresh vegetables, fruit, eggs, chickens. By 1935 Ken Cowley found the district humming with agricultural development. The LNC even employed, and paid from its own funds, a European agricultural officer.

The missions were as active against each other as against the world, the flesh and the devil. Cowley had to settle a holy war.

> The Salvation Army band, in which the location chief, 6 ft 5 in, banged the big drum, was marching round and round the church of the Friends of Africa Mission in which the American minister was trying to preach. I, aged 23, arranged a peace conference between these men of God, at which it was agreed that neither should operate within half a mile of a church or school belonging to the other.

Gold-diggers, Rustlers and Wizards

The Nandi and Kipsigis tribes, living in the highlands of Nyanza Province, were under the baneful influence of their Orkoiyots, generally known by Europeans as Laibons. When 'John Willie' Hosking was DC Nandi, the district was terrorized by a family of Laibons and the chiefs, headmen and all the people begged him to let them exterminate the family. A Laibon did not have to use threats to obtain anything he wanted: women, food or cattle.

One man, who had objected to the Laibon Suter arap Yator walking off with his shoes, drowned himself in a shallow pool in sheer dread of reprisals. But of what crime had arap Yator been guilty, other than being arap Yator? Hosking wrote: 'I applied for his deportation as a menace to the peace of the tribe. The case was heard by a Supreme Court judge in Chambers. The interpreter said, "He pleads Guilty." What he actually said was – I know enough of the local dialect – "Can I help it? It is in my head."'

In the late 1920s the Nandi, who were inclined to be troublesome but not objectionable, were both. Ken Hunter found the moran* truculent and provocative, by day strutting round with their long-bladed war spears and big painted shields, making the nights hideous with their dancing and drumming. There was more stock-theft than ever before and the elders made no attempt to stop it. For this Hunter blamed the influence of the Laibon, Barserion arap Manyi, who was son of the Laibon Meinertzhagen had killed. He was a talented propagandist. The white men, he explained, had built a railway in order to flee the country, but were frustrated when the line could go no further than Lake Victoria. Now they were tunnelling under the earth to make their escape. If anyone doubted this, let him go to Kakamega and he would actually *see* the tunnel, indeed he could help dig it. When they had gone, the Nandi would resume possession of Uasin Gishu and all the white men's cattle. They could start possessing the white men's cattle now, and he would provide them with magical protection.

---

*A misnomer: moran is a Masai/Samburu term. The warrior age-grade in the Nandi are properly called Maina. But non-Nandi generally called them moran, so let it stand.

Hunter wanted Barserion deported but the PC, Cecil Dobbs, by now a wily veteran, suggested that the government's prestige would be better served by keeping him at home and making him behave himself. So the Laibon was ordered to take up residence in Kapsabet *boma*, by day never out of sight of the DC's office, and at night under curfew. Law and order improved. Other wizards Hunter extracted from their forest lairs and made them live beside busy highways, each with a notice outside his house specifying, like a doctor's brass plate, his name and magical powers. Witchcraft which had survived persecution wilted under ridicule.

The Masai were thought to be tricky largely because they had never been made to do anything they did not like. The moran system kept the tribe permanently on a war-footing, with a standing army trained for war but with no fighting to do. Naturally they kept their hand in by stock-theft.

Clarence Buxton, DC Narok in 1935, thought it would do the moran no harm to pay taxes, and a lot of good to earn money by working on roads. He had a strong personality, and managed to persuade some three hundred moran to make a road which would benefit their tribe.

The officer-in-charge,* S. H. Fazan, visited them at work.

> They did not have the demeanour of enthusiasts filled with patriotic fervour for the development of their reserve. A few looked mildly amused, some sheepish and doubtful, some sullen and some nervous. I left somewhat uneasy in mind.

Three factors upset the moran. They had been told to leave their spears behind, and this they resented, for the moran's 'white' long-bladed war-spear was not only a weapon but a status-symbol. They were just about to undergo the *eunoto* ceremony which was the beginning of the end of their moranhood and disposed them to have a final fling. And Buxton brought a laibon to the road camp, both to conduct the ceremony and to exhort the moran to carry on with the good work. Fazan wrote afterwards,

---

*Masai was an Extra-Provincial District, with DCs at Narok and Kajiado, and an officer-in-charge at Ngong.

Gold-diggers, Rustlers and Wizards

The Laibons are not part of the government machinery, and I think it bad policy to call them in when they may be useful and send them away when they are not. [It] cuts across the organization of chiefs.

In order to keep an eye on the road gang Buxton set up camp nearby, with his wife and daughter. In the early morning of 25 June he heard shouting from the direction of the road and rode over to see what it was about. He encountered about a hundred moran, armed with clubs, swords and a few spears, running towards him with shouts and threats. He could detect, he afterwards said, 'no trace of homo sapiens, no light or sense of reason', but an expression of 'demoniacal, insensate fury'. Masai moran working themselves up for battle foam at the mouth and jump up and down quivering like a bowstring. They raised their weapons, and one flourished his sword over Buxton's head.

Swinging round his horse, Buxton galloped back to camp and sent off his wife and daughter in the car. He fired into the air with his shotgun, but the moran came on. He had with him two askaris of the Kenya Police and five of his tribal police, all with rifles. When the moran were a hundred yards off, he ordered a volley and four fell, two dead and two wounded. The remainder dispersed and soon most of them were back at work as though nothing had happened.

The affair petered out in prosecutions for riot and an inquest which found that the firing was justified. Fazan had 'nothing but admiration for the promptitude, firmness and judgement with which Major Buxton had dealt with a very ugly situation', while criticising various misjudgements which had produced that situation. Some of Buxton's colleagues were not so complimentary. He was the only DC between 1917 and 1950 who had to open fire on 'his' own tribe.

Fazan ordered that moran were not to be employed in large numbers on road-work, and then only as drivers of ox-drawn scoops and graders; so the problem of occupying them remained. In football some took a languid interest, and they quite enjoyed running and jumping in the stadium Buxton built at Narok; but all they really wanted to do was to steal cattle; pleasure the unmarried girls; and hang about looking picturesque with their long-bladed spears, braided red locks and shining, lean, muscled bodies – an occupation which became quite profitable as camera-carrying tourists multiplied. If a lion started killing their cattle, they were more likely to send for the game warden than deal with the lion as their fathers would have done.

Buxton was a good DC, at a time when there was no money to spend but his own. As Fazan reported, he 'breathed life' into a district paralysed by the great depression. He got in all the tax, no mean feat; and he got the moran in a better frame of mind so that some enlisted in the tribal police. He dented stock-theft by making it less profitable.

There were two breakthroughs in Buxton's time. The first was that the Masai started spending their own money (and they were very rich in livestock) on water supplies, and even doing the hard work of making small dams and water-tanks. The second was that after long and patient lobbying they agreed to their cattle being inoculated against rinderpest and foot-and-mouth. At first it seemed that this boded nothing but good; but in the long run this could be disastrous, not only for the Masai but through all the African savannah country from the Atlantic to the Indian Ocean. The devoted labour of hundreds of vets made it almost impossible for any animal to die except of old age or starvation, resulting in over-grazing, terrible soil erosion and the steady advance southward of the Sahara.

Buxton's prospects of a governorship ended in the divorce court when an injured husband cited him as co-respondent, alleging misconduct in the Nairobi Game Park. Buxton's denial – 'In the *Game Park*, me Lud? Preposterous! Too many ticks' – failed to convince the judge or the Governor, and he was transferred under a cloud to Palestine. He resigned after two years and bought a farm near Nairobi.

DCs Narok and Kajiado seemed to alternate between those who tried to entice the Masai into the twentieth century and those who became more Masai than the Masai. Among the latter was one of the administration's stars, E. H. Windley, who added to his talents the advantage of ample private means and a wife with royal connections. He spent six years in the two Masai districts and

Gold-diggers, Rustlers and Wizards

spoke the language well. He heard one remarkable case of alleged rape. The accused moran denied penetration. Windley translated from the Masai:

'Yes you did', said the complainant.
'No, I didn't.'
'You did. You went in *this* far,' and she grabbed the offending member.
'Not as far as that.'
'Further,' and she changed her grip.

Windley hastily adjourned the case, lest there be a repeat performance in the courtroom.

Adjacent to the Masai, and at enmity with them, were the Kipsigis (or Lumbwa), just as good cattle-rustlers and much better men. But in the early 1930s they behaved abominably. Here, too, the trouble was the Laibon-moran combination. The DC Kericho was Brumage, a South African of the 'no-nonsense' school of administrators. The DO, R. Armitage, was not much impressed with Kericho.

> The natives are completely under the thumb of the Laibons whose power is due to witchcraft alone, without use of poisons. A man denounced by a Laibon can get no one to do anything for him ... We cannot appoint a new chief, as we cannot find anyone who is not under Laibon influence. The moran obey nobody and set on anyone who obeys the government.

There was a terrific increase in crime in 1932-3, but by the end of 1933, noted the Annual Report, 'the ramifications of the Laibon organization were uncovered. So long as a single Laibon remains, there will be no amelioration'.

Brumage was not the man to put up with this. He persuaded the authorities to pass a Laibons Removal Ordinance which would enable them to be deported to another district, where their magical powers would be at a discount. There were delays before the ordinance was passed, and administrative difficulties in receiving the Laibons in Kisii district. It took a year to get rid of the twelve worst families, during which Brumage sorted out the Kipsigis by methods which he described as 'Blood and Iron'. (Fortunately the Laibons put their trust in magic, not in European lawyers.) But the Laibons were still busy plotting, directing the cattle-raids and casting spells, when Jack Clive took over the district, and 'had to take on the job of school-bully, which I dislike'.

Six young Laibons murdered a farmer and raped his wife near Naivasha. In due course they were sentenced to be hanged. The Laibons spread word that the hangings would not take place, as the government feared their supernatural powers, and the six would return to the tribe. This was generally believed. So I obtained permission to take six of the leading Laibons and six members of the LNC to Nairobi, as I thought to witness the hangings. This was not allowed, but my party saw the bodies in the pit afterwards. I thought that this would have a considerable effect, and when it was over I said to Chief arap Roronya, 'Well, are you satisfied that *they* won't return?' He beamed all over his face and said, 'Yes, they are dead. And now we want to see the Railway Workshops and the Standard Printing Press.'

In 1936–7 Clive managed to get rid of the remaining ninety-three Laibon families, and the whole atmosphere of the district changed.

With a dozen officials in the *boma*, tea-planters nearby and farmers at Sotik, Kericho did not lack social life, and Clive was heart and soul of it. He took on all comers at tennis, showing amazing dexterity in throwing the ball high with his stump to serve. He came from a theatrical family, had a great repertoire of music-hall songs, and could always bang out on the piano an appropriate tune for his light, topical verse. 'Your DC is a bit of a hearty,' said a visiting DO from the Gold Coast, with prim disapproval. But Sir Philip Mitchell, who governed Kenya from 1946 to 1952 after long service in Uganda and Tanganyika, said that Clive was the best DC he had ever known.

He found the Kipsigis moran an alternative to stock-theft in

Gold-diggers, Rustlers and Wizards

athletics. They were perfectly built for running and jumping, light, long in the leg, with a physique and lungs developed by a balanced diet, in a malaria-free area, at 6,000 or 7,000 feet above sea-level. He promoted district sports, built a stadium from the goat bag, and got the moran, who had latent competitive spirit, really keen. The next generation won medals at the Olympic Games.

The Kipsigis were a happy people in the late 1930s, freed from the tyranny of the Laibons. They were very healthy, their women were handsome and fertile, they were not averse to schooling, spoke the prettiest language in East Africa, and had no inferiority complex *vis-à-vis* Masai, Europeans or anyone else. They took to horses and made rather a corner in grooms' and jockeys' jobs; some became quite good polo players. They had enough rain and a rich soil. There was no pressure on land. Because they had taken only recently to agriculture, and their heart was really in stock-raising, bad farming habits had not become ossified into immutable tribal traditions. Many had worked on Boers' farms, learning from these experts the use of ploughs and work-oxen. By 1937 there were several hundred ox-drawn ploughs in the district. Since work with oxen was regarded as men's work, while cultivation with the hoe was women's work, the increase in ploughing shared the work burden more fairly between the sexes than among the Kikuyu. Of course the moran continued to steal cattle, but without malice or spear-blooding. Clive called them 'the gentlemen robbers of East Africa'.

Nandi and Kipsigis made the best athletes; Luo, Baluhya, Kikuyu and Kamba the best footballers. Organized sport was a point of contact between the public schoolboys of the administration and young, educated Africans, otherwise so difficult to approach. At first the competitive spirit was tribal; but Tom Colchester, who as Nairobi Municipal African Affairs Officer was much involved in sport, believes it gave Africans their first awareness of a Kenyan identity.

I took the Kenya football team to Kampala, where we won for the first time, and I shall never forget how all through the night on the way back to Nairobi, hundreds of people turned out at each station, and thousands met us in Nairobi.

Men Who Ruled Kenya

R. G. Turnbull, when Governor of Tanganyika, was asked by Denis Healey, 'Tell me, Sir Richard, what are the enduring legacies which Britain will leave to Africa?'

'Association football', replied His Excellency, 'and the expression "F*** off!"'

Interest in sport did not end with British rule. John Butter, an officer of the administration at the time of independence, got the Nairobi African élite playing golf. Punctually at 4.30 – indeed rather before 4.30 – ministers and permanent secretaries might be seen leaving their offices, leaping into their Mercedes and roaring off to the golf course.

9

Sloth Belt

The Coast Province was Kenya's depressed area, sunk in lethargy, starved of funds, staff and hope. 'It is sad,' wrote the DC Malindi in 1924, 'to see a man rotten with syphilis, inert with leprosy and in agony with yaws, and to be able only to advise him to walk to Mombasa for treatment.' The problems of the coast, said the Native Affairs Report for 1923, were 'inveterate apathy and ineradicable improvidence'. It was extremely unhealthy. Those who served on the coast in the 1920s would have been flabbergasted to see, forty years later, the places where they had sweated and shivered and vomited with malaria, crammed with package tourists from Europe, keenly enjoying the 'Sun, Sand and Sex' guaranteed or implied by their travel agents.

These delights were not apparent to Charles Atkins at Kipini, headquarters of the Lower Tana district, as on his evening stroll he passed the graves of five of his predecessors, of whom one had shot himself, 'which gave food for thought'. But Kipini had one asset, a steam launch in which he chugged up and down the Tana river visiting the villages of the Pokomo tribe.

The S.L. *Tana* was steel-hulled, flat-bottomed and about 40 feet in length. The boiler was fuelled with logs which were cut and stacked at the villages. The African staff sat on the lower deck, where my cook heated his pots on the boiler fire. The forward part had a canopy beneath which were table, chair, bookcase and gun-rack where the DC sat in comfort. In front and at a lower level was the bridge, where stood the quarter-master at a large steering wheel, with an engine telegraph and binnacle facing him, all the brass being highly polished. Nights were spent on shore, in a mosquito-netted cage, so that one could eat, drink and sleep protected against mosquitoes, sausage-flies and other insects which would otherwise be attracted by the Tilley lamp to drown themselves in the soup.

Atkins learned the Pokomo language from a German grammar compiled by a Lutheran missionary who was an ardent Nazi and on whom he had to keep an eye. The Nazi was the only person qualified to examine him, and Atkins passed. 'I never spoke the language since.'

The most attractive coast station was Lamu. The DC's house had in the 1930s no electricity or piped water, a multitude of bats, wide verandas and huge, airy rooms separated by curtained doorless arches, with intricately carved wooden shutters to the windows. The DC, usually a bachelor, roosted in one corner of it. The remainder was occupied by his launch crew, by the *boma* carpenter, and by whole families claiming squatters' rights by virtue of their descent from the Sheikh's slaves.

The DC's right-hand man was the Liwali, the Muslim judge. Since the inhabitants were nearly all Muslims and lived by the Sharia, he did most of the magisterial work. It is difficult to see how a DC and a DO found enough to do. But 'Daddy' Cornell, who regarded Lamu as a sort of eventide home, found that even two or three hours' work a day was an intolerable burden. He therefore ordained that all petitions, complaints, etc, must be submitted in writing. He then had made four official stamps: *Shauri la Liwali* (the Liwali's business), *Shauri la Police* (Police business), *Shauri la Mungu* (God's business) and *Shauri lako* (your own business). With these he was able to get through his work in *much* less time.

Most officers posted to Lamu were bachelors, either on the eve of retirement, or youngsters in charge of their first district. A surprising choice of DO was that of Major Gregory Smith, recently married to a widow with three children. He came into the administration in 1930, older than most cadets but by no means through the back door – Black Watch, ADC to the Viceroy of India

Sloth Belt

and to the Governor of Southern Rhodesia. He might have been an intimidating subordinate, but not for his DC, Shirley Victor Cooke.

For Gregory Smith's step-children there were lessons in the morning, a rest in the afternoon, then a walk with lots to see and smell. The dhows, built without nails, held together by wooden pegs and leather thongs, came bowling in before the monsoon, horns blowing, reeking of dried shark. It was said that the slave trade still flourished: the dhow captains would inveigle Africans aboard, make them drunk and then weigh anchor for Arabia.

Cooke and his PC, H. R. Montgomery (brother and uninhibited critic of the future field marshal), were both Irish, both men of decided and generally opposite opinions. Cooke had the more vitriolic pen, but Montgomery the bigger clout. So in May 1930 Clive was summoned to the PC's office in Mombasa and told to go straight to Lamu and take over. He pointed out that the monsoon was blowing great guns, no dhows were putting to sea, the telegraph line had been broken by elephants, the post could not get through and there was no way of warning Cooke that he was coming. Montgomery replied, 'Can't help that – don't mind a man calling me a swine – but when he calls me a bloody swine, he's for it.' So Clive arrived at Lamu, and Cooke left. (To complete the Cooke saga, he resigned from the administration and went into politics. Despite his reputation as being unduly pro-African, he was elected to the Legislative Council, time and again, by the European voters on the coast. As a parliamentarian he was often inspired, but rarely predictable, except in siding always with the underdog.)

The populace, having little else to do, used to send anonymous complaints to the Governor about the DC. Clive was never accused of anything worse than sodomy, but a petition demanded the removal of the Liwali for raping a lady and then making off with her shoes. This missive was returned to the DC for comment. He showed it to the Liwali, who shook with laughter. 'Who can say, if it were thirty years ago? But look at me now!'

Lamu had no great crime problem, but one day a fisherman was found dead with a fearful spear-wound in his groin. Two other fishermen, known to be on bad terms with the victim, were arrested. Their story was that the three of them had found a huge fish in a trap. Finding itself surrounded, it had backed into the deceased and killed him. Clive went to the fish trap and there found a sting-ray, eight foot long, with a ten inch sting at the end of its whip-like tail. The 'murderer' was hanged publicly on a tree outside his house.

The Gregory Smith family were bathing one day,

> all bobbing about in the sea, when a strange European was sighted. Gregory waded ashore to greet him and soon discovered that they had both been at Rugby. Thus we met John Athelstan Cheese. Jack Clive nicknamed him Saint Ivel, and he was the nearest thing to a saint that any of us ever met.

The son of a wealthy family, he had come out as a missionary many years earlier, and was so taken by Somalis that he determined to live only for and with them. Lamu was his base, to which he returned from time to time. Otherwise he wandered about Jubaland, Ethiopia and the NFD, living always with Somalis and telling them of Jesus Christ. He translated into Somali the New Testament and *Pilgrim's Progress*, undeterred by the fact that there were in Africa probably not a dozen Somali Christians. 'He had a small beard and a rather beautiful face, like many pictures of Jesus.'

There were three other European non-officials, all characters out of Somerset Maughan. Charles Whitton, 'Coconut Charlie', had lived there for sixteen years, and what he didn't know about Lamu wasn't knowledge. 'Pioneer Percy' Petley lived in another coconut plantation. He and his partner, Robert Milne, from time to time set off up the Tana on dubious trading expeditions. Nobody quite knew what they bought and sold, but there was always a market for, and a supply of, poached elephant tusks and rhino horns. They were great favourites with the Gregory Smith family, with whom they usually lunched on their return from a venture to the interior. There was then much winking and nodding, and veiled references (*pas devant les enfants*) to glamorous Somali women.

Sloth Belt

There was a smallpox epidemic. Everyone had to be vaccinated and a medical officer, Alan Howell, arrived to supervise. Clive wrote:

> The Lamu ladies would not be vaccinated by a man, so Jane* took on the job. We looked through the window and saw a squirming, wailing mob of local lovelies with Jane, dead white in the face with suppressed rage and about half the size of most of them, handling them in a way which would have made a Gauleiter look like a pansy. She did 2,000 of them in two days.
>
> It was a time for all good men to come to the aid of the state, and from the adjacent district of Garissa there arrived the DC, Sharpe, torn from his landscape gardening, with his fat butler, offering to vaccinate the border village of Shella. Each person's dose of vaccine was contained in a little glass tube. The procedure was to break the end off the tube, scratch the patient's arm with a needle and blow the vaccine in three blobs onto the scratches.
>
> After a while Sharpie found he could get only two blobs out of his tubes, and asked the butler, 'Are you getting three blobs, Abdi?'
> 'Yessah'
> 'How do you do it?'
> 'If there is not enough for three, I spit the rest.'
>
> In the absence of a DC at Kipini, Clive had to see to the vaccinations there too, and hoped that the Nazi Lutheran missionaries would help with the Pokomo. The *Herrenvolk*, however, barricaded themselves in their house and refused even to help with the station staff, so the responsibility fell on the district clerk, Haji Bilal bin Khamis.
>
> Alan and I went to Kipini where Haji Bilal bustled out of his office, grinning all over his face. I introduced him to Alan who asked if he had vaccinated everybody.

*Clive's wife

'Yes, sir, they are all done, very well done. The needles got blunt and didn't bite at all, so I used this.' He produced from a pocket of his somewhat soiled jacket the office penknife, whetted to a razor-edge.

This shook Alan who said, 'I suppose you didn't put it through a flame, between patients, by any chance?'

'Oh no, sir. That would have been foolhardy. It would have spoilt the edge.'

A. D. Swann was posted first to Kwale district, a little inland from Mombasa. The *boma* was in the Simba hills, 3,000 ft, nice and cool. The rest of the district was nasty and hot.

In the coastal strip everyone suffered from hookworm and every deficiency disease known to man, and they lived mainly on cassava.

Because of hookworm, they had to dig pit-latrines. That was fine so long as you weren't on a coral outcrop. Trying to dig a pit-latrine in coral was beyond belief.

Even when they were dug, people did not like using them. Years before, H. E. Lambert had commented sadly in his annual report on the labour wasted on these 'bottomless pits'.

Excellent coconut and cashew nuts could be grown, for which there was a ready market. But to Swann's distress it was ordained in Nairobi

> that perennial crops were bad for character and physique, and they must grow annual crops. They were made to put in cotton, which was a total disaster. I could not help feeling (being very young and ignorant) that they were far happier with their coconuts and cashew nuts, which thrived with very little effort on their part.

Inland was low-grade cattle and goat country, inhabited by the Duruma tribe. Swann did eighteen months there, and got sodden with suppressed malaria, before being transferred to Nyeri.

Sloth Belt

R. E. Wainwright arrived at Kilifi at an inopportune moment when his DC, Douglas McKean, having been dilatory in tax collection, had been ordered by the PC to go out on safari and stay out until all the tax had been collected. So Wainwright's first three weeks in Kenya were spent in charge of the *boma* with a rudimentary knowledge of classical Swahili and not the slightest idea of what cheques and payment vouchers to sign, and money to be counted. There seemed to be prisoners of some sort, tax-defaulters, he gathered, and miscreants sentenced by the native tribunal for adultery, whom he watched cut grass and firewood, brush dust forward and backward, and throw gravel into potholes in the roads. He inspected the tribal police who guarded them, though they had not the slightest wish to escape. He listened, through an interpreter, to innumerable complaints and petitions, and did his best to satisfy the complainants and petitioners.

Eventually his DC arrived and took him out on safari to show him the ropes.

> Showing the ropes consisted of telling me dirty stories of which he had an unbelievably large and funny repertoire. He was a most forbidding figure with grey hair, heavy black eyebrows and a huge hooked nose. In fact he was the kindest person – too kind, really, to be a good DC.

Wainwright next had to build rest-houses, using communal labour:

> They would go into the forest and cut poles and thin withies, and bark from certain trees to use instead of string and nails, and grass for thatching. The hut would have two main poles planted into the ground with Y-tops, and a ridge-pole to fit into the Ys. Vertical poles would be driven into the ground for walls, and the whole building built up into a sort of basket-like shell with withies tied horizontally onto the upright and the space in between filled with mud and finally plastered with cowdung. This made a hard, smooth surface surprisingly resistant to the weather.

As Third Class Magistrate he had to try a case of rape. The accused admitted meeting the complainant on a forest path. When she made eyes at him, he propositioned her, and they agreed on a fee of one shilling, which she earned then and there. But she was, he said, '*Si tamu sana*' (not so very delicious), so he took back his shilling. Young Wainwright was in a legal and moral dilemma. Clearly the man was in breach of a contract, but to give the girl the shilling would encourage prostitution. 'So I took five shillings off the man for the Goat Bag, and sent the girl away with a scolding.' Robin Wainwright was to go far in the service.

He was transferred to Nairobi after a very bad attack of malaria.

10

Half-Term

As a junior DO in Nairobi Wainwright spent much time settling disputes between 'memsahibs' and servants. Bad employers got bad servants, so one could believe neither. We kept a secret Black Book of the former. The one who started by saying, 'Young man, I've been thirty years in this country, and never had a complaint against me before', usually had four stars after her name.

It was a relief to move to Machakos where his DC, Bailward, told him to start by building his own house, a schoolboy's dream.

Cedar posts were cemented into the ground; wire netting was tacked to the posts; hessian was sewn lightly onto the wire. Then a paste of one sand, one cement, was brushed thickly onto the wire and hessian. When this was dry, a plaster of one cement, three sand, was put on. The wall was very strong.

The district was grossly overstocked, and soil erosion was appalling. An expert from South Africa recommended that each location be restored to fertility by removing from it for several years all the people and all the cattle. He then collected his fee and hurriedly departed.

Bailward was told to get on with it. The first location to have a stock census was found to be capable of holding 4,500 cattle, and to be actually holding 17,000. The elders were given the invidious task of deciding whose cattle must be sold, and were bound by the most solemn oath to be fair. Naturally they nominated as sellers those

Kamba who were furthest away, mainly KAR and police askaris, who hollered blue murder, as did their officers. Soon there was total non-cooperation. Cracking the whip, the government ordered the seizure of 2,500 cattle from a location deemed capable of holding 500. These would be impounded until claimed by their owners, who would be given back only what they were allowed to keep, some 20 per cent. No one claimed them, so the government ordered them to be sold.

Advised, it was believed, by the senior Kamba police inspector, the opposition organized a march of 1,500 women on Government House to express their displeasure to His Excellency. They invaded the grounds and were with difficulty persuaded to go away and camp on the racecourse. There they stayed for a month, perfectly well behaved, and only dispersed when the Governor promised to hold a *baraza* in Machakos. Meanwhile the sale of the impounded cattle was cancelled, owing to a legal error in their seizure. At his *baraza* the Governor said that everyone must keep calm, while the whole matter was re-examined.

In December 1938 it was decided that compulsory destocking should be indefinitely postponed; and that the 2,500 impounded cattle should be returned, unconditionally, to their owners.

Game, set and match to the opposition.

Bailward was selected as scapegoat and transferred. He got Wainwright to photograph him beside the poorest runt of a cow that could be found and used this as a Christmas card over the caption, 'Destocked'. Many recipients were amused; some, including the Governor, were not.

Next door in Kitui, R. Pedraza was DC with two DOs, John Carson and Wally Coutts. Pedraza, recalls Coutts,

> having made a deal with one of the Indian traders to buy and export honey, sent John Carson to raid the bee-hives. John being a dedicated officer did so methodically. When the station was inundated with honey, the Indian refused to take it full of grubs and bee-carcases. Pedraza, whose Swahili was none of the best, was heard berating the poor Indian, '*Wewe hapana* English gentleman.'* The Kamba were up in arms as

---

* *Wewe hapana* is grossly ungrammatical Ki-Settler for 'you are not'.

Half-Term

the main ingredient of their beer is honey and after the age of 40 all Kamba are mildly and habitually sozzled. John Carson was embarrassed and the DC in a rage.

Then Pedraza was replaced by Brian Bond, one of those Protestant Ascendancy Anglo-Irishmen whose affectation it is, when with Englishmen, to put on a tremendous Paddy act, speaking with a brogue and carrying on about the wrongs done to Ireland by the English, i.e., by their own forebears. Coutts's retort

when he taunted me about 'your king' was to ask why he was in his present post serving 'my king' and why he had got an MC and two Bars fighting for him. The Kamba loved him and called him 'Bwana Major Boned'. He had been a DO in Kitui and knew virtually all the inhabitants. When one fellow was giving trouble, BB said, 'That's old Mui's nephew. I'll speak to the old man.' He did so, and there was no more trouble. That seemed to me the best sort of paternalism.

He presented a cup for inter-location football, and when there was a match we had to attend. Towards the end when the gloaming gathered grey, BB would start moving about, then say, 'There won't be another goal now. I have the makin's of a dhrink.'

The 'makin's' took some time while BB told me of all the horrors the English had perpetrated in Ireland. In order to get the ingredients he had to step carefully over two marvellous Dalmatians stretched out on the floor. When their food was ready, the cook gave a low whistle and the dogs disappeared. BB still very carefully stepped both ways over nothing on his repeated journeys to and from the makin's.

Despite this wassailing, next morning he would be seen coming down to the boma at 6.15 a.m. clad in shorts, pyjama jacket and sandals, twirling a fly-whisk, and woe betide any of us who were not by then on boma rounds.

In 1937 Kenya had by no means emerged from the Depression, and there was absolutely no money for development. The preservation of Pax Britannica (or Hibernica in Bond's time) was the main objective.

R. A. Wilkinson was posted to Meru, where the DC was Freddie Jennings, lean and hard, with a bronzed face and a thick shock of prematurely white hair. He was clearly the livest of wires, master of any situation.

He was one of the DCs who were recruited at the end of the First World War, all remarkably colourful characters. Very soon I came to the conclusion that in Kenya the Man in the Clapham Omnibus did not exist. There were no ordinary chaps, almost everyone, no doubt owing to the climate or something, seemed to develop a robust personality. On the first morning I went to the office he called me in and said,

'Wilkinson, you are new here. I expect you will want to know how we do things, the office regulations and division of duties and all that sort of thing.'

And I answered, keen as mustard, 'Yes, sir, certainly, sir.'

And he said, 'Well, Wilkinson, there is only one rule here. I do bugger all.'

This proved to be roughly the case, because I recall being in the office with an absolute host of [Africans] sitting on the grass outside, all with their personal problems to be discussed, and at about 12 Freddie would come in, look round and say, 'Mm, Mm. It's a bit quiet today, isn't it? I think I'll pop up to the house and have a pink gin.' But he was the nicest of men, it was a pleasure to do his work for him.

Anyhow, he knew how to delegate, and very soon he delegated to me the task of going on foot safari, collecting the tax. Porters I always thought rather a relic of the past, and I did not really like seeing these chaps staggering along with their heavy loads. The normal form of exchange was copper cents with a hole in the middle which they carried on a string round their necks, and as a result the tax was extremely heavy. And of course the further we went, the more tax we collected, and the more the porters had to carry.

Taking over Nyeri in 1939, P. Wynn-Harris found over four hundred appeals against native tribunal judgements awaiting his attention. They had been left undone by the outgoing DC, Freddie

Half-Term

Jennings, coasting through the last months of his twenty-year contract.

Wynn-Harris was a shortish, powerful Welshman, full of energy and of keen intelligence. In 1933 and 1935 he had got nearer to the peak of Mount Everest than any since Mallory and Irvine, returning with Mallory's ice-axe. But even he was defeated by the sheer volume of his predecessor's backlog. He and his DO, Robin Wainwright, devised an ingenious plan of offering plaintiff and defendant in each case the alternatives of waiting until the DC or DO could hear their cases, or submitting them to arbitration by a panel of three elders chosen by agreement of the two parties. The latter alternative was popular: elders familiar with Kikuyu law and custom could sort out far quicker than a DO (and interpreter) the complexities of a land dispute going back three generations.

An elephant broke into the Catholic Mission in Nyeri and killed one of their converts. Wynn-Harris quickly collected a heavy rifle, Wainwright and an elderly retired elephant hunter, and set out in search of the marauder.

> We drove along a track out into the steep hillside, left our car and started walking, peering down the hill where we expected the elephant to be. Suddenly P. Wyn called out, 'Look out! Here he comes!' and there he was, coming straight at us, about twenty-five yards away and slightly above us. I had not even loaded my rifle, so slipped over the edge of the almost precipitous wall below. P. Wyn and the old man ran back and up the hill to find a position from which they could shoot. The old man only ran about thirty yards before collapsing, unable to go further. Fortunately the elephant was first attracted to the car, and trumpeting loudly, tried to pick it up on his tusks and throw it over the edge of the cliff, on top of me. My hair stood on end as I heard the trumpeting and the crash as he picked up the car twice, but only managed to move it halfway towards the edge. He then saw the old man's blue shirt and made for that, giving P. Wyn the chance of a shot which dropped him dead.

11

The Silent North

'The Silent North' was Glenday's term for the Northern Frontier District (NFD), implying that its officers were stronger than others. Actually, when two or three were gathered together, they talked non-stop, generally about the NFD. DCs carried on after 1918 just as they did before 1914. At Wajir John Llewellin preserved for the Boran, Sakuye and Ajuran some of their own wells. Nothing can tarnish the lustre of his long lonely years of bluff and bargaining, but he had his blind spots. His right-hand man was the Mohamad Zubair sheikh, Haji Hassan Yera, whom he trusted completely. Others thought him an accomplished con-man. Long Lu's Somali expertise and lean good looks made him as irresistible to Mohamad Zubair girls as they were to him, so he notoriously favoured that section. His successor, Sharpe, taking over in 1920, found that they moved wherever they wished, 'Mr Llewellin said they *could* not be kept in their own areas.' They greatly regretted their patron's departure. 'Sharpie', who did not fancy even Somali girls, rounded up the Mohamad Zubair cattle-owning sections in a difficult and dangerous operation. They were:

> the choicest collection of rogues and ne'er-do-wells I have ever seen. It was six weeks' hard bush work. They paid in fines for the trouble caused, 1,000 people, 10,000 head of stock. The Mohamad Zubair on the Tana river received the same treatment as other roamers in pastures new. I hope it will not be thought that the amount in fines and forfeitures was excessive.

The Silent North

The camel-owning sections, more mobile and truculent than the cattle-owners, could not be dealt with in this brusque way. But in the dry season they had to use their Wajir wells, and 'Sharpie' applied the requisite pressure by blocking these up with tree-trunks.

Most of the Wajir headmen and tribesmen seemed to think that orders should be obeyed only when it was expedient to obey, and that a headman's chief duty is to get as far away from the responsibilities of his tribe and government as possible. Many have been enlightened on this point.

In 1925 Jubaland was ceded to Italy, a reward for deserting her German and Austrian allies in 1915. It was no great loss to Britain, but aggravated the problem of the 'alien Somalis'. These were of tribes properly resident in British Somaliland and Jubaland. Like every Somali, they were perpetually trying to move westward and southward, across the NFD and into Kenya. Taking with alacrity to the life of a city slicker, they gravitated to Nairobi and other towns, where they opened shops, acquired cattle and intrigued ceaselessly for the admission of their friends and relatives. They were extremely unwelcome in the NFD, particularly the Herti from Jubaland: detribalized and acknowledging no chiefs, they were thought to be a thoroughly bad influence. But since those born under the Union Jack were either British subjects or British Protected Persons, it was difficult to keep them out. Moreover many had served in the KAR or Frontier Constabulary, not a few had won the DCM and the MM for gallantry, and could produce wallets full of recommendations from former commanding officers. A great deal of a frontier DC's time was spent countering their machinations and checking their proliferation. Only 'Sharpie' spoke up for them:

> We formed a colony in Kenya, so why not the Herti in the NFD? How many British are tax-dodgers? Why should the Herti be loyal to us? We handed them over to the Italians. Are the British living on the Riviera loyal to France?

Men Who Ruled Kenya

In 1926 the headquarters of the NFD were moved down from Meru to Isiolo, ending the anomaly of the NFD being governed from a *boma* in the Central Province. Isiolo, hot and dusty, swept every day by strong winds and plagued by *shamba*-raiding elephants who placidly ignored small boys hurling curses and stones at them, was a hotbed of alien Somali traders. Long established, they could not be deported. They spent their time plotting, chewing an illegal drug called *miraa*, and evading African poll tax. This they did rather ingeniously, denying that they were Africans and demanding to be taxed at a higher rate as Asians, which was at first refused.

Administration of the NFD and Turkana was based on the Outlying Districts Ordinance (1902) and the Special Districts Ordinance (1934). The former declared them 'closed' to all except their own natives and holders of passes obtainable from the DC. Thus alien Somalis, Ashraf* fleecing the pious, missionaries, inflammatory Muslim holy men, globe-trotters, politicians, investigative journalists and undesirables of all kinds could be kept out, or prosecuted if they slipped in. Under the Special Districts Ordinance, to quote R. G. Turnbull, 'everything was illegal, except when specifically authorized by the DC'. It did in fact give the DC very wide powers, most of which were seldom used but were there in case of need. Its importance lay in giving legal sanction to tribal grazing boundaries, gazetted and marked on the ground after exhaustive research into the needs of cattle, camels and shoats. Their aims were to block Somali migration, and to reduce tribal wars over water and grazing. There was a general Somali Line, west and south of which no Somali might graze his stock on pain of confiscation; and to stop pressure building up from behind, various sectional boundaries, such as the Degodia Line.

D. Storrs-Fox was DC Wajir in 1926. His predecessor

> had installed as Khadi [Muslim judge] the Mad Mullah's son, who had taken on almost all the hearing of shauris, leaving the DC with little contact with the people. The interpreter

---

*Ashraf, singular Sharif, were Arabs, often Somali-ized, claiming descent from the Prophet and generally cashing in on it.

The Silent North

seemed hand-in-glove with the Khadi. 'Holy men' were turning up from nowhere in particular. So I took over all the shauris myself, returned the interpreter, a Somali policeman, to his police duties, and put under arrest any holy man without a pass. The Mad Mullah's son found the atmosphere too cold for his taste and departed.

(It was customary for an incoming DC to find a district in a mess, and for an outgoing DC to hand it over in apple pie order.)

There was an influx of Bartiri, a Jubaland tribe. Storrs-Fox sent out a police patrol which was attacked. Two Bartiri felled an askari and were about to cut his throat when they were shot dead by Constable Guyo. Storrs-Fox wrote:

> Unfortunately there were no defined district boundaries, and the incident occured in the sphere of influence of the DC Bura, Martin Mahony, in whose eyes a Somali could do no wrong. He sent a Somali askari to investigate, who reported that the dead men had been shot in the back at 50 yards. Mahony persuaded the PC, Rupert Hemsted, to commit my policeman for trial on a charge of murder.
>
> I and the Commissioner of Police briefed a European lawyer for the defence. The prosecution case fell to pieces, and the judge said, 'I am inclined to agree with Mr Storrs-Fox that the accused, instead of being tried for his life, should be rewarded.'

The NFD was under military administration from 1921 to 1925. Glenday, taking over from the army in Marsabit, made a study of the tribal structure of the Rendille and Gabbra and set out their grazing boundaries. He was involved, with only the police to back him, in an operation far bigger and more dangerous than ever the soldiers had tackled when a large, rifle-armed incursion of Habash and Gelubba raided the Gabbra as far as halfway down Lake Rudolf. There he intercepted them, killing thirty-four and recovering much of their looted cattle, camels and shoats. He pursued them to just short of the border where he brought them to bay, killing forty more and recovering two hundred livestock. His return to Marsabit was as perilous a feat as can be imagined, encumbered with stock to recapture which the enemy hovered round and followed. He marched along the lake shore, with one flank secure, every night cramming men and animals onto a promontery across the neck of which was built a strong thorn zareba.

On the cession of Jubaland, Harry Thuku, the Kikuyu deportee, was moved from Kismayu to Marsabit. He and Glenday did not hit it off; but with the next DC, Sharpe, Thuku struck up an improbable friendship based on their enthusiasm for growing things.

There was plenty of spare land, so Sharpe set him up on a sizeable farm, got him maize-seed, a plough and work-oxen, gave him advice and helped him to market his produce and trade in shoats, tobacco and buni. Together they planted trees for the DC's garden, and grassed his lawns with Kikuyu grass.

Thuku was not short of money. He bought two Abyssinian horses, writing in his autobiography:

> You could get a good horse for shs 400. There would be race-meetings when Major Sharpe's friends came up, and I would sometimes ride one of my horses against them. People were very kind, and the military officers sold me saddles. I employed a Meru groom.

In 1930 there came the order for his release. Sharpe's successor, 'Bay' Bailward,

> knew me well, and did not simply tell me in the office that I was free. He called me outside, and we went about a hundred yards from his office, under a tree. Then he took the letter from his pocket and asked me to read it.

Thuku was offered a lorry to take him and his belongings back to Kiambu, Bailward promising to look after his horses which Mrs Bailward – 'she was mad about horses' – wished to buy.

The Silent North

'No,' I said, 'I will ride my horses down myself.' Not many detainees ride home on racehorses.

Arriving home Thuku proceeded, by shrewd exchange, sales and purchases of land, to consolidate his fragmented holdings into a viable farm.

Then I could begin large-scale farming of maize, from seed I had brought from Marsabit. I also began to keep cattle, and to sell the milk locally. I slowly built up a good herd, and Chief Muhoya gave me an Ayrshire bull as a present. I constructed one of the first cattle-dips among the Kiambu Kikuyu.

I was very pleased when Major Sharpe came to visit me. 'Now, Major Sharpe,' I told him, 'you can see the fruits of your work back in Marsabit.'

'Sharpie' had his imperfections, increasingly blatant with advancing years. Nevertheless he was a good DC in many ways, but his style had a lightness of touch which baffled and enraged frontier officers of the 'Strength through Misery' school typified by Glenday and Reece, who dismissed him as 'a contemptible creature'. He did a good job in turning the political firebrand into a progressive farmer. He might have risen higher in the service but for the fear in Nairobi that he would be the centre of some reverberating scandal.

1929 was a significant year for the NFD. Vincent Glenday became Officer-in-Charge, and remained very much in charge for eight years. He was the frontier officer *par excellence*, more admired than loved, approving only DCs in his own image, inhuman dynamoes, tireless and pitiless. He nurtured against adulteration the unique character of 'the silent North'; and banned 'sleeping dictionaries' on the grounds that those who slept with them would probably catch VD and would certainly be drawn into tribal intrigues. (Nevertheless Gurreh legend holds that the nickname of his younger days, *Faras Adé*, White Stallion, had a *double entendre*.)

There is a story illustrating his style of informed toughness. He was camping with Eric Dutton, a friend from Zanzibar, in Gurreh country beside an iron water-tank, barely filled from a trickling pump tended by a Kikuyu custodian, which served a team drilling for a borehole. Two tribesmen arrived, emaciated but hard as nails, seeking fresh grazing for their clan. They had been living on game, berries and water secreted in the roots of the red-flowered *Buta worrabessa*. Leaning on their spears in front of Glenday, they asked for a drink from the tank.

'No.'
'Effendi, we ask only for a small drink.'
'No.'
'Effendi, we have a great thirst.'
'No.'

Dutton protested, and Glenday condescended to explain.

'These lads are short of water. That is how they live, always a trifle on the short side. But there is plenty of *Buta worrabessa* about, and the wells at Eil Wak are only sixteen miles away. If I let them drink from that tank, as soon as my back is turned, every camel in the country will be brought in, the tank drunk dry and our Kikuyu friend sent to eternity. They are fine fellows, but that is what they would do; and the borehole drillers, just as they are starting work, would have to pack up and go. But that one word "No" has a potency: they won't do it.'

In 1928 Gerald Reece became DO Mandera. He was to be second in the apostolic succession, after Glenday, of more-than-life-size Officers-in-Charge, NFD. The hard time he had had in Kolossia, and Glenday's guidance, had given him in abundance the self-assurance which at first he had lacked. He was intolerant, and addicted to deluging his colleagues with long memoranda often written between midnight and dawn. He did not much like younger officers having fun, but occasionally unbent with his contemporaries, as when he arrived at a Nairobi fancy-dress party, during Delamere's hey-day, wearing a huge topi and with his hair

The Silent North

down to his shoulders, in the guise of 'Lord Mal-de-Mer'. He was a serious man, and more frivolous junior officers sometimes derided his foibles, his slow speech, punctuated by a fuddy-duddy cough and a twitch of the nose to emphasize a point, being a gift to mimics. But he was greatly respected, indeed feared, and was already, in his early thirties, known as 'Uncle'.

While at Mandera he set the unique style of the NFD tribal police. They would be recruited only from the most respected families, men whose 'power depends on prestige, not prestige on power', serving for honour rather than their very low pay, and because of their families' affluence, not bribe-able – or at least not often, or cheaply. They were responsible only to the DC or DO, who only could punish them. They were trained to shoot well, to report accurately all they saw and heard, and to cover long distances at speed, unburdened by blanket, food or water-bottle (very effete) but living on the country and on nomads' hospitality. Their uniform was a white Somali robe, a red turban and sandals; and they were known as *Dubas*, Red Hats. When on duty they were always armed, a rifle being a symbol of authority on the frontier. They were the pride of every frontier DC, and they knew it. Reece established and guarded the *Dubas* tradition: 'It is the tradition that counts. Men come and go, but the tradition carries on. The police are bitterly jealous, and are always trying to fix a case against a Dubas.' The *Dubas* said smugly that they entered the service rich, while the police entered it poor, but left it rich.

Reece left Mandera to be DC, Moyale, with the DO, Mandera, under him.

In March, 1930, Reece wrote Glenday a letter which summarized the style of NFD administration for the next twenty-five years.

The fact is that now we have our motor transport and wireless it is becoming more and more difficult to do any useful administrative work. I would not have dared say that to R. W. H.[emsted] or Rod [Stone] who thought that motorcars were the hell of a good thing in the NFD, but I believe that you share with me certain old-fashioned ideas about administration. Just as the pace of any army is the pace of its slowest man, so will the pace of the NFD long remain the pace of the camel. At the present time it is more important than ever before that we should get in touch with the natives here and inspire confidence, and that cannot be done from a Buick car . . .

On the strength of motor transport the KAR have been withdrawn from the frontier and replaced by a ridiculously incompetent and inadequate police force – useless as soldiers and policeman, and vastly inferior to the old NFD Constabulary . . .

What I want to do is to travel *amongst the people* – not always along the motor roads in a motor-car. This only makes me constipated and serves no useful purpose.

Two years after Reece, Mandera's DO was Hugh Grant, a big fair Cameron Highlander with two MCs. He was a controversial character who attracted admiration and disparagement in roughly equal proportions.

He was a dead shot with rifle, revolver and long-bow. Dick Turnbull, who could not hit a barn-door with a shot-gun, was laboriously stalking a duck when he heard a shot and his quarry disintegrated in a splash and a flutter of feathers. Forty yards away Hugh Grant nonchalantly returned to its cowboy holster a hair-triggered Colt .45. He had a quick temper, and his mastery of Swahili fell short of perfection: perhaps he did not quite understand the nuances of everything his interpreter told him. Thinking it more important that the tribesmen understand him, he spiced his Swahili with Somali and Boran words, horrifying the purist. One cannot quite envisage him running an advanced down-country district, knee-deep in local native councils and tribunals, district education boards and township committees; but he was just the man for Mandera and Moyale, busy and happy, occupying his leisure by engaging the *Dubas* in quarterstaff-play and taking them pig-sticking. He was intensely proud of being a Grant of Glenmoriston, and was as interested as any Somali in his genealogy. It was sometimes not quite clear whether he was talking of MacGregors or Marehan, Stewarts or Degodia.

His wife was an Oxford Grouper, and from time to time Grant was on the wagon, to the consternation of colleagues who had

The Silent North

walked for a week to foregather with him, only to be regaled with cup after cup of strong coffee. When marital pressure from Nairobi relaxed, his hospitality was uninhibited, and enlivened by shooting competitions, the target a match-box in the corner of the room, the weapon a heavy elephant-rifle, held with only one hand. 'The result,' recalls his clan enemy and personal friend, Colin Campbell,

> was a deafening report and all the oil-lamps extinguished. When light had been restored and the smoke had cleared, there was the match-box generally unscathed, a large chunk of wall blown out and the marksman nursing a bruised shoulder.

Grant found his immediate superior, Reece, 250 miles away, 'a nice bloke, just the same age as myself and the same sort of person'.

As to his predecessor in Mandera:

> I have never seen a man so badly messed up by the bush. He could hardly wait to tell me anything, his nerves had gone completely, young and strong but looking worse than most men after a long spell in the line in France. It is extraordinary how some of them cannot stand it.

In the absence of an assistant superintendent, he was in charge of the Kenya Police. They had no discipline, and askaris when given an order argued with the NCO who gave it. The young European inspectors had no conception of dealing with the problem. Craftily Grant arranged for the worst of the malcontents to accompany him on safari, and when they ignored his and their own NCOs' orders,

> I gave them the fun of a six-mile walk with their kitbags tied to them and they to the crupper of a mule with ropes round their necks. This Prussianism caused the collapse of the mutiny.

The KAR having been withdrawn, the police had a semi-military role. But they had not fired their range-course for three years, and were 'wonderfully bad shots even allowing for that'. So:

> Every day we have been hard at it learning to shoot. The Commissioner is a very clever man, and believing in auto-suggestion, tells the young inspectors they are all wonderfully good, and they tell the troops that they are wonderfully good, with the result that they are. They can neither march nor shoot. Out of twenty men here I have only five who can make even a 12-inch group of five shots at a hundred yards. It came as a shock to them to find someone who told them they were quite useless.

However, after a few weeks unremitting attention:

> they now stand in straight lines, more or less, on parade, answer to their names and move at the double like good boys.

How different, how very different, were his own *Dubas* who on parade were like sandalled, turbanned Guardsmen, who shot (nearly) like Greenjackets and moved through thorn-scrub with the speed and confidence of Cameron Highlanders on a heather-covered mountain! The police depended entirely on them for local information.

> They are a cut above everything we have in the way of an armed force here, and do work the police could never attempt. Nothing must be done to lessen their *heshima*.*

Grant had a ruthless streak, and when he heard of a section having many illegal rifles, impounded a mob of their cattle and held them without food or water to encourage the owners to come clean. An animal-lover, he suffered from the lowing of the distressed beasts, but the owners cracked first.

*Heshima: prestige, honour, self-respect.

Above. R. T. Lambert, DC Kabarnet teaches, or perhaps learns, how to make a seine-net, 1939. *Below*. R. T. Lambert watching pit sawyers at work.

Above. Dubas chatting to local girls during a safari in Garissa District, 1950.
Below. A. D. Swann, DC Kiambu, and the singer Danny Kaye, on a visit to Kenya in 1953, examine a Kikuyu Guard simi early in the Emergency before the Kikuyu Guard had many firearms.

Above. C-in-C (Lathbury) and DC (Trench) inspecting Kenya Police and Dubas at Moyale, 1954. *Below*. D. W. Hall, PC Coastal Province, the Governor, Sir Evelyn Baring and the Liwali of Malindi, Sheikh Salim Ali.

Above. Senior Chief Njiri of Fort Hall harangues acting Governor R. G. Turnbull, 1957. *Below*. Governor Sir Evelyn Baring inspects a tree nursery in Machakos District, accompanied by Provincial Commissioner K. M. Cowley and Divisional Forest Officer P. M. Matthews, May 1958.

The Silent North

It fell to him to break it to a formal *baraza* that they must at last pay tax at shs 20. In the end most agreed to pay, but it was still hard to find nomad villages* in scrub desert country. On a long safari during which he lived on camel's milk and boiled goat, and slept with only a camel-mat between him and the stony ground, he sent *Dubas* scouting for villages as in civilian life they had scouted for grass and water, and got most of the tax in. Hiring camels for safari helped the people pay.

The work Grant enjoyed most was map-making with a cavalry sketching board, prismatic compass, protractor, dividers and a Muslim rosary to help count his paces. To this end he climbed every hill in the district, earning the nickname 'Burful' (Hill Climber) and produced a map which served for many years. He was a fanatic about foot safaris off the main roads, keeping chiefs up to the mark, chatting with people in their villages or herding their stock, arriving suddenly and silently with his *Dubas* to the consternation of ill-doers.

Of his tribes, the Gurreh gave least trouble. The Degodia were a 'wild Somali crowd' and much addicted to stealing the water and grazing of others, 'although nominally they have no rifles'. The Marehan were recent arrivals from Italian Somaliland but allowed to stay (for there was no way of expelling them) provided they behaved themselves. In his Handing Over Report Grant warned his successor:

> It must be remembered that with the force at our command it would be hopeless to try to compel these people to do anything to which they seriously object. Any serious show of force in the presence of large numbers of Marehan would result in a most unpleasant time for the person who ordered it and for those who tried to carry out his orders. Police patrols should be ordered not to play the fool with these people, and a patrol attempting to take stock from them would almost certainly cause an explosion; whereas by talking to the elders a fine could probably be got from them.

*By 'village' is meant a family, their livestock, possessions and moveable huts.

Men Who Ruled Kenya

A great deal of time was taken up with foreign affairs, with Grant, the Italian Residente Pirelli and the Abyssinian Gerazmach Belai writing to one another requesting the arrest and return of absconding murderers, for whom three international boundaries converging near Mandera provided a perfect Tom Tiddler's Ground. On a visit to Pirelli at Dolo he passed

> forts held by the most wild-looking brigands, the Italian frontier police. All the natives you pass halt and give the Fascist salute; the brigands lined up, more or less, presented arms, more or less, and let out a Fascist yell. The Residente met me with a guard of honour of more brigands, and a wonderful beard.

From the Abyssinians there was nothing but 'truculence and broken promises': they should be made to 'follow their own customs and bow'. The Gerazmach was a former *shifta*, one of the gang who had murdered Aylmer.

> He should in theory be treated as the officer of a civilized power. I personally will not have him in my house or eat with him. When he comes here I give him the use of a spare house, send him a meal and talk with him on my verandah.

The situation at Moyale was virtually unchanged since Zaphiro's day.

> Another boy was murdered in Moyale tonight [wrote Reece to the Officer-in-Charge in August 1929]. This is the fifth case of its kind during the past three months. Two of the murderers are actually living with one of the Governor of Borana's own subordinates . . .
> We are attempting to negotiate in a friendly manner with a Christian country which is a member of the League of Nations, but even where the most foul and purposeless outrages are concerned, they neglect to take action.
> I and my brother officers and 60 police constables in a British post are sitting here quite helplessly with the

The Silent North

disembowelled body of an innocent child a few hundred yards away, while the murderer is nearby in the territory of a so-called friendly and civilized nation, where he can boast of his prowess.

Glenday pressed Nairobi for permission to allow our tribesmen to carry rifles again within twenty miles of the border, but this was refused.

It was the hopeless task of the British Consul for Southern Abyssinia, stationed at Mega, some sixty miles north-west of Moyale, to nag the Emperor's officers into paying compensation for *shifta* raids and honouring the treaty which allowed British tribesmen to water from Abyssinian wells. Whenever his salary was in arrears – and it usually was – the Gerazmach charged them exorbitant watering fees. For some years the Consul had been Major A. T. ('Titch') Miles, DSO, a small man, brave as a lion and flamboyant as a peacock despite the tuberculosis which was killing him. In 1932 he was on sick-leave, Reece was his *locum tenens* in Mega and Mullins was Reece's *locum tenens* in Moyale. It was not a happy arrangement, since Reece was incapable of refraining from interference in what he still regarded as his district.

Reece bombarded Mullins with advice.

If you disarm the Dubas, as the Police always urge, you reduce their status to that of messengers, paupers and slaves ... Individual tax receipts must be given if possible, otherwise collective receipts to headmen. You must collect tax from the detribalized sods who live round the township, and generally persecute these shits [ie, alien Somalis]. Anyone who comes for some *shauri* and cannot produce a tax receipt should be ignored ... The Abyssinians hate us and [are] double-faced swine.

Mullins, perfectly capable of running the district, resented backseat driving. 'If you give me orders you'll get my back up.'

Between January 1930 and July 1932, there were 141 murders in two years. On Miles's return from leave (still coughing blood into his handkerchief) he, Glenday and Reece assembled at Moyale to discuss this intolerable situation.

The chiefs tried to coax concessions from Glenday. First, Aden Hassan of the Degodia knew of good grazing, used by nobody, only a few miles west of the Degodia Line. Could they not use it?

Glenday: 'No. It belongs to the Ajuran, and well you know it.'

Hassan Ghersi of the Gelibleh Somalis complained that his people had been fined five hundred camels. Could not this be remitted? Otherwise, how could they pay their tax?

Glenday: 'No. The Gelibleh were fined for a dozen cold-blooded murders. If you think I'll let you off the fine so that you can pay your taxes, you are very much mistaken. You are a menace.'

Ido Robleh of the Ajuran complained that the Habash would not let them use the Gadaduma wells. Would not the government secure for the Boran their treaty rights?

Glenday: 'Major Miles will take it up with the Habash. You will get your rights.'

And so on. About one petition in ten was reasonable, and was granted. On the fourth day Glenday gave out his orders.

'First, the wells must be kept open, and for that we must rely on Miles. Second, disarmament is still our aim, on both sides of the border. Shoot at sight all raiders. Miles will press Addis Ababa for compensation for past raids. No hot pursuit across the border: such cases to be referred to Miles. Free medical attention to Abyssinians, as before. I'll put this all in writing, but don't wait for that.'

Glenday approved of Reece: 'A very good man, but I suppose some woman will get him in the end.' Reece did not approve of Mullins's successor-designate, C. B. Norman, whom he thought unsuitable

> for the most harassing and nerve-wracking post in the colony. He is a decent fellow, but I doubt if he is a NFD wallah. I met him at a London restaurant, and in the first ten minutes, he asked, 'Are you fond of chorus girls?'

What then, in Glenday's and Reece's book, constituted a 'NFD wallah'? Except for that frontier paragon, Grant, he must be

The Silent North

unmarried, indeed indifferent to female charms, black or white; and of course, to boys. He must not be taken in by Somalis. He must work fourteen hours a day while in the *boma*, and be out on foot safari at least half the month. (Lorry safaris did not count.) He must stand loneliness, and rise to a convivial occasion. He must regard a posting to the NFD as a privilege, not a penance. There were few who lived up to these specifications, for officers had an exasperating habit of getting married. In Reece's view, if a young DC left his wife in Nairobi, he pined for her and lost half his efficiency. If he brought her, as he could, to Isiolo or Marsabit, either he did too little safari; or he left her alone and she, bored, hopped into bed with the policemen. But every administrative officer had to do at least one tour in the NFD or Turkana.

The DC Wajir in 1932 was Freddie Jennings whose genius at delegating work to others wilted in Wajir, where there was no one to whom to delegate. He was not really a NFD wallah, but his place in NFD history is secure, as the founder and first Commodore of the Royal Wajir Yacht Club, unique among the yacht clubs of the world in being 250 miles from the nearest navigable water.

Jack Clive came to Isiolo as DC in 1931 while Glenday was on leave and Rodney Stone was officer-in-charge. He wasn't a NFD wallah either.

I like verdant scenery, well watered . . . It seemed to me that in the NFD one spent one's life arriving a week too late to catch the latest murderer.

During a safari in Samburu country there was delivered to him a Habash raider who had been found dying of thirst.

The Abyssinian, a courteous brigand who bowed almost to the ground whenever he addressed the Court, admitted being a member of the gang which had killed three Samburu. But as at the time he was out of touch with them and lost in the bush, he could not be charged with murder . . . He was convicted of being in a closed district without a pass, and possession of an unlicensed rifle.

Clive sentenced him to three years' imprisonment, which the Supreme Court reduced to fourteen months. By Glenday's rules he should have been shot at sight. Miles, on his way to Nairobi, told Clive that up and down the frontier Habash raiders were praising God for the leniency of the British. Why not bestow on the fellow a purse of gold?

Degodia from Wajir district began watering their stock in the Uaso Nyiro well west of the Somali Line, in Boran territory. After thirteen Boran had been murdered at the watering points, Stone, Clive and Jennings met at Habbaswein to sort the matter out. Clive wrote:

We had gone into two or three cases with Salad Mohamad, the Degodia headman, when a young Somali, covered with sweat, ran up and told us he was the sole survivor of twenty-four Degodia attacked by an army of Boran who had decamped with their camels to Arro Dima, eight miles away. We set off in the Wajir lorry. As we approached Arro Dima there was a thumping on the cab's roof and the driver shouted that there were people running away across the river. We ran after them. My Boran headman, Fai Halake, appeared on a white mule and, seeing us, disappeared as though by magic.

Eventually six of the Boran let us come up to them. They said they were part of an army of five hundred and had decided to kill every Degodia in existence to avenge the thirteen Boran murdered. We told them we wanted a *baraza* with the whole army and they went off.

Presently the army started drifting in, all wearing the white war headband. We made them park their spears and knives in a great pile and they all sat down in a semi-circle round us. Last to arrive was the young, self-styled King of the Boran, Galma Dida. Questioned by Rodney, he admitted that they had taken five hundred camels and intended to keep them. When Rodney asked Galma Dida what they had done with

The Silent North

the 24 bodies, he said, 'The spears ate them.' They had been cut into small pieces and the vultures had done the rest.

All the time that old fool, Salad Mohamad, the only Degodia present, was shouting abuse at them.

After a couple of anxious hours we persuaded the Boran army to disband, but not to return the camels. That was the best we could do, and as it was getting dark, we beat it back to Habbaswein.

With the help of a company of KAR, we recovered the Degodia camels and imposed a thumping fine on the Boran. This did not satisfy the Degodia, who slew an entire Boran *manyatta*, men, women and children. But they were indiscreet enough to have a thousand camels watering nearby, and Rodney pinched the lot. When they were auctioned, the amount was far more than the fine a PC could impose, and the Supreme Court got a bit sticky. Fortunately Sir Joseph Byrne was Governor, and congratulated Rodney on 'the vigour and common sense which you all displayed'.

So Clive's NFD tour ended well, but he was glad to leave.

The southernmost district of the NFD was Bura, on the Tana river. The Somali Line here was the river, fordable in many places. Poised along it like runners at the start of a race were three Ogaden sections: Aulihan, Abd Wak and Abdullah. Along the Tana, cultivating the alluvial soil deposited by the river as it frequently changed its course, were settlements of negroid slave tribes collectively known as Pokomo.

There was a form of safari unique to this district, down the Tana river on two canoes tied together like a catamaran with a platform on which sat the DC. The *Dubas*, arrant landlubbers, were apprehensive passengers. Roger Lambert enjoyed

> gliding down the stream with the Pokomo paddlers singing their canoe-song while I did my best with sea-shanties. A woman on the river-bank warned us of bad hippos ahead, so I loaded my heavy rifle. Suddenly two angry hippos emerged from the riverside bush just in front of my canoe. I just had time to scramble to my feet and fire at the bull, who went

off downstream while the cow swam upstream, apparently under the canoe.

Lambert was replaced by Sharpe, who moved headquarters to Garissa, by which name the district was thereafter known. He first laid out a garden, then built his house. For this he had two deep-drop conveniences dug. One, adjacent to the house, was called 'Haraka' (Haste); the other, at the bottom of the garden, surrounded by flowering shrubs, with an idyllic view up and downstream, plentifully supplied with copies of *The Field, Country Life* and *The Tatler*, was called 'Baraka' (Blessing).*

The garden had fertile soil and unlimited water; elephants provided manure, and the detention camp the labour. Like all Sharpie's gardens, it was a thing of beauty. As an animal tamer he was less successful: his baby elephant used to keep herself amused in the forest all day, and come in to bed at night; but his attempts to wean from its nocturnal habits a young hyena failed, despite his hiring a small boy to prod it all day with a stick.

Marsabit was the cream of NFD stations with spectacular scenery, a fertile soil and a lovely climate. When Hale was posted there in 1934, he determined to be a complete 'yessir' to Glenday, so that he could stay forever. Glenday occasionally came for a night or two, sitting up late with the whisky and holding forth about the politics of the North.

'What would you like for breakfast, sir?' Hale would ask.

'Oh – chutney on toast and a pink gin.'

Above the DC's house was a forest full of game, a sanctuary for Greater Kudu which Hale used to stalk with a Leica and telephoto lens. Below was rolling grass downland, beyond which the Diid Galgalla, a lava wilderness, stretched deep-blue to the Abyssinian border.

Gelubba raiders were his main concern.

The RAF flew me and a party of Dubas to Alia Bay on Lake Rudolf to try and catch some . . . The Dubas were so

---

*There is a well-known Swahili proverb, *Haraka, haraka, haina baraka*, Haste, haste has no blessing.

The Silent North

copiously sick that the pilot too was almost overcome. The raiders eluded us by putting out in canoes and lying flat. I took some pot-shots with my .318, but they were a long way off and I don't think I hit any.

On foot safaris near the border, it was prudent to frustrate ill-wishers by leaving the camp-fire after dark and bedding down some distance away.

We slept on the ground in a circle, feet outward; at one's feet two upright sticks on each side of the bed. If attacked, everyone could sit up and shoot, but only between the sticks, not endangering one another. We never were attacked.

12

Ities, Bandas and Shiftas, 1935–1945

In the mid-1930s the NFD confronted fascism eyeball-to-eyeball. Mussolini desired a cheap victory over Abyssinia, a reversion to the 'Scramble for Africa' of the nineteenth century, roundly condemned in the twentieth. It was the policy of His Majesty's Government to pontificate, berate and conduct the chorus of disapproval in the League of Nations; but not to do anything effective, such as closing the Suez Canal. Italians denounced the British and French, with their generous slices of Africa, as hypocrites, and relations between NFD officers and their neighbours in Italian Somaliland turned very sour.

Late in 1935 the legions moved ponderously forward. Aided by tanks, poison gas, artillery and bombers, they entered Addis Ababa without much difficulty. The occupation of the rest of Abyssinia took more time, impeded by distances and bad roads. Only the ruling Amhara really fought the invaders: subject peoples tended to regard them as liberators from Amhara tyranny. The Mandera and Moyale tribes were rather pleased, for the Italians bought all the meat they could sell, at advantageous prices.

Hugh Grant, DC Moyale in 1936, could see their camps just across the border, but was forbidden to hold any communication with them. The Italians were no better neighbours than the Abyssinians, handing out rifles to the tribes in the hope that they would attack the Amhara. 'The tribesmen thought the arms came straight from heaven, and started raiding on our side of the border.'

'The Italians,' exploded Glenday:

Ities, Bandas and Shiftas, 1935–1945

are behaving like complete shits. They have closed their wells to our tribes, as a reprisal for us harbouring Abyssinian refugees. Typical macaroni.

In June Grant wrote to his wife a letter marked SECRET.

Things are a bit hectic. The Ities have come into our area and are using a bit of our country. I had to go and see about it, and ran into one of their patrols which shot two of my men dead close to me, and then fled. You must on no account tell anyone about this.

They have turned the frontier into a complete bear-garden, all the tribesmen are playing off old scores. The government have given orders that we are on no account to go near them even if they come into our territory.

By 1937 things were pretty well back to normal, except that the *shifta* now had modern rifles. Grant had a problem of another kind.

A girl was brought in who had been seven days in labour and the child had started to go bad. The hospital dresser knew nothing, so I had to try. Poor thing, she was near dead; she was too small. I broke up the skull and got the child away from her, and the temperature was normal when I left.

Bob Armitage found Wajir rolling in lira from cattle sales to the Italians. Having some money in the goat bag, he decided to dig a water-hole in a dry river-bed called Lag Bogol, choosing a site where there was a depression and dry, trampled mud. Somalis being allergic to manual labour, he imported a Pokomo gang from Garissa. He measured and marked the outlines of the tank, 50 by 45 feet,

and we hope to make it 20 feet deep, with an entrance channel 6 feet wide. Took sample of earth. Hope it holds water.

Two months later, with the rains due at any time, the tank was 13 feet deep all over. After three more months and heavy rains, he noted sadly,

> Evacuated Lag Bogol. It taught me that one cannot make a tank with perpendicular sides in that soil, the sides fall in.

Dick Turnbull, the DO Mandera, was probably the best-read man in the Administration, and the most musical. Cynical witticisms, known in the trade as 'Turnbulliana', flowed effortlessly from his tongue and his pen. He learned pretty well everything about the NFD – its flora and fauna, its tribes and their notables, tribal customs, grazing habits. But he occasionally pretended to more expertise than he or anyone else could possibly have; as when, striding through the bush in seven-league boots, he stopped, bent down, picked up a bit of goat-dropping and thoughtfully bit it in two. 'H'm – Aulihan, of course. Rer Ali, I should think – 1938 and a hard *jilaal*.'*

On one occasion he walked two hundred miles to confer with Armitage in Wajir. In accordance with NFD etiquette, he camped for the night a mile or two outside the *boma* in order to come in at a civilized hour in the morning. But at dawn he told his *Dubas* sergeant, 'I've changed my mind. We'll go back to Mandera now.'

However, one morning in June he arrived at Wajir to discuss with Armitage the Gurreh-Ogaden grazing boundary.

> Turnbull and I had our usual malicious scandal-talk. We have the same views on many people, though I don't pretend to his wide range of reading nor to his introspective attitude. He is much more simple than I suspected, and a lot of his talk is pose, especially when drunk ... The Gurreh boundary is rather tricky, as he thinks they are shits but cannot let the Ogaden too near Eil Wak.

*Jilaal: the hot, dry months of January to March.

Ities, Bandas and Shiftas, 1935–1945

The DC Isiolo was Rimington, who kept a giraffe and a monkey, and taught the monkey to ride the giraffe before riding it himself. He broke to saddle and bridle a Grevy's zebra, far larger and stronger than the common zebra. Indeed he took Zeb up to Nanyuki to play polo. None of the ponies would go near this apparition, so Rim was able to score as many goals as he pleased before the club passed a rule banning zebras from play. But faced with an influx of two thousand Abyssinian refugees, Rimington was at a loss; so Glenday sent him to Wajir and brought Armitage to Isiolo. Armitage noted austerely, 'R should concentrate on animal training.'

The refugees were first reported by the RAF, a number of straggling columns, shedding casualties from hunger, thirst and fatigue, between Lake Rudolf and Marsabit. They were Amharas of all degrees, aristocrats, fighting men, bureaucrats and priests, all their women and children, and hosts of non-Amhara slaves. They were guided to Marsabit where Alys Reece (for Reece had fallen from grace into matrimony) watched their arrival.

> There were pregnant women on the point of collapse ... and small children swollen-bodied from famine oedema, their feet mis-shapen and rotten with neglected cuts and sores. Worst of all were the smallpox cases.
>
> All had to be vaccinated, cleaned, clothed, fed, nursed and looked after. When an Amhara lady of high standing needed an enema, and announced that she would rather die than have it administered by the Kikuyu dispensary dresser, it was the DC's wife, new to Africa and with only the most rudimentary Swahili, who volunteered.
>
> I withdrew to study the drill from a nursing manual. It seemed simple enough ... We held court round her bed; the husband and his lieutenants, the daughters, the servants and all. I tried to explain exactly what I had in mind, so that there would be no nasty shocks at a crucial point. My statement was handed out in short instalments and went the

round of the interpreters (English to Swahili to Bourji to Amharic) while the lady's dark eyes, beautiful but weary, were fixed on me expressionlessly.

The next difficulty was to get the husband and entourage to withdraw . . . But at last I was left alone with the patient, except for her two daughters. The rest was easy . . .

When those fated to die had died, the remainder were taken to a ramshackle camp at Isiolo, where Armitage had his first look at them.

Slaves are a problem. I suppose we can insist on their doing communal tasks. Must get the organization, their officers and groups going. I think order will come out of chaos . . . Should they have some sort of Tribunal? The children are a problem, and I hope some mission will take charge of them.

Complete chaos in the issue of posho. M——— does not pull his weight. Full of piss and wind when what is wanted is painstaking attention to detail . . . Quarrels and intrigues between camp nobles, who are not co-operating. Shit in places inches deep.

Turnbull arrived on transfer: 'Makes a great to-do about going to Kisumu, wants to come here as DC.' On arrival at Kisumu he made even more of a to-do, declared that nothing would induce him to stay, that he must be sent back to the NFD. He refused to unpack. The CNC, Hosking, found time to talk to this truculent and difficult young man.

'Think of the expense of sending you from the NFD to Kisumu and back again.'

'Tell me what it will cost, and I will be happy to pay.'

The Goan head clerk commiserated with him. 'My poor young man, you have ruined your career. You should have left your posting to me. We have our methods.'

But salvation came from the north, a request came from Glenday that Turnbull take over Isiolo from Armitage, giving special attention to the refugees. Roger Wilkinson was also sent to minister to them.

Ities, Bandas and Shiftas, 1935–1945

The refugees like all refugees were very grateful at first for being helped, but after a bit strong on complaints of how they were treated. They had not the slightest difficulty in quarrelling among themselves, and the usual action they took was to set fire to each other's houses. Anyone who has been to Isiolo knows about the Isiolo wind, so when one house went up, it was likely that a number of others would follow suit, which was very tiresome. The PC was the great Glenday, an absolutely splendid chap. I remember him coming to inspect the camp and immediately starting a fire himself, to see how we would cope with it.

Glenday was appointed Resident of Zanzibar and was succeeded as Officer-in-Charge by Gerald Reece. At the time of the Munich crisis three Wellington bombers arrived at Isiolo to boost morale. With them came the Governor, Sir Robert Brooke-Popham, and his private secretary who handed Wilkinson

> an enormous envelope covered with red seals and marked TOP SECRET and things like that, and addressed to me personally. I could see that Reece looked slightly old-fashioned at his junior officer corresponding direct with Government House and under top security. However, he said nothing, and when I got the chance I removed the seals and opened the envelope, and inside was another, equally sealed and stamped, and I opened that and inside was a pair of kippers, an extremely welcome addition to one's diet at Isiolo.

Reece would not have been amused. Although marriage had slightly mellowed him, he basically disapproved of fun, especially fun with a touch of *lèse majesté*, which he was inclined to equate with disloyalty. His pencilled chits, scrawled on any odd bit of paper, conveying reproof, giving orders, demanding information, were sent out in hundreds, and nothing escaped his attention. Why were the robes of Wajir Dubas two inches longer than those of Marsabit? Had Haji Hassan Mohamad, a Habr Awal alien Somali, a stock-trader's licence to trade in Boran country?

Not even Turnbull, already marked as his successor, escaped the acerbity of his pencil.

> It is generally agreed that you are an arrogant and conceited young man . . . Please explain why you went to Meru in a lorry driven by a man with a disgusting venereal disease. If you didn't know, you ought to have known.

Yet he treated Turnbull, as Glenday had treated him, as heir apparent, even seeking his advice on the delicate matter of Myles North, DC Wajir. North had joined the Administration in 1935, having served four years in the 60th Rifles. An ornithologist of international repute, he was also a very conscientious, very methodical, rather slow administrator, with a painful stammer which made him seem even slower. (Since he stammered only when speaking English, he used to give orders to DOs in Swahili.) He disapproved of NFD-manship, and in long letters told Reece so. Reece reacted strongly, drafting to North a brutal letter on the unwisdom of a newcomer disputing the principles on which the NFD had been run for thirty years and altering

> everything in the district as soon as he arrives . . . Almost as soon as you arrived at Wajir you sought to cancel my written instructions that the interpreter be replaced; and I think that even now you consider that my knowledge (based on Mr Glenday's) of the alien and local Somali character is wrong.

But he sent the draft for comment to Turnbull who saw North

> still in arms against what he calls 'the NFD administration'. A psychologist would probably say he is tired of Wajir and unconsciously using this way of securing a transfer. I liked him immensely, but if he is so set against the NFD, a move seems to be the only answer.

So Reece toned down some of his more astringent expressions, and ended his letter to North on a friendly note:

Ities, Bandas and Shiftas, 1935–1945

I have gone out of my way to praise you to the Secretariat, and I still think highly of your work and your character. I can only conclude that our temperaments are incompatible and that there is no point in our trying to work together.

Turnbull was out on foot safari as much as possible. One day he met

an elderly European dressed in a battered dark suit which had once had a clerical cut, carrying a small Gladstone bag and a groundsheet. He was walking along the road leading to the nearest watering-point.

Stray Europeans were not encouraged near the Italian frontier, so Turnbull politely asked him to explain himself. He was the Reverend John Ethelstan Cheese, on one of his missionary walkabouts.

He told me he was visiting a Somali family at Eil Wak, 120 miles north-east of us. I told him it was not possible for him to undertake this journey without food and water and some means of carrying them. I said he had better abandon his scheme and come back with me.

He was very patient. He said, 'It is really most kind of you, my dear boy, but I am quite accustomed to travelling in this way; and although I will certainly come back with you if you insist, I shall find it a shade inconvenient. You see, I have given my word to seek out the sons of Mohamad Ahmed of the Habr Suliman, and I cannot disappoint the family.'

When I still remonstrated about the risk he was taking, he said, 'Yes, I agree it may seem odd, but I always travel like this. I hope you won't find it embarrassing if I tell you that I just put my trust in God, and God looks after me . . . It has always worked.'

Well, he was old enough to be my father, so I went on my way, and sent a couple of Dubas, not in uniform, to follow at a discreet distance and see that he came to no harm.

Some hours later the *Dubas* reported back. Padre Cheese had joined a Somali village travelling in his direction. They knew of him, made him welcome, gave him milk and a mat to sleep on, and would take him along next day. The *Dubas* were immensely impressed. 'The old man,' they said, 'is not a Believer, but he is very, very holy, and it is the will of God that no harm should come to him.'

In Turkana the 1939 rains, following a long drought, were very heavy. Within hours a wilderness of sand and stone put on an incredible display of grass and wild flowers; and within days the emaciated cattle filled out, their ribs and hip-bones disappeared and they put on condition with amazing speed. With the lorries of the KAR company at Lokitaung bogged down, the Merille mobilized. They had new Italian rifles and automatics, while the Turkana had been disarmed. They took 10,000 head of cattle and slaughtered a hundred and fifty Turkana. Tony Swann, DO Lokitaung, describes their *modus operandi*:

> You waited till the men were out herding cattle, and then you killed the women and children. It was perfectly logical: they were the breeding stock.

Swann then broke every rule. The Turkana had a fair number of old French rifles hidden away, but very little ammunition. He found in the store of a gunshop in Nairobi cases of ancient ammunition, bought the lot from the goat bag and issued it to the Turkana. It did them a power of good.

Eventually the ground dried up and 4th KAR caught up with a Merille *shifta*. Among the dead were some non-Merille, carrying the identity papers of NCOs of the Italian colonial forces, brave men sent to spy out the land. Ken Hunter, officer-in-charge Turkana, with an Italian-speaking settler as interpreter, conferred at Todenyang fort, on the Kenya-Abyssinian boundary, with the Italian Resident of southern Abyssinia.

> We drank and dined under a full moon and by midnight had settled all the affairs of state – punitive action against the

Ities, Bandas and Shiftas, 1935–1945

Merille, compensation to the Turkana, cooperation in the event of further raids. A few days later Britain and Germany were at war, and no more was heard of the Todenyang Agreement.

During the 'phoney war', with Italy still neutral, DOs behaved very much as in peace-time, spending a great deal of time on safari with camels for transport in the plains and donkeys in the hills, and TP escort. The Turkana TPs, equivalent to the NFD *Dubas*, were a fine body of men and magnificent on parade. Their uniform was a cartridge-belt and a blue mini-skirt with TD in large red letters where a Highlander wears his sporran. All other embellishments were to individual taste. The hair was usually dressed in a sort of bun with blue and red clay in different patterns, and one or two ostrich feathers: any who had killed a Merille proclaimed the fact by a different hair-style. Many wore a round ivory ball, nearly the size of a golf-ball, fixed by a stud to the lower lip, and very uncomfortable it must have been; a variety of bracelets, wrist-knife and necklaces completed the ensemble. On safari TPs were often accompanied by their *femmes de campagne*, buxom lasses shining with goats' fat, carrying their men's baggage while the men walked ahead in lordly ease, burdened only by rifles.

John Dowson was DO Lodwar, but on safari most of the time. His interpreter was a veteran named Longacha, after Geoffrey ('Long') Archer, the first DO the Turkana had seen.

> We would start by moonlight, whenever possible, go for about four hours and then halt during the heat of the day to rest the camels and let them browse, and continue for two or three hours in the afternoon. At various places we met the assembled tribesmen with a herd of goats, their tax. Proceedings opened with song and dance. The dancing, by men only, mimed various animals grazing, fighting, copulating and so on. The singing was most impressive, deep bass voices.
> Then to tax-collecting. The owners would encircle the herd of goats and close in. The goats would realize something nasty was pending and make a dash for freedom. There

would be a wild rush to grab horns, leg or any convenient part.

Having caught the goats, the men paraded them past me, one by one. It was my job, advised by Longacha, to set a value on each animal, usually four or five shillings, which was handed to the owner who was then conducted to the tax clerk to be relieved of his shs. 3 tax. Occasionally the price would be disputed and the goat, thrust struggling into a sack, would be weighed on a spring balance hanging from a tree.

Every officer on safari took with him a sack or two of native tobacco which the Turkana loved to chew. At the end of a *baraza* – or in the middle if the subject under discussion was unwelcome – the tribesmen would break into song. 'The tobacco song', Longacha would explain – a hint that the time had come to stop talking and give each man a handful.

Turnbull was moved to Moyale, whence he could watch Italian troops drilling a few hundred yards away.

> Mussolini's Grande Armée
> Extends from here to Melka Ré.
> In opposition to it are
> Penfold (C) and Turnbull (R).

It was an accurate summary of the strategic situation. The army was back at Wajir; on the frontier were only the DC and his *Dubas* and a detachment of Kenya Police under their ASP, Penfold.

Relations with the Italians greatly improved with the arrival as Residente Moyale of Primo Capitano Cav. Giovanni Marconi, a genial and courteous regular cavalry officer, nephew of the inventor of wireless telegraphy, who had fought in the Austrian, Libyan and Abyssinian campaigns and represented his country at show-jumping. English-speaking, friendly and helpful, he was missed when he left in March 1940.

It was obvious that forty or fifty police and a dozen *Dubas*, armed only with rifles, could put up no effective resistance to invasion. It was therefore decided, the instant war was declared, to

Ities, Bandas and Shiftas, 1935–1945

evacuate Moyale and Mandera. No one foresaw that, with Britain and Germany at war, Italy would remain neutral. So Turnbull was given no discretion in the matter: on 9 September 1939, mortified by this 'most discreditable and unhappy withdrawal', he drove off with police, *Dubas*, government servants, cash and office records down the escarpment and back to Wajir. A few days later his humiliation was completed by a sympathetic message from Marconi: would the British please return? He could not keep order on both sides of the border. Turnbull refused to go back: his *heshima*, he said, was destroyed by having to 'run away like a scalded cat'. So Jake Cusack, whom a trifle like that would not embarrass, led the shamefaced return and presided genially over Moyale during the 'phoney war'.

Mandera was also evacuated by the DO, Paul Kelly. When they returned ten days later they found that the Gosha had been using their houses as public conveniences, and pages from *The Laws of Kenya* were blowing about the *boma* like leaves on Vallambrosa. Life soon returned to normal.

Kelly's standby was his Somali district clerk, Ahmed Farah, described by a later DO as

> quite wonderful, very intelligent, quiet and extremely capable and knows the answer to everything ... I would say he is better and far harder working than the average English clerk, with excellent manners, what you might call a gent ... He handles hundreds of pounds of cash a day, and rarely if ever, makes a mistake. One of the wonders of the world.

Kelly was invited for a weekend to Lugh Ferrandi by the Italian Commissario (PC), Bernardelli, later known as 'Twinkletoes' because of his enterprising leadership of Somali Banda (Irregulars).

> He was a smallish, active man, proud of having taken part in the March on Rome in the early days of Fascism. Taking pity on my loneliness, he offered me a holiday in Mogadishu 'where there are 3,000 Italian ladies'.
> At English afternoon tea, in a cage beside us prowled two adult lions, waiting to be fed. The male suddenly whipped his

paw through the bars, and Bernardelli pulled me back just in time.

'Très féroces', I said.

'Non, non, très domestiques.'

The lions' keepers threw their meat into the cage. Bernardelli invited me in for my photo, standing close to the lions as they growled over their dinners. In vain I repeated my incantation, 'Très féroces', as he pressed me inexorably back towards them. I was glad to get out.

A month later they killed their keepers.

In May 1940 the Mandera *boma* became 'peripatetic', in tents with a train of 150 camels, leaving in Mandera only a dozen police with a fast truck. On 10 June Kelly happened to tune in to the Italian radio and heard a bellicose sounding speech by Mussolini. Rightly interpreting this as a declaration of war, he informed Wajir, to which it was news, and withdrew at a dignified pace to Buna. He even collected tax on the way. Intended as a gesture of confidence, this was probably seen as an attempt to line his pockets before departure.

At Buna Kelly's party came under command of Hugh Grant in the double role of DC Wajir and Commandant of Grant's Scouts, an irregular force of 150 local tribesmen raised to counter the Banda, gather information and act as a screen in front of the army. This was just Grant's cup of tea. He trained them in day and night patrols, musketry and simple tactics. The *Dubas* were much in demand as guides, scouts and instructors in bushcraft.

As an honorary lieutenant in Grant's Scouts, Kelly accompanied 6th KAR and 1st Nigerian Regiment in an attack on Dobel, 35 miles north of Buna.

Stray bullets whistled overhead through the tree branches. I was very alarmed and felt we were being surrounded. We could hear the enemy exulting with Islamic shouts. We returned to the road to find groups of our troops streaming back, 'showing little stomach for the fight'. My officer questioned them. How could they abandon their officers and run away? He was very disappointed – 'Can't go into action with troops like these.'

We withdrew to Buna and that night when shots were fired by Bernardelli's Banda the whole perimeter started firing at nothing. Hugh asked me what I thought we should do, I suppose as a sort of IQ test. I said we should form a reserve line across the perimeter, he and I and a few others, to let the fugitives through and stop the enemy. This was done, but there was no attack and the firing petered out.

They were bombed several times by Italian planes at which thousands of rounds were fired without damage on either side. The Scouts patrolled, cross-examined tribesmen at watering-points and in their villages, and returned with a lot of information, much of it accurate. In January 1941 the advance on Kismayu began. The Scouts did quite well as a screen in front of the army, drawing fire and reconnoitring the enemy positions. But they had no motor transport, and were left behind as the advance surged forward against negligible opposition. To Grant's disgust they were relegated to policing Jubaland when the army drove on to Addis Ababa.

It was decided that Moyale should be held until relieved by two battalions of KAR, and throughout the phoney war work continued on the defences – wire, trenches, dugouts, underground water-tanks. Social relations with the Italians became embarrassing when it became clear that Italy was about to make an inglorious entry into the war in the wake of German victories. The last Anglo-Italian bridge party was held on 3 June, after which chits and newspapers continued to be exchanged, and the Residente, whose bridge was not of the best, punctiliously sent over the money he had lost. On Cusack being commissioned as captain, the Residente made him a present of a length of khaki drill for his uniform.

On 10 June the Italians had warning that war was about to be declared; and the ASP, walking near the boundary-cut, still as he thought in peacetime, had the melancholy distinction of being the first British prisoner of war captured by the Italians. Secret files, cash and non-combattant government servants were sent off to

Isiolo, police patrols were called in, and Cusack took command of a mixed force of police and *Dubas* who held a sector of the perimeter under command of the company of 1st KAR which formed the bulk of the garrison. The garrison's orders had been changed from 'Hold on till you are relieved', to 'Hold on as long as you can and then get back to Buna'. Their transport, four lorries and a lot of camels, was kept below the escarpment.

For the first few days there were small air-raids, exchanges of mortar- and machine-gun-fire, aggressive patrols by KAR, police and *Dubas* and a couple of half-hearted enemy night-attacks. On 24 June the DC's party was withdrawn to Buna, except for six *Dubas* who volunteered to stay on as guides. A pensioned KAR sergeant, living in Italian territory, brought warning of enemy reinforcements. By 8 July the enemy strength amounted to three battalions, twenty light tanks and a battery of field artillery; and the garrison was surrounded. During the next five days it was shelled fairly heavily, and the commander was authorized to surrender or to fight his way out. On the night of 12 July, barefooted and guided by *Dubas*, the garrison withdrew silently between the enemy posts and down to the bottom of the hill, whence they went back to Buna.

Moyale was re-occupied in February 1941. Three months later there was a sad postscript to Cusack's monthly report, an obituary notice for Primo Capitano Marconi.

On his liberation Carter, the ASP, obtained compensation for his large stock of drink looted by the Italians. Nearly twenty years later Cusack, at a farewell dinner given him by the Police Mess on his retirement, confessed that his conscience (never a very sensitive organ) had been troubled by this. Actually, it was he, not the Italians, who had consumed Carter's drink supplies, lest they fall into enemy hands.

Immediately after the outbreak of war with Italy, Turkana was reinforced by Roger Wilkinson, who on his way to the front passed through Kenya's last line of defence,

> two chaps they'd sort of lifted from the bar of the Kitale Club, whose duty it was to blow the Nepau Pass if the Italians should be seen approaching. It is doubtful how successful

Ities, Bandas and Shiftas, 1935–1945

this ruse would have been, even if these chaps had been sober enough to press the button.

Another reinforcement was the Duke of Edinburgh's Rifles from Natal.

They were very good chaps indeed, if one is allowed nowadays to say that South Africans are good chaps. Not only did they wear no hats, but they stripped to the waist and exposed themselves to the pitiless Turkana sun. We all shook our heads and pursed our lips and said, 'Oh, they'll pay for this'; but they didn't, and that was the end of the topi.

Except for the DC, Major Gregory Smith, who sported an old-fashioned Wolseley helmet, embellished with a regimental hackle brought by a runner from his old battalion of the Black Watch in the Sudan. His other job was to command the Turkana Irregulars, raised by offering a .303 rifle, cartridge-belt and khaki mini-skirt to anyone who joined up. The Merille being pro-Italian, the Turkana were unshakeable in their attachment to the democratic cause. The Irregulars' officers included several settlers and John Dowson, recently DO, Lodwar. Wilkinson proceeded to the front line

> at a place called Kalin wells, where the KAR had constructed good defences with fields of fire and so on. Gregory Smith made his camp not, as you might expect, behind the soldiers but two or three hundred yards in front of them; so if the Italians had attacked, I don't quite know what would have happened. I camped with him, and he always expected the highest standards: so every evening we dined with a table-cloth and all that, and it was all very dignified and proper. But some of my friends, officers in the Irregulars, were camped about a hundred yards away, and we could hear loud shouts and big roars of conversation, indicating that they were having an extremely pleasant time, which could not be said for me. Gregory Smith used to mutter a bit, you know, saying it wasn't really a good thing that young men should behave in this way when the world was in such a serious position, and I used to go tut-tut

and agree with him in order to advance my career in the administration.

I renewed contact with my old friends the Abyssinian refugees. A party of young men were sent up to Turkana, issued with brand-new .303 rifles, and told to go and shoot some Italians. I don't think their presence affected the war to any great extent. I imagine they sold their rifles to the shiftas, or set up as shiftas themselves.

While the DC was in Lodwar, Mussolini unleashed his aerial might, two Savoya bombers attacking one morning and catching the DC in the outside lavatory: he had to make a run for it, pulling up his trousers. No damage was done except that the walls of the office were pitted with a few stones which was useful afterwards because any awkward questions asked by the Secretariat, the Treasury or the Supreme Court could be parried by the reply that the relevant papers had been destroyed by enemy action.

We used to get lots of light aircraft from Nairobi and kept dumps of aviation fuel hidden in the bush to re-fuel them. The chaps from the detention camp used to hump these 4-gallon tins up to the aircraft and pour the petrol into the tanks. The Turkana are not great dressers but they are extremely well-hung, and it always used to delight me to see the reaction of the pilots when they saw these splendid members swinging down from the chaps pouring in their petrol.

Early in 1941 the forces of democracy invaded Abyssinia with donkeys as their first-line transport. Dowson noted that the KAR:

> had no idea how to load and look after donkeys. They set off ahead of the Irregulars, but we soon caught up, coming upon a lively scene of chaos with donkeys milling about having shed their loads, and one upside down with a mortar-barrel across its belly.

From Bako, 5,000 feet, the Irregulars, having no clothes, had to be sent back because of the cold. Dowson was then transferred to Occupied Enemy Territories Administration (OETA) and stationed

Ities, Bandas and Shiftas, 1935–1945

at Mega. His superior was Gerald Reece who, besides being Officer-in-Charge, NFD, was Governor of Borana Province in Abyssinia. In this role he embarked with zest on the task of extracting from the tribes of Borana compensation for decades of murder, stock-theft and mayhem south of the border. They thought it most unfair when Dowson took down to Moyale a huge herd of their cattle for distribution to their victims. The NFD tribes thought that this was what the war was all about.

During the 10-day interregnum between the departure of the Italians and the British taking over, the pagan-Muslim war erupted in the good old style with hundred of murders and thousands of cattle lifted. The soldiers went on to Addis Ababa leaving the civilians and police to unravel chaos, all tribes now being armed with as many rifles and automatics as they could carry. Between Mandera and Lake Rudolf the only security forces were about a hundred Kenya police and *Dubas*. The chaos became worse in January 1942 when the Abyssinians took over from OETA.

The DO Mandera was 'Wee Willie' Keir who had joined the Administration from St Andrew's in 1935 and spent most of his service in the NFD. On 20 April 1942, he heard of a Somali *shifta* threatening an isolated clan of Gabbra, between Mandera and Moyale. His armed force immediately available consisted of ten Kenya police, of whom he sent five, under a Boran constable Osman Dikka, to look for them. At dawn on the 21st Osman Dikka was told by Gabbra tribesmen that the *shifta* had taken 600 of their camels. He sent word back to Keir, and with some Gabbra followed the tracks.

Osman Dikka was a resourceful tactician. The raiders were moving slowly, cumbered by the camels, and he managed to circle round and set up an ambush in front of them. The country was very 'close', with thick thorn-scrub and a visibility of only about fifteen yards.

The *shifta* consisted of about thirty riflemen, plus spearmen. Osman Dikka let the advanced guard go by and opened rapid fire at the left flank guard. Police markmanship was not as good as his tactics. Only two raiders were killed, but the camels stampeded and were rounded up by their owners. Exchanging fire with the enemy at point-blank range, Osman Dikka's party withdrew slowly as the camels were driven away. His little operation had been very successful.

But unknown to him, Keir and the other five askaris were following the *shifta*. Doubling towards the sound of the guns, they got into a fire fight with an unseen enemy of unknown strength at a few yards range. Keir was heard to say, 'Where are they firing from now? We're surrounded.' At that moment he was shot in the head and neck. The *shifta* than melted away in thick bush, leaving Keir and three askaris dead, and one badly wounded.

Surprisingly Keir's murderers, or some Somalis alleged to be his murderers, were caught by the Ethiopian authorities and hanged in Ethiopian Moyale. Reece and Grant were invited to be present, and could not in politeness refuse. The Ethiopians – experts, one would think – made such a botch of the executions that the British spectators begged them to give the victims the *coup de grace* by shooting, which was done while they still kicked at the end of the ropes.

The war had moved on from Turkana by December 1941 when Paul Kelly became DO Lodwar. Roger Wilkinson put him in the picture: 'There's not much to do here. Your chief task will be to protect Neil from being bullied by Gregory.'

Neil Loudon had come out to the KAR but had been shanghaied by the administration and posted to Lodwar. He was a graduate of St Andrew's (and a scratch golfer) with a Scottish accent. Gregory Smith thought that all members of the administration should be products of Rugby and Sandhurst, or at least Eton and Oxford. Gregory Smith had a great deal of dignity, and stood on it. Loudon on his early-morning rounds used to stop to play with Turkana children. Gregory Smith thought this conduct unbecoming, and used to take it out of Loudon by remarking to his dachshund, 'The district officer was five minutes late again, wasn't he, Messerschmidt?'

Towards Kelly he resorted to Socratic irony,

> telling me that he didn't know about desert affairs, but I was from the NFD, the prestige of which was far higher than that of Turkana, and could therefore enlighten him. Another foible of Gregory's was his belief that the administration

Ities, Bandas and Shiftas, 1935–1945

alone was privy to the *arcana imperii*, secrets denied to other departments. He called them 'our funny little administration shemozzles', which needed neither explanation nor justification.

Gregory Smith was a very capable DC and a great improver. He improved Lodwar no end, replacing houses and offices constructed of termite-ridden palm-trunks and thatch with cool, airy, wide-verandahed buildings, each house having a mosquito-proof sleeping cage on its roof. They were built mainly of bricks baked in kilns which he constructed. He made a swimming pool. He arranged for every officer and clerk to receive from Kapenguria a weekly box of fresh fruit and vegetables.

Every Christmas the houses he had built were invaded by mobs of Turkana women, singing, ullulating, reeking with the goats' fat with which they were bedaubed and flipping their breasts to spray the rooms with it. Not even Gregory Smith could put a stop to this, for it was useless to call the TPs, most of the girls being their wives and sisters.

He improved the Lodwar prison, which was constructed on the most advanced penological principles, with neither locks nor bars. By Turkana standards it was luxurious, and it had to be surrounded by barbed wire, not to keep the prisoners in, but to keep their friends and relations out.

In frontier affairs Gregory Smith, after the withdrawal of the KAR, devised a scheme which stopped large Merille raids for some years. A chain of five forts were built, each garrisoned by fifteen Kenya police and fifteen frontier tribal police. A raiding party could get in between the forts but, when the alarm had been given, would find it difficult to get out again with the stolen cattle. He instructed Kelly to put up a line of stone cairns, each topped with a long angle-iron post, a thousand yards apart. The Turkana were kept well back from this line; anyone found between it and the Ethiopian frontier was presumed to be a raider, and shot at sight. To the angle-iron posts nearest to the Merille Kelly attached some skulls found nearby, scene of a recent massacre. This was intended as a warning, but he felt rather ashamed of it, 'an example of the brutalising influence of the NFD'.

The Frontier Tribal Police were the Turkana Irregulars renamed, instructed and commanded by picked NCOs of the regular tribal police. They were a very useful force, and at first included some Merille. Eventually these deserted, the risk of murder by Turkana being too great; but they honourably left their rifles and ammunition behind.

Kelly, of course, did a lot of safari, camping generally in a place written large on the map but containing no human habitation, a dry laggar junction, perhaps, with a few waterholes dug in the sand and some shady trees. One safari was to Teleki's Volcano, six days from Lodwar. They marched mainly in the cool of the night, and once Kelly was apprised by loud cries of *Otakhoi*! (O, my mother!) that the guide had lost the way. Having been making a study of the stars, he took a chance and insisted on a 90 degree change of course. Dawn, to his triumph, showed that he was bang on target.

The volcano, dormant for some decades, is a cone of clinker, cinders and gravel. The lava-flows from it are shiny black, contrasting with the rust-coloured clinker on either side. In Kelly's year, after good rains, the foot of the volcano was like a rock-garden with clumps of campanula, convolvulus and orchids.

Gregory Smith, having made his mark on Turkana, was rewarded by a transfer to Kericho, and was succeeded by Turnbull. If a man was to remain long in Turkana and stay sane, he must have intellectual interests. Turnbull's included classical music on an expensive gramophone, and compiling a list of NFD and Turkana trees, with their names in Latin, Somali, Boran and Turkana.

One of his earliest safaris, with Kelly, was to the cedar-forested mountain of Lorienatom with shade, rock-pools, log-fires at night. Transport was by donkey.

> Donkey transport is a bit slow, and loading is very disorderly. I sensed Dick Turnbull's growing disgust and, fearing he would make the mistake of interfering, I said, 'The loading of donkeys cannot be done in an orderly fashion as with camels. The best you can do is to turn your back on it, sit down and read a book. The shouting and braying will soon be over.'

Ities, Bandas and Shiftas, 1935–1945

A pleasant Sunday or week-end trip from Lodwar was to Ferguson's Gulf, forty miles by a good lorry track. The gulf is a shallow lagoon separated from the main lake by a long white sand-spit, on which a group of thatched bandas served as a camp. The fluoride-tainted water teems with tiger-fish, tilapia and Nile perch of which the smaller ones, up to 10 lb, are very good eating.

The lake crocodiles grow to an enormous size, sixteen feet or more. They are said not to be man-eaters. (Turkana, however, are croc-eaters.) It would be unwise to count on this. Jake Cusack took a party to the lake. They had a refreshing bathe, knee-deep; then a little beer in the shade; and then called in vain for the cook. A search of the shore produced only his severed arm. He had gone in too deep.

Kelly was exasperated by the failure of the ASP and European inspectors ever to go on foot safaris: they stayed in the forts, occasionally venturing out by lorry. Police patrols invariably followed the same route, like London bobbies on the beat. It was a miracle that none was ambushed. The friction over foot safaris brought a visit from the Commissioner of Police, whose ambition it was to make the police independent of the administration, if not superior. At Kokoru fort the Commissioner said:

'If there was a surprise attack at this moment by the Merille, who would take command?' [thinking it obvious that he would]. Turnbull replied, 'I am in command. I am directly responsible to the Chief Secretary.' In the awkward pause that followed he picked up a bottle of HP Sauce and read the description of the contents, adding embellishments of his own – spices from the mystic orient, etc.

The Turkana had never had it so good as during the war years. The Merille were kept at a distance by Gregory Smith's forts. Many Turkana joined the KAR or the Frontier Tribal Police, or were employed building the new forts or making roads to them. Year after year there were good rains, and an excellent market for Turkana cattle and shoats. The *baraza* held in honour of the CNC, 'John Willie' Hosking:

was a stirring sight, so many fine tall men, the elders with great chignons down their backs, younger men with elaborate coiffures of red and blue clay set off with ostrich plumes, ivory lip-plugs, bracelets and necklaces, squatting on their little stool-pillows, naked and uncircumcised.

Hosking who had fought against them was delighted by their present prosperity, and by the powerful antiphonal humming, swelling into the full-throated 'Tobacco Song', which indicated – like slow handclaps in another environment – that his speech had gone on too long, he should shut up and sit down.

13

Breakthrough

The KAR, after a shaky start in the NFD, fought with great credit in Abyssinia, Madagascar and Burma. There was no lack of volunteers. They returned from the war with pockets full of unspent pay and gratuities; with expectations of priority in the allocation of government jobs, trading and lorry licenses; and with a knowledge of the world that could make them politicians.

In 1943 the Colonial Development and Welfare Act adumbrated funds for post-war development in the colonies, breaking the barren rule that every colony must be financially self-supporting; and in 1946 the Labour government allocated £3 million for African agricultural development in Kenya. The fund was administered, the district schemes vetted, by a board with ever-changing names which will for simplicity be referred to only as the African Land Development Board (ALDEV). Its chairman and secretary were administrative officers, the first chairman being the one-legged Eric Anderson.

The agricultural revolution started in Kipsigis, with the return of hundreds of men from the war. They received, of course, the lion's share of the loaves and fishes. In addition, many defied the tradition that land was the property of the tribe, not of the individual, by clearing and fencing shambas in the bush. Because there was no shortage of land, this was not generally resented.

Taking over as DC from Gregory Smith in 1946 Tony Swann, who had commanded Kipsigis in Abyssinia and was well known to the tribe, pulled out all the stops on soil conservation, terracing and blocking eroded gullies with communal labour. 'We plugged it and plugged it for eighteen months', touring the district and drumming it into the people that all was in vain if their topsoil was washed away. Swann continued:

Fortunately the Kipsigis used ox-drawn ploughs, so the agricola* and his staff marked out strips through their cultivated land along the contours and spaced according to the gradient. These were left to grass over. Between the strips they ploughed, along the contour, not up-and-down, to stop erosion.

Anyone who insisted on ploughing up-and-down was prosecuted for breach of the African District Council (ADC)† by-laws, in African district courts which were very firm on this. But on the whole the Kipsigis were receptive to new ideas. Swann also got the ADC to ban cultivation within thirty yards of any river or swamp. This, too, checked erosion, 'and within a year the women were coming to thank us because for the first time in their lives they had clean water'.

They needed more water, to lessen the concentrations of cattle round permanent water. The ADC hankered after boreholes which never dry up; but Swann preferred dams which did not lower the water-table. At first they were made by communal labour and ox-drawn scoops; soon the ADC was hiring tractors which did the job much quicker.

Nothing delighted the Kipsigis more than the transfer to them of some unused European estates, which were divided into small farms, laid out by Kipsigis surveyors, with enough common pasture for cattle. 'They thought this the most marvellous thing that had ever happened.' Their only crop was maize, introduced by Dobbs in the 1920s, for which there was unlimited demand during the war and for famine relief in Machakos after 1945.

It was maize, maize, maize. We got them onto the simplest rotation – divide your holding into two, half for crops, half

---

*Agricola: a common term for Agricultural Officer.
†African District Council (ADC): the new name for Local Native Council.

Breakthrough

for cattle, changing every three years. It was brought about by endless, saturation propaganda. You put down your chair and started off. Over the years the message got through and they said, 'It works!'

A maize-cess was collected. Part went to the ADC for agricultural purposes; part was used to subsidize the transport of maize from remote areas so that cultivation was not concentrated round roadhead; and part paid as a subsidy to farmers who manured their land properly. It was no more than common sense.

District teams were all the rage, with departmental heads meeting under the DC's chairmanship to plan and co-ordinate development; so that, for instance, the same people would not be required simultaneously to dig a dam, build a school and bring their cattle for inoculation. A district team provided continuity when individuals were transferred.

We in the Administration said, 'It's for you experts to tell us what needs to be done. We will then use all our influence and staff to see it is done.' This was important because when it came to the crunch the African knew that it wasn't the agricola or the vet who carried the day, it was the DC. Kericho was blessed by a wonderful agricola, Graham Gamble. What a splendid chap!

Lower down the scale each location had its agricultural committee of chief, prominent farmers, agricultural instructor and, if possible, embryo politicians who could there be coaxed into being *for* something, instead of against everything. The committee kept a check on manuring, contour-ploughing, etc.

A pilot scheme for improving the cattle was planned for the Belgut division, 40 square miles next to Kericho town. It would include the sale of surplus stock, dipping against tick-borne East Coast fever, inoculation against rinderpest; and finally, when the area was 'clean', the introduction of two Sahiwal bulls and purebred Boran heifers to upgrade the local stock. The scheme was to be based on four large group-farms run by 57 families. At the heart of it was a demonstration collective farm run by five families.

> We took a complete ridge and divided it up into what should be done ecologically. Where it was stony, we put wattle and trees; where the soil was good, we put food crops; where the grass was particularly good, that was the pasture. We rotated, we had machinery which a collective could afford; the cultivation was very well done. Absolutely perfect in theory, a show-piece. People came from miles to look at this wonderful thing. In five years it was stone-dead because the chaps said, 'We don't like it. We see the advantages, but we want our own land.'

So Kipsigis development proceeded on the basis of individual farms.

> We were lucky in that the district, lying fallow for years, had not been mucked up. It's easy to do something from scratch. It's when you have to unscramble everything that life becomes ten times more difficult.

It was ten times more difficult in Machakos, ruined by overstocking and soil erosion. Between the wars some DCs had kept alive a tiny flicker of no-cost development, planting trees on bare hilltops, piling up 'trashlines' of bush and burnt treestumps along the contours; in twenty years 64 dams had been dug, most of which held some water. These puny efforts, however, did not check the destruction of the district. But money was at last available: between 1946 and 1955 ALDEV spent £800,000 on the restoration of Machakos.

Jack Howes, DC 1946–49, and the agricola decided what had to be done, and extracted from the ADC a reluctant consent to give it a trial. Machakos was to be rescued in two ways: by demonstrating what could be made of the worst sheet-eroded land, and by resettling families in an area hitherto closed by wild animals, water shortage and thick bush.

Breakthrough

In 1949 the holders of a square mile of land at Mukaveti were persuaded by J. W. Howard, Howes' successor, to lend their land for five years to the Agricultural Department to see what could be done with it. The bare red earth, dotted with desiccated thorn-trees and seamed with eroded gullies, had a carrying capacity of about one beast to thirty acres. An African betterment team, under the inspired leadership of John Malinda, a Kamba district assistant, moved in. Thirty-two acres were fenced in half-acre paddocks. Experiments showed that grass cover could best be restored by ridging the land and planting two varieties of grass which were found to be colonizing the enclosures spontaneously.

For two years no cattle were allowed to graze on the Mukaveti Square Mile. This was expected to be the snag: where would they go?

Some were sent to the owners' relations elsewhere; most were kept at home, never grazed but fed on grass cut from the roadside, leaves, weeds, maize-trash. 'They got very thin,' said John Malinda, 'but they were thin before.' The point was that they survived, and when they came out they found a feast awaiting them, thick grass, knee-high. In three years it was proved that the worst sheet-eroded land could be restored to fertility, and could then hold one cow to two acres, stall-fed on sileage during the dry months when grazing did most damage. Machakos, properly managed, could hold far more cattle than anyone had imagined.

The Square Mile was only a tiny pilot scheme. When in 1951 Hughes-Rice arrived as district agricultural officer and saw the state of the district as a whole, he sat on a hill and wept. Thousands of miles of terracing were needed to save the topsoil; and as funds were not nearly enough to pay the labour, men had to be pressed to work, a gift to the politicians. But Hughes-Rice had a wonderful power of persuasion. He and successive DCs, Howard and R. J. C. Thorp, achieved a breakthrough. They were abetted by T. G. Askwith, a former DC who as Commissioner for Community Development and Principal of the Jeanes School of Adult Education, turned out men trained in putting across policy by persuasion and example, not by compulsion. The idea caught on of terracing by groups of men and, even more, women, called out not by the chiefs of their locations but by the elders of their clans. It was a return to the traditional Kamba method, known as *mwethya*, of saving the harvest. And it trumped the politicians' ace, because in no way could it be described as colonialist exploitation. Tom Askwith, who had been trying to sell 'self-help' to sceptical DCs, had cause for satisfaction.

The *mwethya* leaders, chosen by the clan itself, were full of ideas. Everyone was brought in to the work – some to bring drinking water to the labourers, old men to mend broken mattock-handles, a retired nurse to treat injuries, drummers and conductors for the song-and-dance which made the work go with a swing to the thump, thump, thump of bare feet, spades and mattocks striking in unison.

First the agricultural staff pegged out the line of the contour. Then the ploughmen cut furrows to mark the line and loosen the parched earth. Men followed with mattocks to loosen the earth yet further; and then the women and girls shovelled it up into a bank. From being a penance introduced by an autocratic government, it became their own enterprise, with clans competing for the best results. The women designed uniforms for themselves, and composed songs so that they could shovel in unison. By working rhythmically the desperately hard work became even enjoyable. They were amazed by the amount of earth they had shifted by the end of the morning.

'This group is very fierce,' an agricultural instructor told Elspeth Huxley, indicating a line of young women throwing the earth above their heads and clinking shovels with tremendous gusto and abandon, keeping time with a rollicking song:

The askaris used to be strong and bold as lions,
They went to fight and they were fierce as lions,
But now it is we who are strong and bold as lions.
Now we are strong as the askaris.
Now we are stronger than the askaris, stronger than lions,
Yeh! Yeh! Yeh! Stronger than askaris or lions.

Breakthrough

The hillsides became striped with contour-terracing, the grass began to grow and long-dry springs to flow again. Dams were built, small ones by ox-scoops and *mwethya* labour, large ones by earth-moving machinery, dozens a year. In Machakos district 269 seasonal and 52 large, permanent dams, were built in sixteen years. Also built were 226 sub-surface dams. This was a concrete wall built up flush with the surface of the sand in a dry river-bed. When the river came down in flood, the sand above the wall became saturated with water which neither flowed away nor evaporated, and could be piped to a trough below. 22 boreholes were also drilled, but the emphasis was on conserving surface water.

The other 'leg' of development was settling the Kamba in empty lands. When Howard arrived in 1946

> Some experts thought that huge areas might have to be closed for ten or twenty years and the people moved elsewhere. But where?
> The obvious area was Makueni, adjacent to the reserve but uninhabitable because of thick bush, tsetse fly and lack of permanent water. Makueni Settlement was originally planned as a temporary relief area for farmers whose land was being re-conditioned. The success of the Mukaveti Square Mile meant that not many people need be moved. Makueni could be a permanent settlement, not just a relief area.

It was the favourite scheme of Sir Philip Mitchell, Governor of Kenya 1944–52. He regarded it as second in importance only to the over-hasty, under-researched, disastrous Tanganyika Groundnuts Scheme. At the end of 1944 he ordered that it must *start* by 1 January 1946.

Anticipating this by some weeks, David Christie-Miller, just out of the Sudan Defence Force, with 20 very sceptical Kamba, 20 shovels, 20 mattocks, 20 pangas and some wheelbarrows, began clearing 50,000 acres of thorn-bush in order to get rid of the tsetse-fly. They soon came upon the first obstacle: rhino.

> The bush was teeming with them, and my men were scared stiff. A charming old man from the Game Department,

John Hunter, was sent to join me, and shot about a hundred in the first month. Every tree was festooned with drying meat and the work-force got fatter than they had been in all their lives.

Altogether 1,078 rhino were shot to make Makueni habitable for Kamba. To us, making out cheques for 'Save the Rhino Fund', this is a horrid slaughter. But no farmer can share his farm with rhino. The Makueni pioneers used to wear no shoes, so that they could get up a tree quicker when chased.

Christie-Miller was 'engaged in this absurd exercise for six weeks', and then transferred.

It was only a token start. In 1946 money was for the first time available, £60,000 for the first two years. In charge was Hugh York, an agricola who pushed the tsetse fly back by the only sure method, clearing by machinery the bush in which the fly lived. York worked out an agricultural plan based on collective farms each worked by twenty families. They drilled a borehole, piped water from it, cleared plots for cultivation and introduced a few cattle.

What was needed was a whole-time administrator, and one was found in J. W. Balfour who came out of the KAR with a reputation for efficiency and the sympathetic handling of Africans. He arrived in January 1947 at the group of tents which was the Makueni Settlement headquarters, 'under the mighty limestone crag of Nzawi with its pair of guardian Verreaux eagles'. He was annoyed when Myles North was brought in over him, as DO Southern Areas. Fortunately they got on well, and North concentrated on four other grazing/ranching schemes, leaving Makueni largely to Balfour.

North used to say that ornithology was his profession, administration his hobby; and he was immersed in his great thesis on *Notation of Bird Song*.

Although he had the worst stammer I [Balfour] ever met, he had the gift of perfect pitch, and could reproduce on his recorder any note he heard, and write it down on

Breakthrough

a blank sheet of music. He seldom used the expensive recording apparatus given him by an American millionaire ornithologist, preferring to sit under a tree, blowing his recorder at little birds and writing down their replies in musical notation.

Soon we were ready to invite the Kamba in to start a better life. They refused. They said that Makueni belonged to the Kamba anyway, which was true; and the only reason why they had not occupied it before was because of rhinos and tsetse fly and lack of water, which was also true. Now that these obstacles were being overcome, they wished to go in with no rules nor stock limitation and (they said) they were quite capable of taking care of it in their own fashion – which was far from true. [They particularly disliked the idea of communal farms.]

The deadlock continued well into 1947, and we felt frustrated by the attitude of the people we were trying to help. But work continued, more bush was cleared, and boreholes were harnessed for water. 1947 was a good year for rains. The experimental crops flourished, the cattle brought in as guinea-pigs grew sleek and fat.

Jomo Kenyatta was brought onto the ALDEV Board in 1947, though he was adamant against any controlled settlement, and his views had been lavishly fed to the ADC. But as they watched from their barren hills, some Kamba began to wonder if their leaders had been right. They needed land, and Makueni looked tempting. Balfour worked on

> the labour force, then on neighbouring chiefs. Finally, after a meal of hard-boiled eggs and beer, the chief and headmen of Masii location undertook to bring a sizeable body of their own people to sign up, provided each had an *individual* right to his own patch of land. The agricolas still hankered after collective farming; but influential members of the Machakos Re-Conditioning Committee, Frank Joyce and F. O'B. Wilson, backed it, and before the end of the year, settlement began. I was called to attend a meeting of the

ALDEV Board. Jomo Kenyatta was there, and Paddy Merrick, a Thika farmer, shouted in his exuberant fashion, 'Hallo, Jomo! I hear Colonel Balfour has beaten you!' Old Jomo didn't bat an eyelid, and with a broad grin replied, 'Jolly good luck to him!'

From the first trickle of settlers the numbers swelled, and by the end of 1950 there were over 2,000 people on land that 'for a cycle of Cathay' had been in sole possession of tsetse fly and rhinos.

Among the new intake was Onesimus Musyoko, an educated Kamba who had been in the Soil Conservation Service, knew how to use a theodolite and to teach others to use it. Within a few weeks we had a small élite team, surveying and marking the 20 acre holdings and linking them by roads following the contours of the land.

Applicants for settlement were interviewed and those selected were brought into 'details camps'. Each then worked on preliminary clearing until allocated his 20-acre holding. Having built a house, he brought in his family and a few milch-cows. His 5 acres of arable land was ploughed for him, and he cleared the remaining 15 acres. When he had stumped the land and fenced it in 2-acre paddocks, he could bring in more cows. He was paid and rationed until he harvested his first crop. It was proved possible to keep ten head of cattle in good health without them ever grazing outside the holding, stall-feeding them on sileage during the dry season. It changed pre-conceived theories of 20 acres to the beast, and was a revelation to the Kamba. By 1962 a total of 2,187 families had been settled on Makueni at a cost of £148 a family.

The agricultural revolution [wrote Howard] was enormously helped by Europeans who farmed on the edge of the Kamba reserve. Several put all their experience and much time and energy into the Machakos Reconditioning Committee and into safaris to inspect progress. Their names should be recorded in letters of gold – Frank Joyce, Sir Robert Shaw and Sir Frank Wilson.

Breakthrough

A new system of administration, started by Jack Howes in Machakos, was spreading to other heavily populated, advanced districts. It is well described by D. W. Hall who introduced it to South Nyanza.

When I took over one DO was responsible for African courts, another for roads and bridges, a third for liaison with the agricolas and vets, and so on, over the whole district. I did not like this. It did not give a DO the general experience he needed, or the chance to know any part of the district well. I divided the district geographically into three 'divisions' with a DO in charge of everything in each division. They were to tour repeatedly in their divisions and get to know all about them. They should compile a divisional gazetteer and map with every road, dam, school, mission, chief's office etc listed and marked; and should visit all these regularly. Any activity or personality in their divisions was their concern. The DOs liked having kingdoms of their own. They really got to know their divisions and their people and could show me things I never knew about, and recognise people we met casually on a road or at a market.

Each division was divided into about four locations, each of which was in charge of a chief. The DO actually lived in his division, instead of at district headquarters.

D. J. Penwill (DSO, Oxford first in history), taking over Machakos from Thorp in 1954, developed the system yet further. Each divisional DO had under him two 'field officers' of the Agricultural Department, each responsible for two locations, whose task was to improve the standards of husbandry, guide the communal effort, organize nurseries for cash-crops and generally implement the Betterment Scheme. Their paperwork was limited to a single monthly report and the payment of their staff on vouchers prepared in the DC's office. All three lived, with their wives, in a sub-station too small to have a club to cut them off from Africans; but the wives had each other's company by day, and it was arranged that one officer should always be in at night to give them confidence. Each field officer had one near and one distant location, which he got to know in detail. In alternate weeks he commuted out and back to the near location, and camped in the more distant.

DOs were relieved of paperwork as far as possible, and complicated court cases were heard in Machakos. Each officer had a land rover and a tent. The land rover took his kit from one camp-site to another while he spent the day 'walking up and down hillsides, talking with headmen and elders, visiting every holding, inspecting communal work, perhaps hearing some land appeals and holding a *baraza*'.

It was an intelligent adaptation of the foot safari to the era of the land rover. In Kangundo the debonaire Peter Derrick, back in Kenya after four years in Aden, by keeping horses, saw more of his division with less toil and sweat.

More heavy machinery was used. At first the bulldozers seemed to spend most of their time in pieces, awaiting spare parts; but the Kamba make good mechanics and soon got the hang of them. Those who thought the bulldozers would do all the work while they drank beer and applauded were soon disillusioned; they created a great deal of hard manual work in levelling and clearing up. Sisal was the most promising cash-crop, and made quick-growing, stock-proof fences. The worst setback was foot-and-mouth disease, just when the Kamba had accepted the need to sell cattle. It was this sort of thing that broke a DC's heart.

In 1955 the first water was delivered from the Yatta Canal, dug by machinery and Mau Mau detainees, which was to make a great loop from the Thika river to the Tana, serving a quarter-million acres of Machakos and Kitui, well grassed but lacking permanent water. A niggling accountant might argue that to spend £324,849 in keeping alive 25,000 skinny cattle was hardly an economic triumph, but as Chief Timothy Murai orated at the opening ceremony

> From today water will flow through country which has been dry since the beginning of the world, from today every householder will have water close by. From today rivers and streams will run instead of being beds of sand and stone. From today we shall not fear the failure of the rains.

Breakthrough

The changes were as much in attitudes as in material developments. In 1954 Penwill reported:

> It is now possible for ADC members to deal with all their committees' reports without my taking the chair, which I only do to clear up the most controversial matters. Committee members seem quite prepared to explain the why and wherefore without throwing the responsibility on a European.

The members' hearts were in education — 4 new intermediate and 12 new primary schools a year. But they actually passed a by-law under which a farmer could be set a limit to the stock on his holding. 'We have come a long way since 1938.'

Two thousand acres a year were planted with trees, to check the run-off during the rains. It was desperate work digging tree-seedlings into concrete-like hilltops with a failure rate of 25–50 per cent. Nevertheless people actually gave the ADC considerable areas of (admittedly useless) land for that purpose. This was indeed progress!

Kitui, the eastern part of Ukambani, is twice as large as Machakos, with a smaller human and animal population. There was not the same urgency to save the land, but development got going in 1948 with the arrival of Paul Kelly. The work was done by pressed gangs of men only. No one liked it, but in 1949 and 1950 9,000 acres a year were protected by terracing, gully-plugging, scratch-ploughing and grass-planting.

The greatest need was for water. The annual rainfall over most of the district varies from 15 to 25 inches, well below that of Machakos, and it is very patchy, so in any year many dams do not fill. A strong advocate of white settlement (he married a settler's daughter) Kelly was also dedicated to African advancement. He took a party of Kitui notables to see the water storage arrangements on the Joyce and Wilson ranches, where the land was similar to Kitui, with an even smaller rainfall.

Joyce was using dam-scoops drawn by oxen, working continually to add dams to valleys already dammed. No rainwater was allowed to flow off the farm; the houses had gutters and rainwater tanks, the rock-catchments had 'garlands'. Wilson's manager showed us wide furrows on a $1/2$ per cent grade draining one catchment into another. They absorbed the lesson.

Between 1927 and 1947 thirty-four dams were made in Kitui disrict. My aim was two dams a year in each of 25 locations. The ADC would pay £50 towards each, in cash or rations for the working parties: ALDEV would pay £1 for £1 and provide the tools.

Sites were selected by chiefs, and vetted by DOs using a Dumpy level. A wide spillway was pegged out to cope with flash-floods. The core-trench was excavated, 6 feet wide, across the stream-bed and up the sides, down to an impermeable layer, the soil being thrown downstream to form part of the wall. The trench was then filled with puddled clay from the dam-basin. The basin was then excavated, the spoil being thrown on the wall which when finished had a crest 6 feet wide, a forward slope of 1 to 3 to the basin and 1 to 2 downstream.

Every chief had a water bailiff, generally an ex-sergeant, supplied with a uniform and an imprest of 135 tools (wheelbarrows, basins, picks, mattocks, shovels, hoes and a string-level). DOs on safari took with them spare tools and wheelbarrow parts. Maintenance was as important as construction. The water bailiff was responsible if a dam failed through neglect of a wall (tree roots, termite nests), or of the hedge surrounding the dam to check silting.

Old people earned their rations by tamping down the dam wall, young men and maidens by shifting the soil, with a leader for their singing. In the evening they practised new dances.

In 1948 10 dams were built; in 1949, 34; thereafter about 50 a year until the total reached 500 in 1958. Of these, 75 were 'permanent', 416 were seasonal; 24 were rock-catchments, usually permanent; and 35 were sub-surface.

Dams and rock-catchments were Kelly's delight, and what better way of finding new sites, for a disciple of Reece and Turnbull, than

Breakthrough

by foot safaris in remote places? Their baggage might be driven from camp to camp by Land-Rover, but he and his DOs walked through the bush to know the people and know the country. Kelly records that for the Governor's visit the Kamba rose to the occasion. It was

> like an Elizabethan royal progress – scouts posted on high rocks to signal the approach of the cavalcade, the route lined with cheering men and ullulating women, drummers and dancers; and a new lane, lined with white-washed stones, leading to the latest dam with fenced and terraced catchment, stone-pitched spillway and stone-pitching on the wall to prevent erosion by waves.

Chief Nzilu of Yatta, a retired sergeant and a talented bullshit artist, had a private bugler to sound the General Salute. As *pièce de résistance*, to the Governor's camp-site flocks of guineafowl had been attracted by millet residue from brewing – slightly intoxicating, so that the birds would not fly too fast or too far when His Excellency opened fire.

14

No Breakthrough

Next to Machakos was the Masai district of Kajiado, 8000 square miles from the outskirts of Nairobi to the Tanganyika border, with an average rainfall of 18 inches, not enough for arable farming. Robin Wainwright found that

> The Masai had a total conviction that their lifestyle was superior to anyone else's, which meant that they never toadied to Europeans, and had excellent manners. Nor did they lie when charged with stocktheft or murder. Being averse to manual labour, many employed Kikuyu. Moreover, Masai women being notoriously infertile, many married Kikuyu girls who became more Masai than the Masai but still nagged their husbands into employing their relatives to do the chores. The large number of Kikuyu caused much annoyance, and at every *baraza* demands would be made that the Government send them all back home. At the end of the *baraza* there would be a queue of Masai, each to say that he supported the demand in principle, but there was just one Kikuyu working for him . . .
> Convicted stock-thieves were employed on road-work. To lessen the degradation of manual labour, they used to hire a bus to take them to and from work, kindly allowing their warders to travel free.

The Masai diet consisted of blood and milk, the latter curdled with cow's urine. To draw the blood, a stopped arrow was shot

No Breakthrough

into the jugular vein, and the flow stemmed as soon as enough blood was drawn. This complicated the provision of education, which the chiefs thought quite a good thing, lest in future the Masai be governed by men of base tribes. For a semi-nomadic people, only boarding schools were of any use. Each pupil had to come with his mother and enough cows to feed them both, which necessitated a great deal of reserved grazing. Not all fathers were convinced of the value of book-learning, so the chiefs used to detail parents to send their sons to school, and fine them if they didn't. They then brought the fines to the DC, who could not credit them to government since African education was not compulsory. So into the goat bag they went.

Wainwright went on leave, and was succeeded by Roger Wilkinson, during whose régime a report came in of two parties of moran, with greased spears, working themselves up for battle. The DC and DO being on safari, the Goan cashier stepped into the breach.

He put down his pen and blotted his copybook and put the money in the safe and locked it, and got hold of a TP and the interpreter and a lorry from somewhere and set off. He eventually came upon the moran who were still making odd noises and jumping up and down and having epileptic fits as was their custom. So he went up to one lot and said, 'I think this is enough. I think you had better go home.' And he spoke similarly to the other lot and they all went home; and the cashier went back too and continued recording the cash transactions in the office.

> Clarence Buxton was an extremely courageous man, I do not doubt that, but I think the danger threatened by collections of moran having fits was perhaps slightly exaggerated.

The DC Narok, the other Masai district, was Hugh Grant, gaining experience of a down-country district before replacing Bailward as officer-in-charge, Masai. Bailward was not the only one who doubted the wisdom of this appointment, writing to Reece, 'I love dear old Hugh, but I don't throw up my cap as high as perhaps I should.'

During the war the Masai, unwilling to take an active part, had sold cattle as their contribution to the war effort. With the hard-won consent of the ADC, sales continued after the war, with chiefs and elders naming those who must bring in cattle for sale. Before a sale on 16 August 1946, a moran named Karambu ole Sendayo ignored their order, and at their request a TP was sent to requisition one of his beasts, returning with a fine black bull, Karambu's favourite beast. Karambu pleaded, more than once, for permission to exchange it for several other animals. Grant brushed him off, saying that he had had his chance to send another animal. Late in the afternoon, with the dust hanging in choking clouds and myriads of flies swarming round, Karambu made a last appeal. Grant, exasperated, told him to get lost. Karambu brooded for a while and then suddenly hurled his heavy spear into Grant's back with such force that it passed through the body and stuck quivering in a fence post. Grant died at once, an unworthy end for a valiant man-at-arms. Karambu was arrested by his fellow moran and, after trial, executed. The Masai, shocked and repentant, held special cattle-sales which contributed £2,000 towards the education of Grant's children.

Wilkinson took over Narok.

> Our policy was simple. It was (a) to prevent stock-theft, which was very difficult as it was a popular way of spending the time; and (b) to try and get across the idea that it is better to have slightly fewer cattle and better ones, and that grazing should be to some extent controlled and preserved so that it had a chance to regenerate. All this fell on deaf ears. We produced logical reasons why they should do this and that, and they paid not the slightest attention. It was all carried on in the most courteous way, everyone was terribly polite and we got on very well together. They just would not play, and who's to say they did not have some right on their side?

Wilkinson was three years in Narok and greatly enjoyed it. A DC could still do foot safaris, his baggage carried by donkeys.

> I used to look at the map and find odd places which no one knew anything about, and go there on foot, and this very much annoyed the locals who used to complain to my orderly,

No Breakthrough

ole Ndutu, that he was allowing me into places which had previously been sanctuaries from interference.

In one camp I went to bed and the chaps twenty or thirty yards away made a big fire and were sitting round it, and from the fire I heard the noises familiar to us all, mutterings of conversation, and little songs, now and again a great roar of laughter indicating that some talented mimic was giving his impression of the DC. The conversation suddenly stopped. I was half asleep and paid no attention, but after a bit the conversation sprung up again in a more animated manner, and a chap came over and told me that a rhino had walked up to my bed, looked down, sniffed it and then gone away.

Sometimes his wife and three sons accompanied him. One night several lions entered the camp, 'causing much excitement. With great presence of mind ole Ndutu took the three little boys out of bed and hoisted them up a tree'.

Kisumu was less fun, with no game, no foot safaris and no agricultural development. The Luo had fairly fertile soil and good rainfall; the land was not overstocked. They saw no reason to change the farming practices of their ancestors. But they were keenly interested in politics-cum-commerce. As the second largest tribe in Kenya (757,043 at the 1948 census) they did not wish to be dominated by the Kikuyu (1,026,341). Charles Atkins, DC, 1945–50, encouraged this interest in public affairs, laying on the elected ADC as much detailed administrative work as possible. Tax collection was solely in the hands of chiefs, with a paid staff to help them; and the African courts were reorganized into a statutory system with written records and a ladder of appeal courts. Atkins had one of the first African DOs, Isaak Okwirri, who had been a company sergeant major and was a very good one. Atkins recalls:

> There were two major factions in Luo politics. One was led by Oginga Odinga whose endeavours to build up a Luo business company had my full support. His reputed Marxism was less than skin-deep: he told me that he went to China and adopted some of the tenets of communism merely to

get financial backing, as his rival for the Luo leadership, Tom Mboya, had tapped the United States for funds. Mboya had his base in the trade unions in Nairobi.

Kisumu had enormously improved since Atkins was last there before the war. No longer was the Kavirondo Gulf regarded as a death-trap.

A man named Rowe of the PWD drew the plans and built a yacht of 16 ft LOA known as the Rainbow Class. Others were built by a Sikh carpenter from his plans. Simply rigged, with only a mainsail and jib, these proved very safe family boats for inexperienced helmsmen, while giving plenty of enjoyable racing for those who wanted the sport.

Atkins was Commodore of the Yacht Club and, by an adroit combination of seamanship and gamesmanship, won most of the races. Crocodiles and hippos added a spice to sailing.

P. M. Gordon was posted to South Nyanza as a cadet. His wife joined him in Kisii and the DC, Eric Davies,

> kindest and most considerate of men, sent us out on a 2-weeks safari under canvas. I think he meant it as a second honeymoon. I was to build a dam. I had not the remotest idea how to do so. However, I selected a site in a small stream, the chief arrived with an eager band of workers and after a week I gazed complacently at a structure which might have served as a model for a barrage across the Nile.
> That night a storm broke, with spectacular lightning, prolonged rolls of thunder and torrential rain. At dawn I walked down the stream. It gurgled merrily, uninterrupted in its flow by a few scattered heaps of mud and stone. The chief and workers appeared. We all gazed at the ruin in silence. Then someone laughed, and the laughter spread, and the women began to move in a swaying dance, clapping their hands. The men joined in, stamping their feet to a chanting chorus. When the celebration ended I dished out the small payments I had been authorised to give 'on completion of the

No Breakthrough

dam'. At last everyone dispersed, still laughing and singing and dancing; and Marianne and I, a bit shamefaced but happy enough, made our way back to the boma.

North Nyanza (formerly Kakamega) was plagued by a sinister religious sect. The Dini ya Msambwa (DYM), Religion of the Spirits of the Departed, a heady mix of African paganism, the Old Testament and hatred of Europeans, originated in the Kitosh tribe in North Nyanza in 1943. In 1948 it was proscribed as an unlawful society, but continued to thrive on grievances relating to district council by-laws for the control of squatters. Its leader then was Lukas Kipkoech, a mission-educated Suk, who after fomenting serious riots was sentenced to two years imprisonment. In 1949 he escaped, and took up his abode in a maze of caves in Elgeyo-Marakwet, proselytizing among the West Suk and causing trouble, including arson and cattle-maiming, on European farms. He claimed to be the Son of God, risen from the dead.

The East Suk of Baringo district seemed to be untroubled by the DYM. In his annual report for 1948 the DC, A. B. Simpson, did not mention it. It was dams and soil erosion and grazing control that he was discussing with his successor, A. J. Stevens, on a handing-over safari on 22 April 1949.

At the African Inland Mission at Nginyang in the northern part of the district, the Reverend T. W. G. Collins, who had been there fourteen years and spoke Suk, told them that he had been harassed by some two hundred tribesmen armed with spears and shields. The shields were significant: Suk warriors always carried one or two long spears, but not shields unless they were going to war. Simpson was confident that with the eight TPs he had with him he could deal with a rowdy mob. He sent two TPs to follow the dancers and, if possible, arrest the leader. Some hours later the TPs arrived back. They had found about two hundred tribesmen dancing in frenzy. It had been impossible to arrest their leader, who proclaimed himself the Son of God, killed by the government and resurrected. They brought a message from this man: 'If you want me, come and get me.'

It was obvious that this was a manifestation of the DYM, led by Lukas Kipkoech himself. Simpson wirelessed for reinforcements and next morning 35 Kenya police arrived, with Superintendent G. M. Taylor and Assistant Inspector R. G. Cameron. On the evening of the 23rd they made plans to arrest Lukas and disperse his followers the following day. The plans were approved by the PC, D. L. Morgan, and the Senior Superintendent of Police who arrived at Nginyang during the night. As the party drove off early next morning, Morgan said to Simpson, 'Now if there's to be any shooting it's your responsibility. Have you settled that with Taylor?' Simpson said he had.

In two lorries with two Suk chiefs, they drove north-west along a very bad road, stopping frequently to repair it, until late afternoon. Near Kolloa they heard drums, and halted. The chiefs went ahead to tell the tribesmen that Lukas was an imposter, they must surrender him and disperse. Meanwhile the police withdrew some two hundred yards to a clearing in the bush athwart the road, and drew up in line in front of the lorries. No one thought of issuing more ammunition from the lorries. The Kenya Police had 20 rounds each, and bayonets; the TPs, 10 rounds and no bayonets.

The chiefs returned with an incoherent letter from Lukas to the effect that his people had come only to pray, and that bullets could not harm them. While Simpson was composing a reply, someone shouted, 'They're coming!' He saw a crowd of tribesmen, heads down, moving diagonally left, right and forward, dancing and shuffling their feet as though coming to a *baraza*. Taylor gave the order to fire, but Simpson, not convinced they were hostile, called, 'No! Wait!' He ran forward with his interpreter, calling on the tribesmen to halt and lay down their spears. Taylor again ordered, 'Fire!' but Simpson shouted, '*Bado*' (not yet). The Suk stopped coming forward, but continued dancing and foot-shuffling. Then they started fanning out right and left, unmistakeably hostile, and Simpson shouted to Taylor, 'Open fire!' He and the interpreter ran back to the police line where his orderly handed him his shotgun. He was on the extreme left of the line.

There were 200–300 Suk, about 90 yards away. As the askaris fired, some fell. Simpson heard a call for more ammunition, and saw about 15 Suk coming for him. A TP ran back past him, and when the Suk were about 30 yards away, he looked to the right and

No Breakthrough

saw he was alone. He then ran himself, falling into a dry river-bed where two or three askaris were fighting the Suk with bayonets. Two spears were thrown at him, and missed. He got up, fired his right barrel at a man with spear raised to stab him, and with his left dropped another who was struggling with an askari. He and the askaris then ran back to the main body, scattered about and firing occasionally but almost out of ammunition. They reorganized, and made their way to the lorries for more, seeing only dead and wounded. The Suk had gone. The bodies of Taylor, Cameron and Stevens were found near the river-bed, together with those of Lukas and 29 Suk. On the government side, besides the three officers, one TP corporal was killed and one Kenya Police askari wounded.

A police levy force was imposed on the Suk, and the trouble in Baringo subsided as quickly as it had flared up.

15

Northern Province

T he years 1945–8 were Gerald Reece's best. He had come out of the shadow of Glenday; the north was his fief, over which he held untrammelled sway; and in 1947 Turkana was added to it, making Northern Province of which he was the first PC. (People still, however, referred to the 'NFD'.) For much of the year he lived in the heat, wind and dust of Isiolo, his wife and young children in Marsabit.

His main preoccupation was with the Somali Youth League (SYL). This had been born in British and Italian Somaliland as the Somali Youth Club, delivered by the midwifery of British officers who saw it as a cross between the Boy Scouts and the Primrose League. It had become violently xenophobic. Its aim was to unite all Somalis – divided between British, Italian and French Somaliland, Kenya and Ethiopia – into a united independent Somalia. Many NFD officers had at heart some sympathy with this, but it was obviously against the interests of Kenya since it would facilitate Somali pressure to the south and west. Most NFD Somalis and semi-Somalis sympathized with the SYL. It inflated Somali racialism, and became the political mouthpiece of Somali migration and opposition to tribal grazing boundaries. Although thoroughly subversive, it was not, in Reece's time, proscribed. The Government ruled through the chiefs so as to upset tribal custom as little as possible, and would not tolerate the SYL undermining chiefs' authority. In no circumstances would the SYL be used as an instrument of government. DCs must constantly put this across, especially on foot safaris. To all DCs Reece wrote:

Northern Province

Officers should travel as much as possible among the people and talk to them in their villages. Adequate escorts must of course be taken, and all officers must be warned not to give any order which cannot be enforced if disobeyed. In times like this the presence of officers among the people has a very steadying effect, and in this territory it is the man in the bush who counts. Always spend plenty of money on intelligence.

He notoriously had his spies in every *boma*, reporting to him on what the DC was up to. T. J. F. Gavaghan in Mandera used to discuss with the spy what should be reported. Reece's hatred of the Kenya Police was notorious, and he even invited DCs to relate police imperfections. They responded with alacrity. T. A. Watts from Marsabit wrote that the askaris were not bad, but the NCOs and European inspectors were. The former were useless as disciplinarians, and the latter knew nothing of their men. The ASP never went on foot patrols and spent far too little time in border outposts where the men's demeanour was one of 'slothful dejection'. Gavaghan in Mandera denounced the lack of severe depot training; indiscipline (citing insolence to NCOs and sit-down strikes); turn-out (long hair, unshaven faces, coloured stockings, dirty buttons); lazing on sentry duty; failing to salute and much else.

A tempest blew up when J. H. Candler, *locum tenens* for Watts in Marsabit, wrote to Reece of the local ASP:

> I have to inform you that he was very abusive to your wife last night and indicated that the administration in Marsabit was a crooked ramp and that you and Mr Watts were implicated in it. I do not wish to dirty my hands with this man, but when I challenged him to repeat his statement to me in the morning, he denied having ever made it. He is unfit to be an officer, and should be removed at the earliest opportunity. I will not allow him to enter my house. Good government is not possible with this man in our midst.

He was not long in their midst.

The *Dubas*, on the other hand, Reece regarded as *sans peur et sans reproche*. Nothing enraged him more than Gavaghan withdrawing rifles from all the Mandera *Dubas* because two men had proved subversive.

What I objected to most strongly was that *all* the men were disarmed. If you thought one or two were dangerous, why did you not deal with them alone? Once before it was done by a DC who was nervous of his Dubas, and in doing so he completely ruined his unit. While the men saw they were feared and distrusted, the Kenya Police and townsfolk and tribesmen wrote them off as mere safari porters.

Terry Gavaghan was as strong as Reece in his opinions. He vigorously defended his action, citing intelligence reports of a plot to pass *Dubas* rifles across the border to the Marehan; but he was soon on his way to a distinguished career in another province. The Mandera *Dubas* unit was not ruined.

But Reece never minded DCs blowing off steam to him in personal letters, off the file; and if one had a good case, it paid to stand up to him. Galton-Fenzi, DC Wajir, even questioned the PC's views on foot safari and the SYL.

I have just received your telegram about foot-safaris. The foot-safaris I propose to do are round the Wajir wells. I can see no point in going further afield. For one whole day's walking, one would probably meet only thirty people. If the SYL situation is as dangerous as you say, surely the place for me is in Wajir where the trouble will probably start, if there is any, not some six days' march away in the bush. Though there appears to be no confidence in my judgement, I feel sure that trouble is not as imminent as you suggest.

He got away with it.

In July 1948 Reece became Governor of British Somaliland and was replaced as PC by Dick Turnbull.

Rotational grazing and stock limitation were neither necessary nor practicable in the NFD. Without inoculations, the stock was

Northern Province

limited by natural wastage, and the survival of the fittest produced fine, hardy beef cattle, much in demand on Kenya farms. But DCs spent a great deal of time enforcing tribal grazing boundaries. It was done by impounding the trespassing stock. In no other way could the owner be brought to court: he *had* to attend trial, or he would get back nothing. If found guilty (he could hardly deny it) he was fined 10 per cent of the trespassing stock. (20 per cent in the case of the Degodia, persistent and truculent grass- and water-poachers.)

The most significant development on the frontier was the provision of more water so that the stock could stay away longer from the permanent wells and rivers, giving the grass a fair chance. After the war 24 good boreholes, drilled for military purposes, were made available for tribal stock. Between 1950 and 1958 50 large dams and tanks were constructed with heavy machinery at a cost of £393,000. DCs with modest help from ALDEV and the goat bag produced 55 smaller dams and pans between 1948 and 1952, dug by ox-drawn scoops and light tractors. Gavaghan, for instance, in Mandera, with no resources but the goat bag, straightened the zigzag Eil Wak wells, thus speeding the hauling up of water in buckets, and made many rock catchment pools. Gavaghan reported:

> Catchment areas of smooth rock were used to gather water in clefts at the foot. Small stone walls blocked exits and bitumen (collected from the Strada Italiana in Somalia) was used as a sealant. Concrete garlands across the face of the rock channelled water into the clefts. A small success, but popular.

By 'administrative pressure' and without prosecutions cattle sales were increased from 2,963 in 1948 to 13,807 in 1953. It was monopoly buying, by experts from the African Livestock Marketing Organisation (ALMO), but prices were subject to lengthy oriental bargaining, and were generally thought to be pretty fair.

An ambitious 'flood irrigation' scheme was started in 1951 in Turkana. Beside the Nakutan dry riverbed, near Lodwar, a chequer-board of ten one-acre plots were constructed, each surrounded by an earth bank five feet high with a gap through which water entered when the Nakutan came down in spate. When the water was in, the gap would be plugged, and the water would sink slowly into the ground, producing enough moisture to grow a crop of millet. The DC was L. E. Whitehouse, *the* Turkana expert, who governed them for years and years. I took over when 'Whouse' went home on leave, and spotted with unerring eye the flaw in his scheme: the digging and bank-building were done by tractors. But the object of the scheme was to show the Turkana how to do it, not to do it for them, and never in a thousand years could they learn to manage a tractor. I therefore bought oxen and scoops. But I was wrong; Whouse was right; the Turkana ate the oxen. The Nakutan scheme came to naught when the river changed its course, leaving the ten plots high and dry. So Whouse tried again, on the Turkwell, and that changed its course too.

In 1950 Italian Somaliland, now know as Somalia, was handed back to the Italians under United Nations trusteeship. The Italians were supervised by a commission consisting of an Egyptian, a Peruvian and a Filipino, all keenly anti-colonial. If ever the Italians tried to take a strong line over anything, they countermanded it. After ten years the Somalis would choose between continued trusteeship and independence. In the vain hope of winning the referendum, the Italians pandered to the SYL which made things difficult for the British in the NFD. There was a certain amount of trade across the border, mainly illegal. Thus tea and sugar were smuggled into Somalia, and from Somalia came Lugh Ferrandi salt and Marehan prostitutes, both – Turnbull assured the Foreign Office – of poor quality and tampered with in transit. Of more importance was Somalia cattle smuggled into the NFD.

Officers' wives were allowed in all stations except Lodwar, Wajir and Mandera; and even to Mandera access was sometimes permitted. Peter Gordon, DC in 1951, wishing to add to his family, obtained special permission for his wife to fly up for a fortnight, an enterprise known throughout the NFD as 'Operation Toto'. The Italians entered into the spirit of it with Latin abandon, inviting the happy couple to Lugh Ferrandi for a weekend.

Northern Province

It was a mini-Roma with a triumphal arch (cracking) and an enormous fountain (dry) embellished with statuary (chipped). The official residences were palazzi, but with peeling walls and most of the bathroom tiles missing. The WC had to be filled from a bucket. After we had retired for the night, we were serenaded with guitars and were obliged to put in an appearance on the balcony of our room, Marianne being loudly applauded.

F. A. Peet's wife joined him in Garissa in 1949–50 and accompanied him on a safari to the edge of the Boni forest on the Lamu border. This was Africa as Livingstone saw it, unexplored, unadministered, inhabited by a tribe of little hunters who wanted only to be left alone. She wrote to her mother:

> Today two enormous elephants came down to bathe. They were so funny to watch, wallowing in the mud and sploshing it over them. There were three or four chaps watering sheep who tried to get the elephants off by throwing mud at them. One elephant thought this a bit cheeky and started to charge through the water; but when the man ran away, turned back and continued his bath.
>
> *Next day.* It's a lovely part of the district, completely wild and much greener with lots of game of all kinds. We had a glorious campsite by a spreading tree, but were woken up at 3.30 by two very persistent lions grunting and roaring fifty yards from the tent. Tony went out with his gun and they went when he flashed a torch on them.

Soon after taking over from Reece, Turnbull had the Somali Youth League proscribed and seven Somali 'youths', considered to be veteran troublemakers in their forties, deported to Lodwar. It was a classic example of the minimum force exerted at exactly the right moment, when the tribesmen were beginning to wonder what they got from all the money collected by the SYL. It gave little more trouble for several years, but had always to be watched.

Turnbull ruled Northern Province on the same lines as Glenday and Reece, but with a lighter touch, and without Reece's animus against the Kenya Police. Asked by a too earnest enquirer what were the principal problems on the frontier, he replied, 'Ingrowing greens and hangovers.' But when Elspeth Huxley asked him what he found so fascinating about it, he replied with patent sincerity, 'The romance.'

He insisted on DCs doing a lot of foot safari, and reporting each month how much they had done. The author once said to him, 'I've been walking for three days and saw nobody but my own *Dubas*. Was it really necessary?' He replied, 'It doesn't in the least matter that you didn't see them. The point is that they should see you. In fact it's enough if they saw your footprints in the sand.'

He greatly enjoyed foot safaris himself, striding along at a punishing pace, a handkerchief dangling from his mouth, the well-chewed corner of which he sucked to keep his mouth moist. No one might drink water during the march, but milk at a village was permissible, lest the host be offended. He thought 25 miles a reasonable day's stroll. As he led the single file through the bush, he tossed over his shoulder scraps of NFD lore. 'That tree over there – *lebi* in Somali – they make camel-bells of it . . . Never turn aside for thorn: bash straight through, it's quicker.' So saying, he ducked down and, with a noise of rending cloth, forced his way between two wait-a-bit bushes.

'I like Somalis,' I said, on a safari in Garissa.

'Oh, you do, do you? Then I must keep an eye on you. If ever I find they like you, you're out!'

'Any way, I'm learning their language.'

'Certainly. No harm in that at all. Start with a few common, everyday expressions such as "Good day to you, madam", "After you, my dear fellow", and "I'm so sorry, I didn't know it was loaded." '

It was important to be well briefed in the particular subject which engaged his present interest. One month it would be stock sales. 'Why haven't the Rer Musa section of the Abd Wak filled their quota? That headman needs chasing . . . I see the Rer Farah Jibrail sold a lot last month. Was it their own, or brought over from Somalia?'

Another month it was the hides and skins trade, developed to bring money into the NFD which produces the world's best

Northern Province

goatskins, used for making kid-gloves. At every dealer's premises he would inspect the store, drying racks, washing and cleaning arrangement, stock books and receipts.

'This bloody fellow, Haji Abdullahi! Just look at his grading! Call this a second-grade skin? Cancel his licence!'

Off he strode fuming through the bush. Twenty minutes later he suddenly remarked, 'There's nothing like an occasional resounding injustice. Does all the good in the world.' After another twenty minutes: 'That poor bugger Haji Abdullahi. Not his fault at all, really. You can give his licence back in a couple of months.'

A scrap of paper left on the camp-site, a slipping camel-load, an unshaven head among the *Dubas*, would earn the DC a searing rebuke. But in the evening, stretched out on a canvas chair, a whisky and water beside him, witty, erudite and scandalous, ranging from Stravinsky to hill-climbing, from tribal genealogies to *Hamlet*, he made up for everything.

He was a well-informed contributor to the 'District Noted Blokes Book', in which was recorded all that was suspected of every person who had attracted unfavourable attention. Thus:

'A financial twister involved with Abdi Dualeh in black market sugar deals.'

'Suspected Italian spy 1936–41. Visits Kismayu on SYL business.'

'Fiddles his elephant licence. A game scout should be attached to his camp.'

'An inexhaustible mine of inaccurate information about events in Somalia.'

'Forever collecting money for a pilgrimage to Mecca which he never makes. He and all his brothers would be better dead.'

A feature of down-country districts in which he took no interest was democratic local government. The tribes were perfectly capable of running their own affairs without ADCs and such. An ADC was established, experimentally, in Garissa, and abolished itself by voting no rates. Its demise caused the PC not a pang.

A tiresome feature of the NFD in his day was the proliferation of experts, lavishly funded by some subsidiary of the United Nations, researching or reporting or investigating something-or-other. Even Turnbull could not keep them all out, but he kept out an American team which proposed to take blood samples from a thousand Turkana: 'You will be taken for a coven of Government-sponsored necromancers in search of blood for obscene rites and detestable practices.'

A more welcome post-war novelty was the locust officer in every district. Some were alcoholics, some fiddled their travelling claims, some were too attracted to Somali girls; most were decent rolling stones doing a tough job. All were provided with apparently unlimited funds, jeeps or Land-Rovers galore and 4-wheel-drive trucks fitted with winches with which to pull oneself across a flooded river. In the absence of locusts, they were usually glad to make a road or a bridge to oblige the DC. A locust officer in Garissa was an elderly Boer, communication with whom was difficult because he could neither read nor write and would not admit it. A colleague had to do his accounts.

On safari in Moyale you could ride instead of walk, on tough unshod ponies bred in Ethiopia. A horse safari had every advantage: you could cross country impassable for vehicles twice as fast as on foot; to dismount, have a drink of milk and a chat with a tribesman was a pleasant break in a long ride, whereas on a lorry safari it was a nuisance, so you tended to drive past in a cloud of dust. Thirty-five miles was an easy day's ride, but a very hard day's walk; at a pinch seventy miles could be covered in a day; and with the horse's speed you could round up trespassing stock far easier than on foot. The *Dubas* were put through riding school, and were issued with leather cowboy chaps to protect their legs against wait-a-bit thorns.

On a safari near Buna an Ajuran brought word of hundreds of Degodia camels trespassing far to the west of the Degodia Line. The author had sixteen *Dubas* and an unarmed syce, a splendid old pagan Boran from Ethiopia, an ex-*shifta* and a great horse-coper. The Degodia were about forty-five miles away, on an open plain beyond a belt of lava. One or two *Dubas* knew the area, as did Aba Dida, who guaranteed to lead us through the lava, even at night.

Northern Province

Having arranged for the lorry to meet us next day, we rode twenty-five miles by daylight and then halted for several hours to rest, water and feed. We set off again at midnight, under a full moon. Once we were through the lava, it was a lovely ride, along a white sandy track in the cool of the night. Aba Dida timed it perfectly: at first light we were on top of a low ridge overlooking a plain dotted with Degodia villages and camel-*bomas*. The *Dubas* had taken off their red turbans and wound them round their waists, lest they be identified from afar. We rode slowly towards the nearest village until with shouts of alarm men started driving camels away. Then we rode hard.

As we came up to each camel-herd, Sergeant Major Yusuf Abdullah dropped off two *Dubas* to take it to the nearest water, about five miles away. It was a long and thirsty ride to the winding river-bed with its few stagnant pools, with the camels unwilling to be driven, and the Degodia hovering round, hoping for a chance to recover their stock. We watered and fed the horses and made tea, the Degodia in a sullen group a couple of hundred yards away. Then under an umbrella-shaped acacia tree I set up a first class magistrate's court and recorded its proceedings in a notebook. Each herd-owner identified his camels, I charged him under the Special Districts Ordinance and solemnly wrote:

> Abdi Hilole, Degodia, Fai, pleads Guilty as charged and is fined 20 per cent of his trespassing stock, *viz* 16 camels.

The sergeant major was worried lest they try something at night, for we were too few to cut bushes for a *boma* and guard our horses and the confiscated camels. But in the late afternoon the lorry appeared with a dozen more *Dubas*.

Driving the camels home next day the *Dubas* were exultant. The Degodia were their blood-enemies from whom they had suffered much. Now over three hundred Degodia camels were being driven to Moyale where they would be sold at knock-down prices. I was sorry for the Degodia women, standing beside the track watching us drive away their transport and their milk. But if they had got away with this flagrant theft of grass and water, our people would have suffered cruelly in the dry season.

16

Nairobi's Fair City

A stint in the Secretariat was essential for the ambitious, and gave officers a wide view of policy-making.

G. J. Ellerton, having served his apprenticeship in Turkana and Kisumu, was posted to the Secretariat in 1951 because the officials team wanted a 'middle-order bat who could bowl a bit.' He went to A.1 Section dealing with law and order and immigration; and serving the Attorney General's office which linked the executive with the judiciary. Immigration was a delicate issue because he had to implement, without ever admitting to, a policy of letting Europeans into Kenya while keeping Indians out. He wrote:

> Most of A.1's work went to the Secretary for Law and Order, Jake Cusack, and to the Member for Law and Order who was also Attorney General. Jake had charm, wit, intelligence and style. Tall, rather over-weight (he took no exercise), always dressed as though for a fashionable point-to-point, he smoked heavily from a gold cigarette-case and had an enviable capacity for strong waters. He did not drive, and if his long-suffering wife could not collect him, rather early, from the office, I had to take him home. If this failed, he would ring for a taxi and charge it to government funds. I would then have to fend off the Treasury query, inventing an 'urgent meeting at Government House'. The difficulty was to get him to apply his undoubted brains to the business of the office: if he could opt out and leave the matter to others, he opted out. But working for Jake was fun. He never flapped,

Nairobi's Fair City

said 'Thank you' on the file, and protected one from the criticisms and sarcasm of the Attorney General. He had acute political antennae, and could sense trouble (to himself) from afar.

In 1952 I was transferred to Section D which dealt with constitutional affairs and finance. Included in the former was the job of Clerk to the Legislative Council. My principal duty was to don a (borrowed) wig and gown; walk in procession with Mr Speaker to the hall; shout 'Mr Speaker' as he approached the entrance; and read aloud the items of business on the Agenda. I sat at the Clerk's table with my back to the Speaker. In front of me was a low-tech lighting arrangement worked by him. A white light meant that he wanted a word, usually to ask the name of a backbencher jumping up and down in his anxiety to speak; a red light meant that he wanted to answer the call of nature, and would I quickly catch the Deputy Speaker's eye?

There was a full-time Assistant Clerk to do the real work – until one fatal day when, as the procession approached the entrance, a police inspector pushed through the members and asked me, 'Are you Mr X?' 'No,' I replied, 'this is Mr X. But you can't speak to him now as Mr Speaker will be late for prayers.' He did not quite say, 'F--- Mr Speaker' but, addressing the assistant clerk, said, 'Mr X, I have a warrant for your arrest.' X was escorted away, and until he could be replaced I worked harder than ever before, or since.

During this time the Council experimented with evening sessions, but not for long. No sooner did the sitting start than half the European elected members, and as many on the official side as dared, crept off to the bar of Torr's Hotel, returning an hour or two later in an unparliamentary condition.

The administration of Nairobi was bedevilled by responsibility divided between the government and the municipal council*. The DC Nairobi had overall responsibility for law and order, but no

---

*In 1950 Nairobi became a city, administered by a city council.

TPs, chiefs or headmen. He licensed or banned political meetings, and occasionally had to read the Riot Act. He supervised the African Courts and took a few cases himself, though most petty cases were taken by the DO and serious cases by the Resident Magistrate. He administered a few government African housing estates and ran the detention camp. Charles Atkins found that he

> had very little executive authority as the municipality was administered by the municipal council through its own officers. However, as a member of the municipal council and some of its committees, I had the opportunity to try to influence its policy as it affected Africans. Every afternoon was taken up with committees or board meetings. I was on over eighty bodies, governmental, local authority or unofficial. I was also Registrar of Marriages, and there were two or three weddings every week, generally on Saturday afternoons.

(Atkins's successor, Roger Wilkinson, had the embarrassment of presiding over the nuptials of a couple whom he had for years assumed to be man and wife.)

The vast majority of Nairobi Africans lived in municipal housing estates or 'locations', foetid slums served by a water supply that was often disrupted and public lavatories with choked drains and floors deep in excrement. Pumwani, Kariokor, Kaloleni – their names are a roll-call of infamy. These were the responsibility of the municipal (later city) council which was run by and for European and Asian business interests, with no great concern for Africans so long as disease and crime did not spill over into European and Asian areas. Its agent was the Municipal African Affairs Officer, a senior DC seconded to the service of the council, independent of the DC Nairobi. He was not responsible for law and order, and had no judicial powers. He administered the locations through a superintendent in each; he allocated housing, ran African social welfare and sports, and gave the council good advice which was occasionally taken. He in turn was advised by an African advisory council, of which he was chairman: it was purely advisory, with no power to pass by-laws or levy rates. Like the DC, he lacked the basic means of administration, having neither TPs nor chiefs. From 1945 to 1949 this post was filled by Tom Askwith with dedication and increasing frustration. He was more liberal in his views than most of his colleagues, and saw as a challenge a job which they would have done anything to avoid.

It was a flaw in the administration that it had little contact with educated, articulate, urban Africans, stigmatized as 'politicians'. This word was invariably used in a pejorative sense: white politicians were assumed to be anti-African and anti-administration, black politicians to be anti-everything. One had as little as possible to do with both kinds. But in his job Askwith was

> in contact with urban Africans most of the working day and much of the night, and aware of their feelings – an extremely educative process. The first impression was of the bitterness felt by the better educated against racial discrimination.

He persuaded the council to give him a very high-paid African assistant, Dedan Githegi, an outstanding Kikuyu who kept him well informed of African affairs.

The African population of Nairobi, 55 per cent Kikuyu, had increased eight-fold in twenty-five years. For the landless, the unemployed, the unemployable and the discontented it was reputedly paved with gold. But for those who had jobs wages trailed far behind inflation, and for those who hadn't, there was no dole. Insofar as the locations were controlled by anyone, it was by Kikuyu armed gangs thriving on crime, prostitution and protection rackets.

The housing was unspeakable. The considerable building programme pushed through by Askwith's predecessor, Tom Colchester, was swamped by the tidal wave of new arrivals. By 1947 the putative deficit of 26,000 beds was increasing by 10,000 every year. In his 1948 Annual Report Askwith complained:

> It was disheartening for those concerned with African welfare to see legitimately employed Africans sleeping under the verandahs on River Road, in noisome shacks in the Swamp,

in buses parked by the road, and fourteen to a room in Pumwani, two to a bed and the rest on the floor.

The cost of a new housing programme in permanent materials was so daunting that he proposed helping Africans build their own houses, to approved standards but of traditional materials – walls of mud and wattle, floors of polished mud mixed with cowdung, roof of thatch or corrugated iron. Despite opposition by the medical authorities, 600 houses were so built, and were a great success. But what were these among so many?

So Nairobi got worse every year, and the criminal gangs more powerful. Many were associated with subversive politics, notably the infamous 'Forty Group'. The militant trade unions also had links with the gangs. So tribal enmities sharpened with every other tribe hating and fearing the Kikuyu. This was not to the liking of Kikuyu political leaders who claimed that their Kenya African Union (KAU) represented *all* tribes, whereas it was really the latest embodiment of the Kikuyu Central Association.

In 1948 there was danger of a rail strike among the Luo and Baluhya who formed the bulk of the railway workforce. Askwith got the tip-off from Dedan Githegi.

He was worried because he had heard that the railway authorities intended to dismiss all strikers and replace them with Kikuyu, which would aggravate inter-tribal animosities. He had a suggestion to make. Jomo Kenyatta, who had recently returned after years abroad, was holding a big political meeting at the week-end. If he could be persuaded to speak against the strike, it might be averted. I shall always remember my first meeting with this remarkable man and the stir among the onlookers when his car drew up and he strode majestically towards Dedan's office twirling his fly-whisk in one hand and carrying in the other his famous ebony walking-stick with the ivory handle. After a suitable interval I invited them into my office, and in due course we came round to the problem of the strike. The upshot was that at the political meeting Jomo waved his stick and thundered, 'If anyone talks of striking, I'll knock his block off!'

Nairobi's Fair City

There was no strike; and Askwith was left with the conviction, shared by few of his colleagues, that Kenyatta was a moderate who might have been a force for good if the government had 'tried to work with him or meet him halfway'.

One continued to write reports of increasing unrest, largely the result of economic hardship and racial discrimination, but apparently to no avail.

Among these reports was one by Dedan Githegi of the first Mau Mau oathing ceremony in Nairobi, in 1948.

17

The Heart of the Matter

❧

After the war there were changes in a DC's position, particularly in the advanced districts. There were more departmental officers, and *vis-à-vis* the heads of departments in his district – agriculture, veterinary, education, police and others – the DC was no more than *primus inter pares*. There was more continuity than before the war: most Central Province DCs stayed several years in one post, and when they went on leave, they were replaced by their senior DOs who knew their districts. An unwelcome product of more sophisticated administration was the prodigious increase in 'bumf', the proliferation of reports and returns demanded by an insatiable Secretariat. In 1918 the DC, Embu, complained of 375 official communications in a year: in 1947 he received 200 in a week. In his history of Nyeri District 1949–52 O. E. B. Hughes wrote of 'that drag-anchor, the DC's office'.

> The DC himself was President of the ADC whose receipts and payments were checked daily in detail by himself or a DO; he was chairman and executive officer of the township committee; he was responsible for a considerable amount of miscellaneous revenue collection; he was chairman of the district team, and district education board, the local land board etc. He had no private secretary; he typed and filed all his secret and confidential letters (a Sunday morning job.) He could afford the time for no more than seven or eight days, and no nights, a month on safari.

As for being on safari:

The Heart of the Matter

None of us stayed long enough in one place to hear an echo of local news, or get to know individual Africans other than chiefs, sub-headmen, court elders etc. We were all back in the boma religiously writing our safari reports on Saturday morning. We should have skipped the report-writing and stayed out till Sunday and met some of the hundreds of weekend visitors up from Nairobi. I cannot remember seeing a foot safari set out from the boma, though the furthest corner of the district was less than 25 miles away.

As Hall had remarked fifty years earlier, the more sophisticated the administration, the more advanced a district, the less the DC knew his people. Tied to the office by paperwork and routine duties, he depended more than in the past on his chiefs.

Some academic and other critics thought that it was a grevious error to rely on chiefs, since the older ones were ignorant and reactionary, and the younger ones mere government stooges. They should have been ditched in favour of the new élite – progressive farmers, proto-capitalists, school teachers, some of whom were not hostile to the system as such and if rejected went into opposition. But apart from the fact that most of the younger chiefs *were* members of the élite, it was out of the question to ditch them. Although invented by the British, they had in half a century acquired authority which was quasi-traditional. Underpaid, some had to some extent feathered their own nests and looked after their families. But F. A. Loyd, who served many years in Kikuyu districts, found them

> far from yes-men. Many were very good representatives of their people, and argued a good case. The younger ones, of course, were better educated and more able to cope with the smart new generation of politically-minded Kikuyu.

As for the new élite, they were being brought into the governmental machine and trained for higher office as fast as suitable men could be found. We were looking for education, ability – and integrity.

The administration worked most closely with the Agricultural

Department. Before the war Colin Maher, an agricola with a one-track mind, had loudly and repeatedly predicted ruin unless something was done to save the topsoil from erosion. During the war, when staff was reduced to a minimum while maize production was boosted to meet war needs, his prophecies were catastrophically vindicated, especially in the Kikuyu districts which contained the most fertile land in the country. After the war Sir Philip Mitchell, who became Governor in 1944, directed that soil conservation be given top priority: the steep slopes of Kikuyuland must be terraced *at once*. But how could the Kikuyu be induced to turn out in thousands for work which, although entirely for their benefit, they detested and thought quite unnecessary?

It had to be a combined operation of agricola and DC, the former deciding what needed doing, and the latter providing the man- and woman-power to do it. DCs replied mainly on the chiefs and sub-headmen who were used to providing communal labour for roads and grass-planting. Because it was the Kikuyu custom, and because so many of the young men had drifted off to Nairobi, much of the work was done by women. It was far from popular, but it was essential, and was done at an increasing rate through 1946 and the first half of 1947. The efficiency of a chief was judged largely by the terrace-miles completed in his location, which did not add to his popularity.

The idea of this work being done by communal labour fitted an anthropologist's philosophy on African society and land usage. This held that land was the property of the tribe, a cultivator holding it only on trust; that tribal society, grievously threatened by modern ideas, was egalitarian; that hopelessly fragmented holdings* could be cultivated properly only when grouped into large collective farms; and that the prosperous private farmer was divisive, a danger to society, a miner of the tribe's soil, who should be given no encouragement. The most authoritative exponent of

---

*For instance in the middle altitudes of Fort Hall the average farmer cultivated between 4 and 5 acres divided into several tiny plots. A survey of 80 families in Nyeri showed that each farmed on an average 10 plots, to which the aggregate distance from the family house was 10 miles.

The Heart of the Matter

this philosophy was the CNC, P. Wynn-Harris, strongly influenced by H. E. Lambert, his adviser on African land tenure. A secretariat circular laid down

> the duty of the land authorities to resuscitate this [communal] interpretation and to make the individual who disregards the welfare of the tribe's posterity and exploits a piece of tribal land for personal gain realise that he is committing a very grievous offence against the tribe.

A conference of agricultural officers in 1947 passed a resolution that

> The policy shall in general be based on encouraging cooperative effort and organisation rather than individual holdings.

In this the hand of H. E. Lambert can be seen. But he was the most dangerous kind of adviser, the expert whose knowledge is a trifle out of date. During the war – indeed with Harry Thuku and a few others before the war – individual ownership of quite big farms had caught on. Agricultural and anthropological theory might favour collectives, but human nature would have none of them. In Nyeri two go-ahead chiefs, Nderi and Muhoya, by purchase and the exchange of small plots within their own families had built up excellent mixed farms of about 150 acres. These were the pace-setters. In 1950 Swann found over sixty private farms in Nyeri district, mainly along the boundary with the settled area where people could see how Europeans did it. Swann wrote: 'Most were between ten and twenty acres, but bench-terraced, beautifully farmed, heavily manured and giving jolly good yields.' By 1950 they were growing coffee and, in the higher altitudes, pyrethrum: profitable cash-crops.

Whatever the party line put out from Nairobi on the advantages of collectives over the 'kulak', no field officer of the Administration or the agricultural department paid the smallest attention to it. Frank Loyd was DC Nyeri 1948–9 and Fort Hall 1949–53. He wrote:

There were lots of progressive farmers all over Fort Hall to whom the Administration and agricolas gave strong support. A committee was appointed, of which I was 'field member', to investigate means of increasing the scale of loans to them. We never went in for collective farming with the Kikuyu, who were individualist through and through. We were all for the 'kulak'.

Tony Swann, DC Nyeri, then Kiambu, wrote: 'The administration *never* wanted collective farming. I cannot remember the subject being discussed at any DCs' meeting.'
Robin Wainwright, DC Embu 1946–51,

> cannot remember at any time or anywhere any suggestion that ordinary farming in African reserves should be collective. Everyone, administration and agricolas, were entirely sold on individual holdings and farming.

His successor, Roger Wilkinson, 'never heard of anyone giving a moment's consideration to communal or collective farming'.

The whole matter is an example of how the DC, provided he carried with him his departmental officers, could ignore the party line put out from the highest authority in Nairobi.

There were two types of terrace, narrow-based and broad-based or 'bench' terraces.

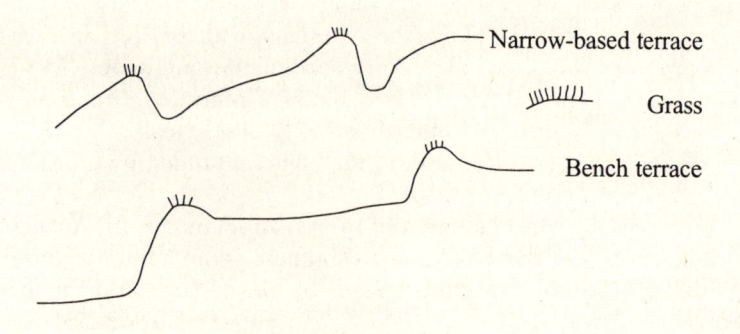

Narrow-based terrace
Grass
Bench terrace

The Heart of the Matter

At first all were narrow-based, for these were easier to dig. But they needed a lot of maintenance, for the ditches had to be re-dug when they silted up. In the late 1940s bench terracing became more popular (though not with the diggers). It required the shifting of more earth, but the result was easier to plough and cultivate, and needed little maintenance. Eventually the practice was to put narrow-based terraces only along the steepest slopes, bench terraces elsewhere.

Whatever the type of terracing, the Kikuyu hated being made to do it. The work was extremely hard, and the benefit could not be quantified. On the contrary, for every 3 foot drop on narrow-terraced land a strip 4–6 feet wide was lost to cultivation. All one could say was, 'Well, if you hadn't been terraced, in the end you'd lose far more' – never a convincing argument. It created prodigious resentment against the administration and the chiefs, and was a gift to the propagandists of KAU: 'The DC *says* your land will benefit from this toil. But who will reap the benefit? The Europeans, to whom it will be handed over.'

Nevertheless in Kikuyuland things seemed to be going quite well. Wally Coutts, perhaps the only DC who spoke Kikuyu well enough to hold a *baraza* without the help of an interpreter, took over Fort Hall in May 1947. On 20 July 1947, Jomo Kenyatta addressing a meeting of 10,000 people in Fort Hall denounced not the concept of terracing, but the employment of women on it. Next day no women turned up. In a few minutes he had wrecked the most important work in Fort Hall. The issue was well-chosen. The idea of women being pressed to hard labour sent shudders of horror through the British Labour government, the United Nations and the International Labour Organisation. The labour department in Nairobi warned the PC that it would be impossible to defend the practice at the ILO.

In January 1947 a general strike in Mombasa paralysed the city and port for several days. Its chief organizer was Chege Kibachia, a smiling little Kikuyu too gentle personally to hurt anyone. Reputedly – and the repute was enough – he made his point by arranging for African Workers' Federation 'askaris' to slice the ears off non-strikers. In August he was restricted to Kabarnet, in Baringo district*. In the same month there returned to Kenya from India an inflexible, card-carrying Sikh communist, Makhan Singh. He immediately aligned himself with the most militant trade unionists who staged a violent strike and riot at the Upland Bacon Factory in Kiambu district. The DC was Edward Windley. In September 1947 a new DO arrived, F. R. Wilson. He wrote:

> On my first day I was involved in the Uplands strike. The factory lay astride the railway. A senior official of the African Workers' Federation had been travelling along the line drumming up support and collecting subscriptions, but a clerk at the factory would not subscribe. A strike was called to bring about the clerk's dismissal, and the labour force assembled on the line, many with pangas. I telephoned Windley who soon arrived with about thirty Kenya police armed with truncheons and a few rifles. After an unsuccessful attempt to disperse the mob, the DC read the Riot Act. Stones were thrown at us from ballast on the line and the police moved in to make arrests. The mob used pangas, and one constable had his arm nearly severed. The police then opened fire; there were some casualties and the mob fled. When we took the dead and wounded back to Kiambu Hospital the Kikuyu doctor on duty refused to treat the constable.

It was not legally possible to impose a general ban on all KAU meetings. Only a specific meeting could be banned if the DC thought it would endanger good order. KAU tactics were, therefore, for star rabble-rousers to drive up from Nairobi at week-ends, hold meetings and return to Nairobi before they could be banned. On 24 August 1947, such a KAU meeting was held in Fort Hall district in the location of Chief Ignatio Murai. Forty-five years old, a former teacher, he was one of the best of the new type

---

*Bored there with nothing to do, he asked for a job as tax clerk. When the author was DC in 1954 'Mr Chege', still under a detention order, was district clerk, and a very good one. The only duty he evaded was accompanying the Kabarnet football team, as goalkeeper, to play against the inmates of a nearby Mau Mau work-camp. After one experience, he found that meeting his old cronies, 'Hya, Chege!' was too embarrassing.

The Heart of the Matter

of chief, and a very brave man. Speaker after speaker poured out hatred against the government, the chiefs and the Europeans, to the menacing shouts of the crowd. Clearly this was incitement to riot. Ignatio had with him only two TPs, but they boldly pushed their way through the crowd, arrested the two most inflammatory orators and were taking them to his headquarters, half a mile down the road, when the mob recovered from its surprise and with a hail of stones moved in to the attack. Ignatio ordered the TPs each to fire one round. One rioter fell dead, another wounded, and the remainder withdrew. KAU never forgave the TPs this, and at every subsequent meeting they were subjected to the vilest abuse and horrific threats, which was one reason for the stubborn TP loyalty in later years.

Nevertheless 'Mug' Mullins in his Annual Report on Central Province described 1947 as quite a good year. The ADCs were satisfactory, though given to interminable debates led by young councillors who denounced in open session what they had approved in committee. More responsibility was being given to Africans, though the need to check carefully their accounts laid an increasing burden on European officers. Such was the demand for education that ADCs spent 90 per cent of their rates on it; and it was futile to try to stop KISA schools for which large sums were being collected. As for soil conservation, even in Fort Hall the momentum was picking up again by the end of the year. The prospects for 1948 were good. Sir Philip Mitchell agreed with this optimism. On soil conservation he felt that if DCs kept their nerve, the benefits would become apparent, and opposition would die down.

Coutts in Fort Hall, in *baraza* after *baraza*, harangued the Kikuyu in Kikuyu, on the folly of KAU propaganda against terracing. He had several talks with Kenyatta himself on the subject. John Cumber, a new DO, met Kenyatta at a tea-party in the DC's house.

I asked him which of the other beneficial measures in the district he would oppose now, in order to ruin his supporters' economic future. He looked at me in disbelief, roared with laughter and asked me to repeat what I had said. I did so;

but added that, having just left India, where Gandhi and Congress were now clinching the deal for independence, I could not recall any occasion when a responsible Gandhi-ite had opposed the Raj's agricultural measures in order to further their cause. It seemed to me strange, therefore, that a man of his standing should oppose terracing, which was essential to the interests of the local farmers. I went on to claim that I had some idea of Indians' mental processes, but had not been here long enough to grasp those of the Kikuyu, unless it was to cut off the nose to spite the face.

Old JK had stopped grinning by now, content to rest his buck-teeth on his lower lip and drool a little while he pondered. Eventually he said, 'So that's how you feel about it?' I said, 'Yes, and many others too.' He then said quietly, 'You may be right. I'll think about it.' In the event, his opposition to terracing was switched off, but I am sure it was the result of Wally's constant haranguing.

In 1948 Coutts reported the existence of a new subversive Kikuyu secret society, the object of which was to kill Europeans. Also in that year the term Mau Mau appeared for the first time in an intelligence report.

Even in Fort Hall it was not all work and no play. Indeed a visit by a distinguished American author, collecting material for his Kenya book, made Wally Coutts almost wish it was. He was a good writer when sober and a great bore when drunk. He was drunk for most of his three-day visit, starting on his return from a drive round the district when he insisted on stopping at Filo's Bar to order two double whiskies and a bottle of gin. That night he was fairly pickled and next morning Coutts had to extract him from Filo's and tell him to behave himself as his visit was government-sponsored. He said:

'Now SIT DOWN. Are yah listening? I'm sure as hell NOT sponsored. I told 'em to put their fee where the monkey puts the nuts.'

Coutts took him back to the house and went to his office to resume the hearing of a murder committal. Translating in his mind from Kikuyu and recording in English every word of the

The Heart of the Matter

evidence, he was appalled to see his guest stagger in and embark on a one-sided conversation with a chief whose English was limited to 'Yes' and 'No'. He adjourned the case in despair, just as the native courts adviser arrived from Nairobi to see how he was getting on. Coutts introduced them. Gratified by this contact with a wider literary world, the adviser proffered a hand, only to be told, 'Now SIT DOWN. Are yah listening?' Eventually Coutts took a bemused adviser and a staggering author back to the house where his wife, realising the situation, prescribed immediate luncheon.

'Are yah going to give me a drink?'
'Not until you have eaten something.'
'NOW LISTEN. Are yah going to give me a drink?'
'When you have eaten what is before you.'

After a lengthy silence he rounded on the adviser. 'Have yah ever borne the burden of the day? Have yah ever felt the heat of the sun?'

'Well, I served in the NFD . . .'
'Where were yah in the war?'
'Well, Wally and I both volun . . .'
'So yah weren't in the war!'

Muttering that it was all very disgraceful and he'd report it to the CNC, the adviser returned to Nairobi.

The next involuntary host was Gerald Reece, to whom Coutts sent a coded signal recommending prohibition during his tour round the NFD. At Mandera Terry Gavaghan met his guests with profuse apologies, 'I'm terribly sorry, we're out of drink', and directed their attention to the lime-juice. To Reece he muttered: 'Gin in the left-hand water-bottle.' They had a cheerful evening, with the author in surprisingly good form. After a while he lurched out 'to water Africa' and Gavaghan, keeping him under observation, saw him look furtively round, take a huge flask from his hip-pocket and hold it gurgling to his mouth.

Robin Wainwright took over Embu in 1946. There he was blissfully happy building court houses, TP lines, and a guest-house for visiting chiefs and ADC members. In his spare time he made for the Corydon Museum a table from fifty-nine varieties of Kenya timber.

I was fortunate in having as ADC Foreman of Works Jagat Ram, a gentle and knowledgeable Punjabi. Together we trained a skilled team of African masons and carpenters. We found a good clay not far from the boma with which we made bricks, burning them in simple open kilns. The bricks were so good that we experimented with tiles, perfecting an extremely strong and attractive 'brosely' tile.

The people and I were agitating for a secondary school. After having this turned down because there was no money, I was told on the last day of the year that if I could provide buildings, at no cost to the government, by 14 January, the first day of the term, we could have our school and the government would pay its recurrent costs. So we had fourteen days in which to build boarding and teaching accommodation for thirty boys, and houses for the teachers. Thousands turned up to work, most being sent into the forest to cut poles, withies and thatching-grass; others dug holes as fast as Jagat Ram and I could mark out the buildings. Vast quantities of mud had to be mixed to fill in the walls. The school was completed in thirteen days.

The district agricultural officer was Leslie Brown, an extremely intelligent and efficient but disagreeable man, hated by the people because he would never even shake hands with a black man. Often I had to hold a *baraza* the day after his, to calm the people down and tell them to ignore his atrocious manners and do as he advised, because he really knew his stuff.

Brown and his less abrasive colleague in Meru, Jack Benson, brought about an important change in departmental policy: that press-gang terracing should be supplemented by giving farmers as inducements to terrace help in growing high-priced cash-crops, especially coffee.

The situation in Embu and Meru was much easier than in the three Kikuyu districts. Except in Kerugoya, the south-western division of Embu which was inhabited by Kikuyu, the people were less politicized, suspicious and litigious. Wainwright found the ADC extremely friendly and co-operative: 'We never had an

The Heart of the Matter

acrimonious debate, though they were inclined to speak too long and repetitively.'

There was no land shortage and very little feeling against white settlers who bordered on Meru only for a few miles and on Embu not at all. Meru had empty, fertile land going spare.

P. M. Brothers was DO in Meru in 1947. A Battle of Britain pilot, complete with DSO and DFC, he lobbied the Secretariat for the use of a light aircraft.

While my visions were not shared by the Boot-and-Saddle brigade, I had the backing of P. Wyn Harris, that intrepid CNC who learned to fly, bought his own aircraft and terrified experienced aviators by his ardent but unskilled efforts.

A foot safari, skilfully misled by local guides, had pronounced the Kionyu area uninhabited and suitable for occupation by those who had over-grazed their own areas. A decision to move them was taken. The DC, Noel Kennaway, and the agricola, Benson, decided that an aerial survey might be profitable. It was. Never had we seen so many hidden, untaxed and contented people. Collecting the years of outstanding tax made Bwana Ndege*, me of the all-seeing eye, unpopular in some quarters. But one cannot have the wife drunk and the bottle full. From the air a more suitable grazing area was found and the move made. The two flights totalled one and three-quarter hours, a profitable exercise.

Partly because of the risk of diseases spreading to European farms, the Kikuyu were not allowed to grow coffee until 1947, or tea until 1949. But a greater difficulty in introducing cash-crops was the fragmentation of Kikuyu holdings. The countryside, wrote R. O. Hennings who in 1951 became executive officer of ALDEV

> was higgledy-piggledy with thousands of small scattered plots. Clearly the key to agricultural progress was the gathering of fragments into farms of reasonable size, a prolonged and complicated process. In the years before

*Ndege: bird. Hence, by association, a plane, and its pilot.

Mau Mau there was no hope of gaining the co-operation and consent of right-holders.

To have planted coffee-trees on small fragmented holdings would have made their gathering together forever impossible. Leslie Brown went round grumbling, 'I've done my part in working out the potential of well-farmed smallholdings. Now it's up to the administration to make the people get on with it.' But you cannot (as Turnbull remarked) make a man a good farmer by putting him in prison for farming badly.

In Embu and Meru, less fragmented, the people had been exhorted to grow coffee since 1947. Embu conservatism was stubborn. But in Meru coffee caught on. The soil and climate were perfect, and under supervision by perfectionist agricolas, the Meru grew superb coffee. Only those who bench-terraced, *boma*-ed their cattle, manured their land and rotated their crops were allowed, as a reward, to plant up to a hundred coffee-trees. In 1948 there were over a thousand Meru coffee-growers; in 1952, this had increased to 6,473. By that time the Embu had realized what they were missing, and were planting madly. Wainwright finds it 'infuriating to read so often that the colonial government prevented people from growing coffee and tea, and that it has all been grown since independence.' Tea was more difficult, but came later. A man could make £18–£20 a year, growing only food-crops on twelve acres – a modest return which made the case for collectives. Brown calculated that he could make £100 a year (a very handsome income then), plus subsistence, on 8 to 10 acres including a half-acre of coffee.

In 1949 P. Wynn-Harris, the outstanding administrative officer of his generation, went to be Governor of Gambia, and was succeeded by Eric Davies, than whom no nicer man ever ran a district.

18

Mau Mau

Before 1948 only the Kikuyu had heard of Mau Mau. By 1951 everyone seemed to be talking about it. But neither the Labour government, in office until 26 October 1951, nor the Conservative government thereafter, was officially informed of it until August 1952.

No one knows the origin of the name. Its essence was resentment at European settlement of land which the Kikuyu believed to be theirs. This was aggravated by grievances of unemployed and landless Kikuyu, by a distaste for communal terracing and by the feeling among the more educated that they were denied the status and salaries for which they were qualified. All these threads of resentment were drawn together and manipulated with consummate skill by Jomo Kenyatta. This he did quite legally through the Kenya African Union and the KISA schools, of which he was respectively chairman and head of the KISA* teacher-training college at Githunguri.

In August 1950 Mau Mau was proscribed as an unlawful society, the members, managers and oath-administrators of which could be prosecuted – provided anyone dared give evidence in open court against them.

KAU gave Mau Mau a legal front and machinery for support by political action, funds and propaganda. They had the same aims: Europeans out, and Kenya for the Kikuyu. They differed only in method – KAU operating by mass agitation which did not exclude intimidation; Mau Mau by intimidation and murder,

*See p 211

ensuring obedience and secrecy by requiring members to take oaths which at first were not objectionable to the Kikuyu, being sworn by men only, with none of the obscenity associated with later Mau Mau oathing.

Was Jomo Kenyatta, Chairman of KAU, also the creator and manager of Mau Mau? His record as Prime Minister immediately before, and as President after, independence, and his magnanimity to his former foes, have promoted a belief that, so far from being the Mau Mau leader, he was clinging to the tiger's tail. But throughout the 1950s nearly everyone in Kenya, white, black or brown, believed that he led Mau Mau. It would be hard to find a Kikuyu, then or now, who in his heart did not and does not think so. The contrary belief was held until well into 1952 by several senior headquarters officers of the administration and police. It was based on wishful thinking: they did not *want* Kenyatta to be involved in Mau Mau. He was given several opportunities to denounce publicly and unequivocally Mau Mau and its many murders of Crown witnesses and government servants, all Kikuyu, which took place (*pace* his apologists) *before* his arrest. He never did so. His apologists say he dared not. Most administrative officers believed then, and believe now, that he chose not to do so lest he thereby be devalued among the Kikuyu. Probably this belief was valid, though the evidence is conflicting.

Although much was made of Kenyatta's visits to Moscow during his long sojourn in Europe, Mau Mau was not communist-inspired. Nor was it truly a nationalist movement, for attempts to spread it beyond the Kikuyu, Embu and Meru had very little success.

The collection of political intelligence was the responsibility of the Special Branch of the Kenya Police, a two-man band in Nairobi, working under the Director of Intelligence and Security (DIS), and reporting through the Commissioner of Police to the Member for Law and Order.* In 1951 a Special Branch officer was posted to Nyeri. Otherwise, the Kenya police had no presence in the reserves, so most political intelligence emanated in fact from DCs, whether it was passed up through administrative channels to the PC and the CNC, or through police channels to the Member for

---

*Member of the Executive Council, responsible for law and order.

Law and Order. The relevant files were circulated between the Member for Law and Order, the CNC and the Chief Secretary. But F. D. Corfield, author of the thorough and detailed *Origin and Growth of Mau Mau* (1960), was 'left with the inescapable conclusion that they just "disappeared" into the central secretariat because there was no one responsible for the regular sifting of intelligence reports and assessing their long- and short-term implications'. In 1950 an internal security working committee was set up under the Secretary for Law and Order, Cusack. It might have been given that duty, but was not: its responsibility was mainly with internal security schemes and operations.

A DC's secret intelligence report (typed every month by himself) went to neighbouring DCs, the PC, CNC, DIS; but precious little came down to him from them. 'Ozzie' Hughes recalls one letter from the Member for Law and Order about the situation in Malaya, and a long memorandum from the Governor about communism. That was all. Hughes relied for information on

> DOs, chiefs, perhaps the TP sergeant and interpreter, and occasional informers for whom he had to ask the PC for small sums. The best sources were DOs on safari with two or three TPs, but these never stayed long enough in any place to get to the root of local doings.

DCs heard rumours of Mau Mau oathings, but not until they had taken place. An experienced officer, however, could tell there had been an oathing from the sullen demeanour of the people, the blank stares and backs turned as he passed by, the poor turn-out for terracing, and in some cases by a tendency for chiefs to keep their heads down. George Hampson, a DO in Nyeri 1949–54, who spoke Kikuyu, recalls of the years 1950–1:

> With weekend visitors from Nairobi – KAU agitators and thugs of the 40 Group and Cowboy gangs – administration became increasingly difficult. Reports proliferated of underground opposition to the government. Mau Mau oaths, in theory voluntary, were based on traditional initiation ceremonies with the addition of magic designed to bind

initiates to obedience and secrecy. By 1951 oaths were being administered at night, to women as well as men, gross breaches of tribal custom. There was an increase in arson and murder, and a darkening, tangible atmosphere of fear. People were too scared to bring to court complaints of malicious damage to crops and property. Prosecution witnesses fell silent, or disappeared.

In August 1950 Hampson was in charge, in the absence of the DC, Swann. His Sunday morning lie-in was interrupted by the arrival of Senior Chief Nderi and two men, somewhat battered but reasonably calm, who said they had escaped from a Mau Mau oathing having been beaten up for refusing to take the oath. Hampson collected ten TPs and fifteen Kenya Police from the Nyeri township station and drove at top speed to Kyando where the oathing had taken place. On the way they arrested two men whom the informers identified: one had under his shirt the bloody pelvis of a sacrificed goat into which every male initiate had to insert his penis, an essential part of the ceremony. But they arrived at Kyando too late, finding only oathing paraphernalia of banana-leaf arches and the remains of the goat.

Frank Loyd, DC Fort Hall from January 1949 to August 1953, looks back upon the twelve months from September 1951 as by far the worst.

We had no special emergency powers, and intimidation meant that murders, increasing every month, were impossible to deal with. Nobody would give evidence because he would be killed if he did. When a headman and two TPs were murdered, no one had seen it, no one knew anything about it. A mild form of intimidation was hanging disembowelled cats outside chiefs' houses. I had been in Fort Hall, as DO and DC, a good many years, and knew the people fairly well, and it was really frightening to see their appearance: you could tell where there had been an oathing, simply by driving through.

DCs sent frequent reports on the growth of Mau Mau to the PC, Windley. These reports are not now available, but they were available to Corfield who quoted many of them. S. E. Napier-Bax, in the office of the Director of Intelligence and Security (DIS),

> spent days reading all the reports from people in the field. The emergence of Mau Mau was no secret. From DCs, a few other field officers and the odd settler came repeated warnings of the impending storm.

All these warning were ignored. Why?
Sir Philip Mitchell, in poor health and coasting downhill towards retirement, was naturally influenced by the man who had been DIS since 1946, whose knowledge of subversive trade unions had been of the utmost value during the Mombasa general strike. So was H. S. Potter, who became chief secretary in January, 1951. The DIS was a little inclined to discount administration warnings about Mau Mau, which was outside his own special interests and expertise. Geoffrey Ellerton, in the department concerned with law and order, remembers far more anxiety about communism in trade unions than about Mau Mau. The real weakness, however, was not in personalities, but in the lack of any machinery for the regular sifting and assessment of political intelligence. This was done, says Corfield, if at all, by the 'unintegrated efforts of the Member for Law and Order and the CNC'.

In July 1950 Swann reported from Nyeri a dangerous revolutionary organization centrally controlled. Ian Henderson, the Kikuyu-speaking, Kikuyu-thinking Special Branch officer in Nyeri, confirmed this in greater detail, as did two Kikuyu-speaking missionaries. Windley urged that Mau Mau leaders be prosecuted, but this was not done. Corfield found that the main inhibiting factor

> was the interpretation given to the law of sedition by the courts. In the five years before the Emergency there were only five successful prosecutions for sedition. The sentences of fines usually awarded by the courts were quite useless. The fines were paid without difficulty from the accumulated funds of Mau Mau.

Men Who Ruled Kenya

At a KAU mass meeting in Nyeri in March 1951, the conveners of which had undertaken to denounce Mau Mau, not a word was said against it, and a resolution was passed condemning the prosecution of oath administrators. Henderson commented: 'It would have been suicidal for anyone to pass a remark in favour of the government'.

Swann then returned to the charge:

> This has confirmed the complete identity of the Nyeri branch of KAU with Mau Mau. All moderates were dismissed from office, and replaced by extremists. Jomo Kenyatta is usually named as the head of both bodies.

After another KAU meeting in May, Swann forecast that chiefs would soon be murdered. But the Senior Superintendent of Police (SSP) in Nyeri described his views, although endorsed by Henderson, as 'exaggerated', and the DIS shared his scepticism. Swann stuck to his story and Windley wrote to the CNC on 27 June: 'There has been a swing to the extremists who have gained control of KAU committees in Nyeri and Fort Hall (also Nairobi) during the past six months.' But eight days later the DIS forwarded to the Member for Law and Order, without comment, a paper from the SSP Nyeri which discounted the administration's warnings as 'over-painted'; and the member, K. K. O'Connor, described them to the CNC as 'alarmist, not accepted at their face value by the DIS'.

The situation in the Rift Valley Province was described by the DIS in February as 'greatly improved lately. It would appear that the Mau Mau is cracking up.' In October the PC said it was not, and cited the impossibility of finding witnesses to oathing ceremonies.

In the second half of 1951 Loyd sent repeated reports of the growth of Mau Mau and its close connection with KAU and KISA. In December Swann again forecast that 'blood will soon be shed'. Even Windley asked him: 'Are you sure you're not exaggerating a little?' Swann was sure. Unfortunately the SSP (but not Henderson) discounted these warnings, and the Member for Law and Order chose to believe him rather than the administration.

On 27 November an attempt was made at last to evaluate the disparate reports. The internal security working committee, chaired by Cusack, presented its first, and last, report to the Governor. It reached what Corfield describes as 'an astonishing conclusion' that

> As soon as the shs 60 entrance fees are no longer forthcoming, little more will be heard of Mau Mau ...[which] remains a possible instrument of mischief in the hands of agitators, though one of which the potentialities appear to be waning.

A PC's Annual Report was not supposed to include contentious arguments, clarion calls to action or dire warnings of troubles to come, all subjects for special secret letters and private talks. Windley's Central Province Report for 1951 was fairly optimistic. There were a few paragraphs on KAU, KISA and Mau Mau, but 'in the interests of brevity' these were removed from the report by the CNC's office. It was this bowdlerized version which was presented to Mitchell in January 1952, causing him to minute on it: 'A very good report of an excellent and encouraging year's work'. Corfield commented:

> It is not easy to escape the impression that this reflected a definite policy on the part of the central government to play down the prominent part played by Kikuyu leaders in fomenting the unrest. That was the impression left with the provincial commissioner.

Moreover it was this bowdlerized version which was published, confirming the belief of settler politicians (many of whom knew of the DCs' warnings) that the Government was shutting its eyes to the danger.

The Kenya Intelligence Summary for 1951, compiled by Cusack, recorded 'a general improvement in the situation in regard to Mau Mau'. Mitchell had been receiving also the district secret intelligence reports, forty of them every month. But he cannot have been paying them much attention because in March 1952 he directed that they no longer be sent to him.

The further one is from the fire, the less one feels the heat: and it is in human nature, particularly perhaps in the English nature, to deprecate 'flap' and over-reaction to hypothetical perils. There is therefore a tendency for intelligence reports from officers in the field to be toned down at each stage as they pass up the corridors of power. There was in the secretariat a sort of resistence to DCs' warnings, disparaged as they were by the SSP in Nyeri and by the DIS. The mental block may have been in the CNC's office, or in the MLO's or in both. All one can say for certain is that the field administration gave ample warnings about Mau Mau; that these warnings were diluted on their way to the Governor; and that he was sure he knew far more about Africa than all the PCs and DCs put together.

Throughout 1951 the senior officers dealing with internal security had been the Chief Secretary, J. D. Rankine; the Member for Law and Order and Attorney-General, K. K. O'Connor; and the CNC, Eric Davies, a much-liked man and a good DC, but hardly one for 'the day when heaven was falling'. In January 1952 Rankine was replaced by Henry Potter, a kindly, competent, somewhat colourless individual who after eighteen years in Kenya had spent the last eight in the Uganda secretariat. O'Connor was replaced by John Whyatt.

A much stronger character than Potter or Davies, Whyatt was a stranger to Africa. Where the duties of his two portfolios of Law and Order and Attorney-General conflicted, he saw himself only as Attorney-General. He was a very sincere man, a devout Catholic; but his real god was the English Common Law, and he fought to the last twist and turn against pressure to adapt this to the needs of a colony in a state of rebellion. Unfortunately he was rude and inconsiderate, making enemies wherever he went. His Secretary for Law and Order was Jake Cusack who some considered to be a crafty, idle, able, cynical Irish hedonist. They made a curious team.

The Commissioner of Police was Michael Sylvester O'Rorke, most of whose service had been with the Palestine Police. A charming character and a talented water-colour artist, he was a man for the broad brush rather than for detail, out of his depth commanding a force the strength of an infantry division, scattered in many small detachments, with no trained staff officers. He was jealous of the administration, and believed that the police should be responsible for law and order. Cusack introduced the author to him with the words, 'This is Charles Trench, Michael. His ancestors sent yours to hell or Connaught.' We remained on the best of terms.

Neither Potter, Davies nor Cusack had recent experience of the Kikuyu; Whyatt and O'Rorke had none. The administration's greatest Kikuyu expert, Coutts, spent the years 1949 to 1957 administering St Vincent in the West Indies.

Mitchell wanted to go down in history as one of the great colonial governors. The peak of his career would be the visit to Kenya of Princess Elizabeth and Prince Philip, soon after which he would retire to a well-merited seat in the House of Lords. He resolutely closed eyes and ears to the hideous possibility that his governorship might end not in glory but in bloodshed. Neither Potter nor Davies were the men to press unwelcome advice on a strong character; and Whyatt could be discounted as a man who knew nothing of Africa. Still less would he listen to settlers, whom he loathed; and they him.

Yet the European elected members were well informed about Mau Mau. They had among their constituents farmers who had spoken Kikuyu since boyhood and were in close touch with their labour. Doyen of the settlers was the Member for Agriculture, Cavendish Bentinck, with a finger in every pie and a constitutional inability to pull it out. Their spokesmen on law and order were Michael Blundell, a Rift Valley farmer and leader of the European elected members; Wilfrid Havelock, a Kiambu coffee-farmer; and Humphrey Slade, a Nairobi lawyer who had a farm on the Kinangop. All were elected members of the Legislative Council (Legco) and reasonable, intelligent men, but endowed in Potter's and Whyatt's minds with horns, forked tails and cloven feet. The most the official side would concede to them was an occasional discussion in an informal law and order committee, not for mutual enlightenment but, in Cusack's words, 'to keep the buggers quiet'. Corfield noted that Whyatt's dislike of European politicians had a 'baleful effect on his judgement'.

PCs and DCs had more contact with Michael Blundell than with any other settler politician, so his view of the service is of interest:

I always found officers up to district level most friendly and co-operative. However a great change took place at provincial level. Most PCs, with the exception of Robin Wainwright, were remote, rather inaccessible and I often felt suspicious of a political Minister.

While I think the administration was remarkably fair and dedicated, with officers of high quality, there was a touch of celestialism about it, engendered partly by the Union Jacks, official pith helmets, brass buttons, the myth of the Queen's Representative etc which made it remote from the people.*

Although liking and working with individual officers, I did not like the system. I felt we ought to run our own country.

Sir Evelyn Baring wrote of Blundell:

> He was good with young officers. A number of senior officers were suspicious of him. He was equally suspicious of them, and not at all good at bringing them round to his point of view.

During six nights in January and February 1952, the huts of eighteen headmen, Crown witnesses and conspicuous loyalists in Nyeri were set alight, with the occupants inside and the doors wired up. They managed to escape through doors and windows. There then arose the agonizing dilemma of the royal visit in February. To cancel it would hand a propaganda victory to the Mau Mau and end Mitchell's hopes of a peerage. To allow the royal couple to drive through the heart of Kikuyuland to the Royal Lodge in Nyeri district (a wedding present from the colony) seemed an appalling risk. Swann was 'sweating in a cold perspiration lest anything happen'. In the event nothing did. It was at the Royal Lodge that Princess Elizabeth learned that her father had died and she was Queen.

---

*Some DCs, including the author, never wore pith helmets or brass buttons except perhaps for a Governor's visit.

After the visit Swann attended a conference of the CNC, the Member for Law and Order, the Commissioner of Police, the PC and DCs of Central Province.

All of us stressed the danger of the situation, but the officers from Nairobi thought we were exaggerating . . .[Some weeks later] Sir Philip Mitchell, having announced to the Press that he 'knew nothing of Mau Mau', collapsed with 'exhaustion neurosis' and was invalided home in June.

His successor was Sir Evelyn Baring who was receiving treatment after an accident and could not take over for several months. Potter became Acting Governor.

Meanwhile there had arrived a new Director of Intelligence and Security, Trevor Jenkins, a Kenya police officer who had enlarged his experience of sophisticated African politicians during a secondment to the Gold Coast. He immediately started a detailed investigation into KAU, KISA, Mau Mau, the links between them and Kenyatta's role in all three, and produced his report on 30 April. It was, wrote Corfield, 'by any standards a first class document, but the most interesting thing about it was what did not happen to it'. The report was addressed to the Member for Law and Order, with copies to the CNC and the Commissioner of Police. The latter received it on 14 May. Cusack, the Secretary for Law and Order, acknowledged receipt of the MLO's copy on 16 May. On 15 June he sent a copy to the Chief Secretary, Potter. But no copy was sent to Government House, either while Mitchell was Governor until 26 June, or when Potter was Acting Governor thereafter, until 12 August when Potter asked for a copy which Cusack sent him with the minute:

> Your Excellency may care to peruse the attached memorandum on Mau Mau which was prepared by the DIS in April.

The omission to send a copy to the Governor defies rational explanation. The CNC's failure to send copies of the memorandum to PCs before 25 September is also extraordinary but of less moment, since most of the information on which the memorandum was based came from the DCs in Central and Rift Valley Provinces.

(*A personal note.* In April I took over from Geoffrey Ellerton in Section A.1 of the secretariat, having scarcely heard of Mau Mau and expecting to be concerned mainly with Asians and alien Somalis. At first as a sideline, I acted as Secretary to the Law and Order Committee, chaired by Whyatt and attended usually by Cusack, O'Rorke, Blundell, Slade and Havelock. Of course I took no part in its deliberations, my role being merely to 'record and report what they think that they think that they ought to have thought'. Later I performed a similar service for the Colony Emergency Committee, chaired by Potter, attended by Whyatt, Davies, Cusack, O'Rorke and others at need, but no non-officials. So my observations on these people and events are for the most part those of a silent eye-witness.)

In July and August the situation deteriorated very quickly. John Pinney, a DO in Fort Hall, saw the rot set in.

On August Bank Holiday an old man in Ruathia was chopped in two because he had given evidence in court. Further down the road the whole family of a chief's retainer was murdered for the same reason. And in the river below Gituge was found the strangled corpse of an African court process server who had given evidence in a Mau Mau case. Hardly a day passed without a report of a corpse or a missing person, and always they had informed or given evidence of early Mau Mau oathing.

The chiefs and headmen were frightened, except chiefs Njiri and Ignatio. If an officer went on safari, the young men would turn their backs and spit. They were beginning to wear Kenyatta beards and long hair. In KISA schools Kenyatta hymns* were sung, and nearly every teacher was rotten to the core. I visited Chui school and the headmaster said, 'What do you Europeans want here? I am busy educating Kikuyu children. Go away.'

A church elder took me to see a Mau Mau oathing ceremony. I had as escort one TP, and our only weapon

*Christian hymns with Kenyatta's name substituted for that of Jesus.

was a walking stick. We sat on a hill and watched about 900 people oathing. There was nothing we could do. The people laughed at us and spat.

The oath now being administered was the 'double killing oath', which may be summarized as, 'I swear to kill whomsoever I am ordered to kill, and if I fail, may this oath kill me.' They swore also to rescue Kenyatta should he be arrested. A man who had taken the first oath was committed, and could only go on taking more and more horrifying and disgusting oaths, allegedly involving the consumption of human flesh, faeces, semen and menstrual fluid. This was supposed to put initiates beyond the pale of tribal society: they could never go back. (Turnbull, however, 'never thought oathing was particularly horrifying to the Kikuyu. They probably thought it a nice day out'.)

The Mau Mau murdered scores of Christian martyrs, men and women who may not have been pro-government but refused to betray their faith by these disgusting rituals, knowing that refusal would be followed by death in unspeakable agony. The Christian churches should be proud of those Kikuyu.

In the chiefs' meeting at Nyeri in May Hughes, who had succeeded Swann as DC, suggested that there be revived the traditional *Athiegani* (scout) system of the Masai wars. A few chiefs responded, as did the Consolate Catholic Mission, and in July the first rudiments of the Home Guard came into being, armed with spears, bows and simis'.*

Kenyatta was debarred from holding meetings in the reserves, though he could hold them in the settled areas, whence came wild rumours of what he had said. 'Ozzie' Hughes thought he should be allowed a meeting in Nyeri to bring the thing into the open, give him a chance to denounce Mau Mau, and lest a continued ban be reversed by the British government 'which would make us look pretty fools'.

Sanction was given, and he addressed a meeting 30,000-strong, from a platform well bedecked with Mau Mau paraphernalia. A noticeable feature was the number of young

---

*Simi: a short sword.

men and prostitutes who had accompanied him from Nairobi. After the meeting he told me that if he had known that the crowd would get so nearly out of hand through hysteria, he would not have asked for permission to hold it. He was at that moment a very frightened and worried man. The district was thereafter in compete turmoil.

Kenyatta's speech contained nothing that could be held against him in court, and nothing that the Mau Mau could interpret as reneging on them. In the hope that he would commit himself against Mau Mau, he was allowed another big meeting near Kiambu, and was again equivocal. (One who did denounce Mau Mau bravely, and publicly, was Harry Thuku. But he was yesterday's man, not worth killing).

A debate in Legco on 10 July revealed the unbridgeable gulf between Whyatt, who dominated the official side, and his *bêtes noires*, the European elected members. The more they orated about incipient rebellion, the more he denied it.

The attitude of Whyatt was crucial. He was fully convinced of the dangers of Mau Mau; but, urged by Potter and Davies to have Kenyatta and his henchmen despatched (like Harry Thuku and others) under deportation orders to distant places, he would reply, 'Where is the evidence that will induce a judge to make a deportation order?'

'Then why not declare an emergency and have him detained under a Governor's order?'

'Because there is no emergency.'

The law, he would explain as though to a class of retarded children, provides for the arrest, trial and imprisonment of malefactors, and even for potential trouble-makers to be bound over, with sureties, to keep the peace. Let DCs get on with it. He could not be made to understand that where there are no witnesses, the law is powerless; and that while the Mau Mau leaders were at large, there would be no witnesses.

Potter was far from complacent. Although he told the Colonial Secretary that Blundell's representations were 'hysterical, unbalanced and emotional', he was well aware of the danger. Taking the minutes at meetings of the emergency committee, I gained the impression that what inhibited him was his conviction that the British government, for fear of liberal opinion in Britain and of ructions in the United Nations, would never authorize tough action against African nationalists. Three generations of colonial administrators had believed, 'When it comes to the crunch, HMG will let us down.' A stronger man than Potter, sure of HMG's support, might have persuaded Whyatt to worry less about the niceties of the law and more about keeping order. But Potter was only a fairly obscure civil servant, temporarily acting as Governor. Light is thrown on his and Mitchell's attitudes by a remark which the latter made some months later, to David Christie-Miller, DC Nakuru: 'You must realize that the British government will do nothing to help a colony *before* a row breaks out. But the moment there are corpses in the streets, it will do everything.'

On 17 August, after perusing the Jenkins memorandum at an emergency committee meeting, Potter asked its author, 'Well, is Kenyatta our man?'

Trevor Jenkins replied, not without regret, 'I'm afraid so.'

Potter then sent the Colonial Office the first official warning of trouble to come.

In the early morning of 26 September Ken Robertson, a Nanyuki farmer, went out to look round his beloved Jersey herd and Corriedals ewes. He found over 250 dead, disembowelled but still alive, or staggering about on two legs and two bloody stumps. There had been an oathing on his farm that night. On 3 October Mrs A. M. Wright was stabbed to death on her farm near Thika. Two days later Mr and Mrs K. Bindloss were shot and stabbed on their coffee-plantation near Kiambu. These were the first Mau Mau crimes against Europeans.

Swann, on leave, had a long interview with the Governor designate, and was surprised by Baring's grasp of the situation. Baring flew to Nairobi at the end of September, and the atmosphere was transformed. He was no obscure civil servant, but a personage in England, with an intimate knowledge of the Conservative government and party. He never doubted that, if he needed emergency powers, he would get them. In an unpublished account of these events, written probably in 1964, he related:

I arrived in Kenya on 29 September and within five days went on a tour of the Kikuyu country. On return, on 29 October, I sent a letter and telegram to the Secretary of State. The gist of these documents was that there had been a complete breakdown of criminal justice. During the last three months in the Kikuyu reserve thirty-six witnesses subpoenaed by the Crown in murder cases had been assassinated before they could come to court. In the same period twenty-four Kikuyu headmen had also been assassinated. Kenyatta made no attempt to stop the murder campaign.

There was an attack on all sources of authority by the Mau Mau . . . Kikuyu chiefs and headmen, African administrative officers, Kikuyu teachers, European missionaries of all denominations, leading farmers and all African government officers pressed the point on me that without the removal of Kenyatta and other Mau Mau leaders there would be absolute chaos.

During my tour, one of the most respected chiefs in the Kikuyu country, Waruhiu, was assassinated by a gunman on the high road between Nairobi and Kiambu.

This murder, wrote Baring, 'was the occasion to declare an emergency and arrest the leaders of the Mau Mau movement'.

The Colony emergency committee began planning the operation which was given the code-name 'Jock Scott', the core of which was to be the arrest of Jomo Kenyatta and 127 other prominent Mau Mau. One problem was the date for the declaration of the State of Emergency. Factors affecting it included the state of the moon, so that the police making the arrests could drive without headlights through the Kikuyu reserve; a British infantry battalion must be flown in at dawn next day, just in case . . . [This had to come from Cyprus, and would not be available until the end of a current operation against EOKA terrorists.] There must be a cruiser at Mombasa, not (as the wags suggested) because the administration thought it could sail up the Athi river and bombard Pumwani, but because it was the smallest warship which could put ashore a landing party with enough technicians to run Mombasa docks in the event of a general strike.

Mau Mau

The meeting at which these details were finalized ended about 10 p.m. As I was preparing to take home the notes from which I would type the minutes, Cusack asked, 'Have you got a gun?'

'Of course not,' I replied.

'Do you mean to say you're driving through Nairobi at night with those papers and no gun? Here, take this.' He handed me a .45 Webley which I put awkwardly in my pocket.

During the night of the 20 October Jomo Kenyatta and nearly all those on the 'pick-up list' were arrested.

19

State of Emergency, I

It was generally assumed that Kenyatta's arrest would provoke a violent explosion, quickly suppressed. Indeed on 22 October Senior Chief Nderi and his police escort were chopped into small pieces by a mob assembled for oathing. There followed a 'phoney war' for several weeks. The government was blamed, by those not burdened by responsibility, for losing the initiative. The difficulty was that, although the law had been strengthened, the forces available for its enforcement had not. There were murders and other atrocities which will be related in due course; but the burning question was, 'What should be done with Kenyatta?'

Settlers favoured hanging him from the nearest tree or, failing that, he should be detained indefinitely without trial; the worst possible outcome was that he should be brought to trial and acquitted. Whyatt would not have this. 'This man is guilty as hell,' he said, 'and I'm going to prove it in open court. If I can't prove it, he can go free.'

There were two major difficulties. The first, of course, was to find witnesses who could give first-hand evidence of Kenyatta's membership and management of Mau Mau. Before his arrest that would have been impossible. Now a bold though desperately scared young man named Rawson Macharia came forward who said he had actually seen Kenyatta take part in a Mau Mau oathing. He would go into the witness box only if, as soon as he had given evidence, he were flown to Britain for a course in higher education: if he remained in Kenya, he was certain to be murdered. Other witnesses could give supporting evidence, but Rawson Macharia's was vital.

State of Emergency, I

The other problem was, who should hear the case? If it was heard by a judge, there must be a preliminary enquiry by a magistrate; terrified witnesses would have to give the same evidence in open court twice over. If he was tried by a mere magistrate, it would seem like a put-up job. The Deputy Crown Prosecutor had an inspiration. 'There's a recently retired judge, R. S. Thacker, QC. Appoint him First Class Magistrate and he can try the case without a preliminary enquiry. No one can say he isn't qualified.'

Thacker said he would hear the case, but would be in danger for the rest of his life, and must be paid a realistic sum, *per diem*. On the assumption that the case would soon be over, this was agreed. Unfortunately – fortunately for Mr Justice Thacker – a brilliant delaying action by Kenyatta's Counsel, D. N. Pritt, QC, spun it out for several months.

In November Dick Wilson was told in great secrecy that Kenyatta and five others were to be tried in Kapenguria, and he was to go there as DC and do a hundred and one things in two days to prepare for this. He was then to charge them with the management of an unlawful society, and transfer the case to a specially appointed resident magistrate, R. S. Thacker. There followed forty-eight hours' non-stop work, clearing the jail for its new inmates, converting the school into a court-house, pitching camps for witnesses and police. On the third day Wilson arraigned the accused in his office and duly passed the case on to Thacker.

The strategy of the defence counsel, D. N. Pritt, was to provoke Thacker into losing his temper or throwing his hand in, and then claim a new trial. He continually accused Wilson of refusing him facilities to consult his clients; and would turn his back on the magistrate and harangue the press, while Thacker was hard put to keep his temper.

However Rawson Macharia and the other Crown witnesses gave their evidence well and stood up to formidable cross-examination. In early April all the accused were found guilty and sentenced to seven years' imprisonment, which they served at Lokitaung. Rawson Macharia was packed off to his studies in England, and the other Kikuyu Crown witnesses provided with *shambas* a long way from Kikuyuland.

There are three postscripts to the trial. The first was related by Malcolm Macdonald, Kenya's last Governor, in a radio interview after Kenyatta's death. Asked if he believed in Kenyatta's guilt, he replied:

> I can best answer that by repeating what Kenyatta said to me during internal self-government when he was Prime Minister. I told him that the Chief Justice was leaving, and asked who we should appoint in his place. He replied, 'I think we should appoint the judge who convicted me at Kapenguria. I thought he was a very good judge. Certainly he did listen to lying evidence about me, but he wasn't to know they were lies.'

The second postscript is by Baring, who visited Kenya after independence and met Kenyatta in the President's Office. Baring said, 'I was sitting at that table when I signed your Detention Order twenty years ago.' Kenyatta replied, 'I know. In your shoes, at that time, I'd have done exactly the same. And I've signed a good few Detention Orders on it myself.'

The third postscript is my story. There was in Nairobi a judge of the East Africa Court of Appeal, Burkitt Rudd. He was a keen polo player, but suddenly sold his ponies and never came to the ground again. Years later we were neighbours, and I asked why he did this. He replied, 'It was at the time of Jomo's appeal. Everyone was talking about it, and in order to keep an open mind, I gave up all my social life, including polo.' It was a high-minded thing to do: there are many sacrifices to principle more easily made than one's favourite pastime. I asked him, 'Having seen JK as a pretty good President, do you now have any doubt about the justice of his conviction?'

'None whatever,' said Burkitt Rudd.

The East Africa Court of Appeal was not noted for partiality to the prosecution or for allowing political expediency to muddy the wells of justice. Nor was the Privy Council, which came to the same conclusion.

Some years later, when the Emergency was all over, Rawson Macharia returned home. It was obvious that Kenya would soon be independent, and Kenyatta its first President. Rawson, wishing

State of Emergency, I

to go on living there, announced that the evidence he had given contained not a word of truth. Well, he would, wouldn't he?

After Kapenguria Dick Wilson was made personal assistant to the Governor's intelligence adviser, a senior officer from the UK intelligence services, brought out to organize proper intelligence services for Kenya.

The 'phoney war' period did not last long. The Mau Mau organization seems to have been cellular, not hierarchical. Some of the cell leaders had been picked up; others, unknown to the government, were regrouping in the forests of the Aberdares and Mount Kenya. In the first three months of the Emergency eight European farmers were killed or badly hacked about. Over Christmas and the New Year thirty-five Kikuyu loyalists were murdered. A police patrol was ambushed and lost all its rifles. The murders of isolated farmers set off a disastrous movement to get rid of Kikuyu labour from Rift Valley farms. The unexpected influx of 50–60,000 Kikuyu for whom no preparations had been made added immensely to the difficulties of Nyeri, Kiambu and Fort Hall.

The campaign against the Mau Mau was conducted by John Whyatt, Member for Law and Order, markedly impeded by John Whyatt, Attorney-General. But some useful things were done. More DOs were posted to Kikuyu districts; and, the increase in numbers making it possible, the 'divisional system' was introduced there, so that in every division there was a resident DO with TPs. Kenya police posts were established in Central Province districts. Owing to the shortage of police officers, these were commanded by NCOs of the Kenya Regiment*. These had no police experience, and none of the askaris were Kikuyu, so they were deaf and blind in Kikuyuland; but they made loyalists feel safer.

KISA was proscribed, and its children distributed among mission schools. A beginning was made in getting anti-Mau Mau witch-doctors to hold 'cleansing ceremonies' in which, with appropriate ritual and the sacrifice of goats, those who had taken the Mau

---

*The Kenya Regiment was a territorial battalion, all European, composed mainly of young farmers most of whom were 'officer material'.

Mau oath could be purged of it. At least they provided colourful copy for the media. One ceremony was filmed. The camera stopped – and so did the ritual, not to be resumed until the camera started again. The witchdoctor was not going to miss a moment's publicity. The Mau Mau upped the stakes by eviscerating dogs, bigger magic than goats.

A Home Guard was built up. At first its object was just survival. Guards lived in huts clustered round the missions and the stouter-hearted chiefs, and were armed with native weapons, fire-power being provided by TPs. They were little more than a symbol of resistance. Expansion could not be hurried, for it was far better to have no home guard at all than to enlist unreliable men. Selection was by chiefs and guard leaders themselves, whose lives depended on choosing reliable men: 'Well, I'm sure of Njeroge, but a bit doubtful of Nyaga.'

Gradually in Fort Hall the selection was systematized by the 'confession' procedure devised by Jerome Kihori, a Kikuyu, a Makerere University College graduate and an outstanding DO. Most Kikuyu men had taken at least one oath. Before anyone was accepted into the home guard he had, as the Kikuyu say, to 'have his lungs cleansed' by confessing all he knew. This had two objects. Once it became obvious that those who broke the Mau Mau oath by disclosing its secrets were not immediately struck dead, others were emboldened to do likewise; and the confessions, methodically filed and cross-referenced by Jerome Kihori and his clerk, built up dossiers on Mau Mau oath administrators, treasurers and hit-men, a major intelligence breakthrough. A similar system was followed in Nyeri, the most important step, recalls Hampson, being the *public* denunciation of Mau Mau and the checking of a recruit's *bona fides*. 'To establish a home guard post of twelve reliable men could take months.'

Since farm raids seemed to be mainly to secure firearms, Baring foresaw that the police operation would develop into a small-scale guerrilla war. He asked for a general to be sent out as director of operations, and on 1 February 1953 there arrived Major-General Sir Robert (W.R.N.) Hinde.

'Looney' Hinde was an Eighth Army paladin who since the war had been Military Governor of West Berlin and of Cyrenaica. He

State of Emergency, I

knew Kenya, having a settler brother. Behind the mask of a genial cavalryman was a keen intelligence, sensitive political antennae and remarkably liberal opinions. He thought, for instance, even in 1953 that Africans should be admitted to Muthaiga Club. Within a week of his arrival, he remarked, 'Sooner or later they'll have to take this fellow Kenyatta out of prison and make him Prime Minister.' Anyone else expressing such views would have been tarred and feathered by the settlers; but 'General Looney', because of his war record, of his brother Robert, and of the fact that he had played polo for England, got away with it. He had neither troops nor police under his command: they continued to be commanded and administered by their own officers. His job was to recommend to the Governor (*ex-officio* Commander-in-Chief) a plan of action, and to co-ordinate the actions of the various security forces. In this he excelled because, although a soldier, he never undervalued the administration and Kenya police. 'This Mau Mau thing,' he said, 'can *only* be beaten by the Kikuyu themselves. The tribal police and the home guards are the key to it.'

He arrived with his *eminence grise*, Lieutenant-Colonel A. D. Bevan, a super-efficient staff officer whose speciality was chain-of-command. He formed a small staff consisting of a GSO I (Bevan); staff officer, police (Peter Reilly); and staff officer, civil, (myself); the last two having roughly the status of GSO II. At the head of his modest secretarial staff was the most ferociously efficient shorthand typist in Kenya, the terror of the office but devoted to 'the General' for whom she would gladly type until three in the morning. After the Emergency was over, we lunched together. 'And do you know,' she said, her ample bosom heaving with emotion, 'when the General left, he kissed me.'

A few weeks later I met him in London. 'I hear you've been kissing Miss Somen,' I said.

'The least I could do for her,' he replied.

On arrival he found functioning, 'but not very well', the emergency committee system, copied from Malaya. At every level – province, district, division – there was a 'troika' consisting of the PC, DC or DO, the senior local police officer and the senior army officer. The administrative officer was always in the chair. The committee's job was to devise policy and co-ordinate action.

Executive orders were issued to the military, police, home guard, etc, by their own officers. As revised by Hinde, it was a war-winner of which many claimed paternity.

I believe that David Bevan, Hinde's GSO I, if not the true begetter of the system, gave it the kiss of life. In General Hinde's Directive on Chain-of-Command and Control, issued on 15 April, a procedure was laid down to ensure that someone was responsible for taking action on every committee decision. Furthermore executive officers were appointed to emergency committees. They were co-ordinators, chaser-uppers, and were key men. Most were settlers, ex-regulars with staff college qualifications, personally selected by Hinde. On the same lines – PC/DC in the chair, army and police members, and a Special Branch officer where there was one – intelligence committees were formed, to collate intelligence from all quarters and present a coherent picture to the newly-formed Kenya Intelligence Committee of which Dick Wilson was Secretary.

One of the executive officers, who later joined the administration, was Jon Wainwright, brother of Robin, formerly of the Indian cavalry. He left his farm to form a mounted section of the Kenya Police Reserve, young farmers with their Kipsigis and Nandi syces. This operated with remarkable success in the big ranches northeast of the Aberdares, never sleeping twice in the same place, giving isolated farmers and their wives at least one night's undisturbed rest.

With troopers such as his, there were problems.

> Sometimes discipline had to be enforced. My method was to ride up behind the offender, put my arm round his neck and yank him off his horse, giving it a smack on the rump to speed it on its way. General Hinde spent a day with us, and expressed appreciation of my methods.

Shortly after this, Hinde ordered Wainwright to quit his 'corporal's job' and be executive officer, Fort Hall.

> Having been a settler for a number of years, I had the impression that most administrative officers were anti-settler

State of Emergency, I

and thought Africans could do no wrong. In Fort Hall I found them great people to work with. The only effective gang-trackers were the TPs, a remarkable body of local Kikuyu who remained loyal due to the personalities and powers of leadership of their administrative officers.

An emergency fund was set up, with a 'quick release' mechanism administered in the Treasury by Geoffrey Ellerton.

It was an enormous goat bag from which disbursements could be made without prior legislative approval. This stood on its head the principle that every public servant is a potential peculator. Instead, the assumption was that civil servants could be trusted. I was knowingly let down only once: a district 'lost' £50,000 in a week. Sometimes I had a twinge of conscience, as when we re-stocked all the trout stream because someone had thrown a grenade into the Sagana killing a few fish.

Dick Wilson 'had only to ring up and say, "Now I want something yesterday", and Geoffrey Ellerton would reply, "I'll confirm this afternoon, but I think it will be OK" – and it was.'

Conscription was brought in for Europeans, and at their own request for Asians. Despite Whyatt's reluctance, hundreds of emergency regulations were promulgated: imposing a curfew; gazetting prohibited areas; authorizing DCs to detain Mau Mau suspects without trial; and enabling resident magistrates to try capital cases. The possession of arms and ammunition, attempted murder, sabotage, administering Mau Mau oaths were made capital offences. Blundell, never backward in pressing for these draconic measures, afterwards questioned whether they had any real effect.

When these great psychological convulsions take place in the human mind, shooting and hanging cannot deal with the ideas that are generated ... It was the steady build-up of the constructive work of the administration in the field, as well as the pressure of military operations, that enabled the ideas of the Kikuyu resistance leaders to triumph in the minds of the people . . . It is no exaggeration to say that a first-class DC was worth a brigade.

Kiambu was comparatively quiet, perhaps because Mau Mau wished it to remain so, as their transit area between Nairobi and Fort Hall. On his return from leave early in 1953, Tony Swann was posted to Kiambu.

Just when I got there, they shot another chief, Hinga. He was brought wounded into hospital and, by God, a taxi-driver from Nairobi shot him there again. By sheer luck I had been in Nairobi and was driving back when I saw ahead of me a Nairobi taxi going towards Kiambu. It was near curfew-time, and I thought this rather strange, so I wrote the number down. I told the police, who went to his house in Pumwani – he was a Fort Hall chap – and as they went in, he said, 'I've never been to Kiambu and I don't know Hinga.' It was our man, sheer luck.

Then we had the Lari massacre, near Uplands. At dawn they locked ex-chief Lukas and God knows how many loyalists in their huts and set fire to them. It was the most terrible scene.

Between eighty and a hundred were killed. Men, women and children were so burned and chopped up that an accurate count was impossible.

I was looking at Lukas and his three wives all burned to a frazzle, looking at children mutilated and crucified, when a train drew up at the station and about a thousand people got off, squatters evicted from the Rift Valley. I almost burst into tears. Oliver Lyttleton came out soon afterwards and I said, '*Please*, no more for two months. We will willy-nilly take back the chaps of Kiambu origin, but for two months we really can't, we'll go under if this goes on.' So for two months it was stopped.

State of Emergency, I

In Fort Hall and Nyeri, too, squatters from the Rift Valley poured in who had no land, no jobs and precious little welcome. Most of the young men went off to Nairobi or joined the forest gangs.

On the same night as the Lari massacre a well-led gang attacked Naivasha police station, caught the garrison napping and got away with over a hundred rifles, bren-guns, sub-machine guns and boxes of ammunition, which were taken by lorry into the forest. It was the worst single reverse of the whole emergency. Hinde wrote that it made the police more alert and caused them to strengthen their defences, but promoted a fortress mentality, and a reluctance to go out on patrol. But the Lari massacre did the Mau Mau no good, turning against it many Kikuyu fence-sitters.

The Lancashire Fusiliers and the KAR had no early success against the forest gangs. Swann, an ex-infantryman, remarked:

> In the early days the military plan was the 'grouse-drive'. You started in a long line and swept through the Aberdares from top to bottom. Well, of course, before you had gone fifty yards in the thick stuff it was no longer a line, and the enemy lay low until you had passed. It was the most terrible waste of men, ammunition and everything else. Then General Hinde found the answer, although no credit was ever given him for it. Instead of the 'grouse-drive' you divided the forest into sections, and everyone patrolled his little area non-stop. The terrorist could lie low while you thundered over his head, but if you sat there for two or three weeks, he had to come up for food and water. It worked like a charm. It was the Kikuyu Guard* who won the war in the reserves, and this won the war against the forest gangs.

By May the military force had grown to 70th Infantry Brigade (KAR) and 39th Infantry Brigade (British). 70th Brigade was in the reserves, covering the build-up of the Home Guard and police; 39th Brigade was protecting exposed farms in the Rift Valley. Hinde put

---

*The Kikuyu Guard was the name later given to the Home Guard.

them into the Aberdares, to sort out the forest gangs, leaving farm protection to the police. Unfortunately he did not get on with the General Officer Commanding all the troops in East Africa, so Baring asked for a Commander-in-Chief who would outrank them both. The man chosen was Lieutenant-General Sir Robert Erskine, who arrived in June just when the Aberdares operation was getting under way. In his brief for the Commander-in-Chief, dated 5 June, Hinde put him in the picture.

> Any form of sweep hits the air. I never expected quick or spectacular results from the present operations. We are, however, causing the gangs some casualties and losses of food supply. We are keeping them on the move, increasingly hungry and unable to plan raids at will. If further intensification of the forest offensive seems advisable, we can bring the Kikuyu Guard into the hunt in a big way – using them by hundreds, not just as guides.

It all came about very much as Hinde predicted, but it took longer than he expected.

Erskine, with a full corps staff, assumed command of troops and police, and Hinde became Deputy Director of Operations. It was a development deplored by nearly every administrative officer, settler and policeman. They felt that Hinde had a far better understanding of the situation than Erskine, who had as little as possible to do with the administration and took no interest in the emergency committee system.

Said Robin Wainwright, PC Rift Valley Province,

> We were very lucky that our first general was Looney Hinde, who was a very unpompous sort of chap, who never went round with a huge entourage like Erskine and, as a result, got to know individual DOs, Kikuyu guards and police. He really did understand the problem and how to cope with it, and a lot of us felt that he'd just got to the stage when the troops were trained to be more useful when Erskine arrived and got all the credit for it.

State of Emergency, I

(However, Baring and Blundell believed that in the orthodox handling of two, later three brigades, Erskine was the more effective.)

Hinde was still in charge of the Emergency Committee set-up, co-ordination between administration, police and army, Kikuyu Guard, protection of farms, and various sidelines. He still, said Wilson,

> did a tremendously useful job because we all knew him well; we all knew we could drop a word in his ear, and he was particularly good at nosing out the areas where things weren't going too well. A rather idle policeman on getting up in the morning would find Looney Hinde camped on his verandah waiting for breakfast. He was very good, and worked well with the Commissioner of Police.

One day at the Deputy Director of Operations Committee he asked the Commissioner for his strength in Fort Hall district. O'Rorke replied, 'I'll need notice of that question.' A week later Hinde asked again.

'I'll let you have it in a day or two,' was the reply.

A week later, 'Fort Hall, Michael?'

While all watched with bated breath, the Commissioner rummaged through his pockets, pulled out a scrap of paper, adjusted his spectacles, peered at the paper and announced with a seraphic smile, 'Something to the order of two to four hundred.' It brought the house down.

Shortly after this, in pursuance of his campaign to free the police from the administration's control, O'Rorke staggered a meeting of the DCs of the Kikuyu districts by his bland suggestion, 'Why don't you lot get back to soil conservation, and leave the Mau Mau to us?'

O'Rorke resigned, and was replaced by Colonel Arthur Young, from the City of London Police. He was a total disaster. He was obsessed with his desire to make police askaris the equivalent of the 'common constable' in England, independent of the administration and answerable to no one but their own officers, a concept totally unrealistic for Kenya at that time. In this he was abetted by Whyatt, who suspected DCs of acting *ultra vires*. Baring ruled firmly that DCs were in charge of law and order. This recognized the fact that defeating Mau Mau was not simply a matter of arresting malefactors: it was a battle for the hearts and minds of the Kikuyu, and to win it the DC was infinitely better equipped than any police officer. The DC had behind him fifty years' tradition in the Kikuyu reserves, and the back-up of chiefs, headmen, TPs, African district council, African courts: the Kenya police, having had no presence in the reserves (save for an occasional levy force) had none of these advantages. But as a sop to Whyatt and Young, Baring ruled that the CID should be directly responsible to the Attorney General, which facilitated the investigation of abuses of power by DOs and security forces into which Whyatt threw himself with zest. Blundell asked him, 'Why do we have to protect our enemies so well? Why do you put our troops and forest terrorists on the same footing?' Whyatt's eyes filled with tears. According to his principles, they were on the same footing, equally subject to the law. Young resigned because he did not get his way, and was succeeded by Richard Catling, calm and competent.

A lamentable feature of the rapid expansion of the Kenya Police under Young was the over-hasty recruitment of hundreds of 'contract inspectors' from the UK. Napier Bax, who served both in the administration and in the police, found

> some excellent, but most terrible. How can you take a beach-photographer off Brighton pier and turn him into a police officer in five minutes? I can forgive their ignorance, but I cannot forgive their complete lack of compassion. Many were very brutal.

In the reserves the most important work was the build-up of the home guard, described by John Pinney, a DO in Fort Hall. They were trained, stiffened and given firepower by the TPs, of whom there were thirty in Fort Hall at the beginning of the emergency.

Twenty-eight was the number of casualties they were to suffer in the ensuing months. The Mau Mau made a dead set at them and butchered their wives and children. Their worth

State of Emergency, I

was soon recognized, and they were expanded to 240, later to 400. No unit in the security forces paid better dividends than the Kikuyu TPs.

The worst division was Kangema, of which the DO was Jimmy Candler. Elsewhere it was possible to find a nucleus for the guard among well-disposed mission school teachers, agricultural instructors and such. But in Kangema no one was well-disposed and Candler took the risk of persuading some hardened thugs to 'turn'. Once they had made public confessions and committed themselves to the government side, they became some of his best fighters. Posts for the guard, not as yet properly fortified, were built by communal labour.

On 3 April General Hinde held a meeting in Nyeri and decided that 20 per cent of the guards should have rifles or shotguns (more effective at close range); and that European DOs should be posted to train and lead them. For this he took the pick of the Kenya Regiment. Fifty rifles, and fifty sten-guns for these DOs were issued immediately, and hundreds of cheap single-barrelled shotguns were ordered from Belgium. In the middle of the month the DOs began to arrive. These young farmers lived in conditions of great danger, in pairs, in posts that were far from strong, among Kikuyu whose loyalty could only be hoped for. On 20 April Hinde issued a directive which bestowed on the home guard the more imaginative title of Kikuyu Guard (KG) and defined its tasks as:

1. In co-operation with the army and police, so to deny to the Mau Mau the Kikuyu reserves that they become in due course a secure base from which regular forces can be withdrawn to hunt down the Mau Mau in the forests and mountains.
2. To provide information on Mau Mau.

No longer was their only concern to save their own skins.

By the end of April the KG in Fort Hall had strength of 1,908, in 39 posts, armed with 74 rifles and shotguns. On the night of the 28th the post at Ruathia was overrun by a gang of about fifty, with at least one Bren-gun. Using proper tactics of fire and movement, they swarmed over the flimsy defences. Four TPs and four KGs were killed when ammunition ran out, and eight firearms lost. From this were learned two lessons: each post must have at least fifteen firearms and ample ammunition, and must be properly fortified so that it could not be rushed. Four days later Headman William and Sergeant White, a DO KG, were killed in an ambush.

There was fighting almost every week between the expanding KG and well-armed gangs who were pretty good at guerrilla tactics. To set against several reverses and quite heavy losses of TPs, KGs and headmen, were some remarkable successes achieved by Sam Githu, a prosperous trader of the type the administration is supposed to have cold-shouldered. He was a natural for the KG, was awarded the Queen's Commendation for bravery and made chief of his location. Pinney wrote at the time:

> Life in the posts has a more or less settled routine. The defences are standardised with a wide, deep moat filled with needle-sharp *panjis*.* Inside rise bullet-proof parapets with 'blisters' at opposite corners to allow enfilade fire. Narrow drawbridges span the moat by day, and outside it is a barbed wire entanglement. The buildings are roofed with corrugated iron, rather than inflammable thatch.

Every day patrols scoured the neighbourhood and the headmen, suitably escorted, supervised terracing, or whatever communal work was in progress. The wives attached to the post brought in water and cooked. The divisional DO and the DO KG arrived and issued orders for next day. At dusk everyone manned his alarm-post, the gate was closed, the drawbridge lifted, sentries posted, reliefs arranged. It was a strange mixture of barrack-room life and active service, totally alien to the Kikuyu who took to it only to stay alive.

On 27 July a gang armed with rifles and a Bren-gun attacked a post in Location 1. The KG there was of poor quality, and many bolted. TP Miguel Chege:

Panjis were a device learned in the war in Burma – sharp, thin bamboo stakes varying from ankle- to knee-high, stuck in the ground to transfix anyone bumping into them at night.

State of Emergency, I

posted himself at the main gate and almost single-handed kept the enemy out. Under fire from the Bren, he coolly shot at any terrorist who appeared, and killed several. His action was alone responsible for all the arms being saved. The gang disappeared when they saw the headlights of a relief force.

Miguel Chege was awarded the George Medal, as was Sam Githu for gallantry in the forest, guiding a KAR patrol.

The worst loss was at the end of July when the Kikuyu DO, Jerome Kihori, was killed. Brave, resourceful and intelligent, he had started the 'confession tests' for KG recruits. He was replaced as DO by Sam Githu. By August 1953 the KG strength in Fort Hall was 4,620, in 84 posts, with 747 firearms. They were fighting for their lives, with no end in sight.

A KG was on full-time duty and could not visit his home unless a patrol was passing that way. His wife and family dared not cultivate his shamba but must live near his post. He had no income from his shamba, and no pay because that would make him a mercenary.

The first big victory for KG on their own, without troops in support, was in October. A gang swooped out of the forest on Mariani, and massacred two guards' families who refused them food. Four days later a sweep by 400 KG with police in support surrounded the gang, who still had with them the raped and strangled bodies of some of the Mariani women. 43 terrorists were killed and 20 captured, of whom 15 were later hanged. Soon after this two terrorists came in voluntarily and surrendered to Chief Ignatio, the shape of things to come.

George Hampson saw similar events in Nyeri. 1953 was a year of painful reverses, despite help from the KAR. In the only case of deliberate KG treachery, a gate sentry at Gatumbiro post let in a gang at night to massacre the sleeping garrison. Hampson arrived next morning to a scene of terrible carnage, with nuns from the Consolata Mission tending the few wounded. TPs and KG, and indeed their enemies, dispelled the illusion that Kikuyu could not fight. They fought with the greatest valour; there were no white flags, and precious few prisoners. Hampson's son was born to the sound of rifle-fire, his daughter's school-teacher was murdered.

The KG was still a peculiar army. It had no uniform, only coloured arm- and hat-bands for identification in specific operations. Because of the paramount need to lose no firearms, every man carrying a rifle or shotgun had to be escorted by four spearmen by day, eight by night. Hughes, the DC, laid down:

> No effort should be made to regiment them beyond the point necessary for their own security. Every effort should be made to connect what they are taught with their tribal system of warfare.

Fortunately the DOs KG were all picked men. Most spoke fluent Swahili, or at least Ki-Settler, which served the purpose, and some had spoken Kikuyu since boyhood. There was no more dangerous or more valuable job.

In the last four months of 1953 in Nyeri district, 451 terrorists were killed and, more surprisingly, 294 captured. They were beginning to run short of precision weapons, 28 being captured during these three months. With commendable ingenuity they were manufacturing home-made guns, firing 12-bore cartridges, with barrels made of water-piping or cycle frames, and firing-pins actuated by strong rubber bands. At close range they were almost as effective as the shotguns of the KG.

In the darkest days thought was being given to post-war reconstruction. By late 1953 Richard Hennings, Chairman of ALDEV, was touring Kikuyu districts to make preliminary plans for post-emergency agricultural development. His diary, of one not involved in but close to the fighting, captures the spirit of those days.

> 16 Nov.53. Fort Hall. Talk with John Pinney* and Rimington (Agricola), John in heavy gumboots and sweater with a broad

---

*Pinney and Butler had recently taken over Fort Hall and Nyeri respectively.

State of Emergency, I

belt slung with a large holster. Gangs driven out of the forests and broken up by police and KG in the reserve have now split into twos and threes and emerge to murder at night. Most nights some unfortunate chap gets chopped. They send a couple of little tarts who invite the askaris into the bush. When they get to work, the gang kills them.
17 Nov.53. Jimmy Butler's for the night. Butler on ambushes: 'Travel in an open vehicle. Get out and take cover as soon as you come under fire. If you return fire after the first burst, they fade away. Its when you stop for some time, or go up a road you will have to return along later, that you run into trouble. It's happened half a dozen times, always the same.'
18 Nov.53. After breakfast came onto verandah to meet police officer with Patchett gun greeting Jimmy with, 'We had a bad night. Rigby killed in an ambush' . . . Some miles away Kigondu KG post attacked. Kariuki with defenders held fire until attackers surged in, then let them have it at close range. Two killed, the rest fled leaving four home-made rifles and a number of home-made bombs, cans of petrol stopped with maize-cobs and a fuse attached . . . Butler overworked but bearing up well. On the job 6.30 a.m. to 7.30 p.m., a hundred things to do. All these DCs should get medals out of this.

Mau Mau made some gains in Embu district, particularly in Kerugoya division inhabited by Kikuyu. From Embu it moved round the mountain, with diminishing virulence, to Meru. Someone devised a convenient abbreviation, KEM, for Kikuyu, Embu and Meru. In Embu Hennings found an old man making quite good guns of ALDEV water-piping. He defended himself vigorously, 'I don't *give* these to the Mau Mau, bwana, I sell them.'
An assistant agricultural officer named Alan McConnell, stationed at Kerugoya, spent a merry evening, as was his wont, at the Izaak Walton Inn in Embu. On his way home, he pulled into the roadside to sleep it off. He was awakened by rough hands hauling him out of his car and, finding himself surrounded by Mau Mau, thought his last hour had come. But the dreadlocked gang-leader

peered at him closely and said, 'It's Bwana Alan. Put him back.' Which they did, and vanished into the night.

Evidently the time was not yet ripe for the great agricultural changes which ALDEV was planning.

20

State of Emergency, II

Neil Loudon moved the headquarters of Laikipia district from Rumuruti to Thomson's Falls. There the great event of 1951 was the visit of the golf professional, Dai Rees, against whom he played in an exhibition match. The Governor on a visit urged him to choose the best possible site for his house, even if it were in the Forest Reserve. Nothing loth, the Loudons selected an idyllic site surrounded by huge trees, through which a gap was cut out to give a view of the Falls. Loudon wrote:

> In March 1952, Mau Mau oathing started, and the police began to bring cases in court. Witnesses were not yet afraid to come forward.
>
> Jomo Kenyatta held a KAU mass meeting in June, and appointed a Shell Company clerk, Dedan Kimathi, as secretary of the local branch of KAU. Soon after this he left his job in Shell and became the local oath administrator. The activities of Mau Mau were stepped up from that time. The Kikuyu became sullen and unco-operative, witnesses in previous cases were murdered and people were decapitated for refusing to take the oath.

David Christie-Miller became DC Nakuru in 1950. The farmers ran the district; few of them knew or wanted to know the DC. He first heard of Mau Mau from Kikuyu moving between reserves and settled areas, and from certain Kikuyu-speaking settlers who in great secrecy told him a great deal. He heard a lot more at settlers' meetings which he was obliged to attend to hear himself denounced for wetness, complacency, near-communism and refusal to see facts which stared him in the face. The declaration of the State of Emergency and the Jock Scott pick-up came as an enormous relief: at last someone was doing something. Then, as nothing much seemed to happen, it was business as usual.

With the formation of emergency committees, official-settler relations were improved by the appointment of a settler to each. These were important as an assurance to the settlers that something was being done, and as advisers to the PC/DCs on what reasonable farmers wanted, and what could reasonably be asked of them. Later executive officers, all settlers, were appointed, key-men in the emergency.

The 'phoney war' came to a bloody end with attacks on isolated farms, culminating at the end of January 1953 with the horrifying murders of Roger Ruck, his pregnant wife, who had been called out by the syce to treat a farm labourer's sick wife, and their six-year-old son dragged screaming from under his bed and slashed to pieces. Many farmers reacted by sacking all their Kikuyu labour for whom transit camps and transport to the reserves had to be arranged at short notice. Christie-Miller had to send away a whole trainload, 'which caused endless trouble in Central Province which resented us chucking our rubbish over their wall.' About 60,000 Kikuyu left. Said General Hinde to Blundell, 'Your people are mad, Michael. Their only hope is to have a reasonably contented population round them. If we fill up the roads with hungry, resentful people, it's asking for trouble.'

But how could a farmer, close to the forest and miles from any help, keep scores of Kikuyu on his farm, knowing that the Rucks had been lured to their deaths by their own people, and that the Meiklejohns' houseboy had let in the gang which chopped them up? Farm workers might have no personal hatred for their employers, but had sworn the 'double killing oath'. There was a rush to engage Nandi, Kipsigis, Luo labour, although these were generally not as good workers as 'Kukes'.

Loudon went to the Meiklejohns' farm after it had been attacked. It was an appalling sight. Commander Meiklejohn was hacked to pieces; his wife, left for dead, had come to, crawled to the car and driven in to Thomson's Falls. After giving her 125 stitches, the

State of Emergency, II

doctors lost count. Both she and Mrs Ruck were doctors who had given devoted service, free, to Kikuyu. It was against Europeans such as these that the Mau Mau made a dead set, since they were the refutation of Mau Mau propaganda. The only bright feature of these raids was the spirited defence by two middle-aged ladies, who shot dead three of their assailants.

Christie-Miller was transferred to Naivasha, the most disturbed district in the province. It had 'bandit country' on three sides, and a number of very difficult farmers, including a South African Scot named Bruce Mackenzie

> who used to rush round shooting any Kuke he believed involved in Mau Mau. I warned him to watch his step. He ended up as Kenyatta's favourite Cabinet Minister.
>
> I had an excellent ASP, John Toft, brave, energetic and much liked by the farmers. We made the shrewd move of bringing Humphrey Slade into the emergency committee. With a farm on the Kinangop, he had a real understanding of the farmers' predicaments; and as a first rate solicitor he could interpret for us Whyatt's excruciatingly tortuous emergency regulations.

Slade had the reputation of a fanatical white supremacist, but became the first Speaker of the Parliament of independent Kenya.

Most Europeans between sixteen and sixty, if not called up for the Kenya Regiment, joined the Kenya Police Reserve and embarked on what some thought an exciting experience of manning roadblocks, laying ambushes, patrolling other people's farms and checking other people's labour lines. When anyone was on night duty, someone else had to guard his house and family. The KPR commander in Molo thoughtfully arranged one night for all the ex-husbands to guard their ex-wives – an event known in Molo history as 'The Night of the Wrong Wives'.

Nearly every European, most Asians and many loyal Africans carried handguns on the belt; precariously in a handbag which could be easily snatched; most securely, and without social embarrassment, in a shoulder-holster under the jacket or bush-shirt. When one had a bath, or went to the lavatory, the revolver was placed on a chair within reach, and under the pillow at night. At dinner it lay beside the plate, in the drawing-room on the arm of the chair. On more than one occasion, when a dinner-party had adjourned to the drawing-room for coffee, the Kikuyu houseboy brought round a silver tray on which lay a pistol or two inadvertently left on the dining-table.

Gradually the farms most at risk from the Aberdares on one side of the Rift and the Mau Escarpment on the other became strongpoints protected by barbed wire, sandbags, flood-lighting, rocket alarm signals and, later, two-way radio sets. Farm workers were brought in from their scattered huts and concentrated in labour lines where the good were safer from intimidation, and the bad could be supervised. Kikuyu house-staff were shut out at dusk. You then drew the curtains and sat facing the door. What did you do about a tap on the window and an urgent plea to come to a child scalded by boiling water? Generally you went, pistol in one hand, torch in the other, heart pounding. But sometimes the tap at the window and the agitated message was from the Kikuyu houseboy taking his life in his hands by reporting an oathing ceremony taking place at this very minute in the labour lines. Then you telephoned the police, if the line had not been cut, and waited in a fever of anxiety for their arrival.

Farm guards were enlisted to guard livestock, houses, crops. These were generally of other tribes, but sometimes loyal Kikuyu. Wainwright, who became PC Rift Valley in August 1953, took an all-Party group of MPs, without warning, to the Thomson's Falls mortuary where on slabs lay the mutilated bodies of three Samburu farm guards. Deeply shocked, they uttered hardly a word for the rest of the day, 'which is very unusual for MPs'.

District assistants were in charge of recruiting and training farm guards. Among these was David Lambert, who was one day visiting the guards on the farm of an elderly lady, Mrs Gamble, who expected the highest standards from those detailed to protect her. He found a spitting cobra in the outside loo, and it seemed appropriate to lob in a phosphor-grenade.

There was a flash, and an explosion, doubtless of methane gas. The wooden lid of the thunderbox flew out of the roof

State of Emergency, II

and disappeared into the night, while pieces of the apparatus sprayed through the walls. This was followed by a flame of volcanic proportions. The flames died down, and with a sigh the remains of the building subsided into the pit.

At that moment my dressing-gowned hostess appeared, and in a quavering voice asked, 'What has happened, Mr Lambert?'

'Well, you see, Mrs Gamble, it was like this. . .'

It was no fun with young children. The Loudons moved into their 'idyllic' forest house a month after the start of the emergency. They had it wired and sand-bagged, a Kenya police guard at night and by day a TP always in the garden. (The children believed he was there to see they behaved themselves.) In their only serious, but false, alarm, their defence was impeded by Mrs Loudon's revolver getting caught up in the knitting-wool. The Kikuyu Christian community was very staunch and gave much information. Loudon used to drive out to a quiet place with the informer hidden in the back of his panel-van. The Loudons' fourth child was born in their house in Thomson's Falls. They thought the doctor rather over-reacted to the emergency by carrying on his cartridge belt not one, but two six-shooters.

Others tended to under-react. Near Nyeri there was a group of four 'Island Farms', entirely surrounded by forest that teemed with terrorists. A forest officer was ambushed and killed on the road to the Island Farms, and General Hinde went up next day to examine the situation, taking the author with him.

As our car crawled slowly up the narrow, winding forest road, I felt very nervous: we would have to return this way. The driver did not like it either, peering right and left, with only half his attention on the road. Suddenly the General exclaimed, 'Good God! What's that?'

Down the road towards us, slithering through the mud and bumping over the ruts and elephants' foot pot-holes, came a large, elderly, black limousine, in which sat a large, elderly, white couple, he wearing a morning coat and Old Etonian tie, she in lacy dress and flowery hat. As we drew respectfully to one side to let them pass, she favoured us with a gracious nod and smile, he lifted his hand in courteous acknowledgement, and they proceeded slowly on to a wedding in Nyeri.

Not all Kikuyu were re-patriated. Thousands remained in Rift Valley farms, for they were the best workers. Early in 1953 Christie-Miller heard of two Kikuyu-speaking farmers systematically questioning and 'screening' first their own, then their neighbours' Kikuyu, recording tales of Mau Mau oathing and money-collecting. Unofficially he encouraged them. 'Screening' increased, with 'screening teams' of Kikuyu Christian elders doing most of the questioning. Chiefs and TPs were appointed to settled areas, and spent much of their time with screening teams. As the teams filed and cross-referenced and exchanged information, dossiers were built up of Mau Mau oath administrators, treasurers and executioners. It was largely a matter of meticulous paperwork which would now be done by computer, but was then done by Kikuyu clerks of the screening teams. In January 1954 Wainwright asked all farmers to co-operate. He wrote:

> Efficient screening has amply demonstrated its worth. Prodigious amounts of accurate information, active opposition to terrorist gangs by those who have confessed, [and] loyal and happier labour forces are among its benefits.
>
> Every possible step has been taken to counteract the Kikuyu love of *fitina** and false denunciation, and to prevent the use of threats or torture to extract confessions and information. I have made it very clear that no such brutality whatsoever will be tolerated. The weapons employed in interrogation are using information already known, psychological fear, doubt, ridicule and religion, and these really do produce results. If you have a complaint which you believe to be true of brutal methods being used, please help by bringing the complainant to the administration or police so that he can quickly be medically examined and a proper investigation made.
>
> On the return of your labour there is much that you can do to help. They will be in a worried and bewildered state, and a friendly and sympathetic approach by you will

---

Fitina: intrigue, tale-bearing.

State of Emergency, II

help them resolve their doubts and prevent their backsliding. Encourage them by helping them raise a home guard unit for the protection of your farm, and by assisting African padres and lay readers to make contact with them.

Farmers' attitudes to the screening of their labour, and the removal of some under detention orders, varied. Some took the line, 'Take the whole bloody lot. Shoot 'em if you like, I don't care.' A more common reaction was, 'OK, take 'em all – except old Njeroge, he's my best cowman, been with me twenty years and I'd trust him anywhere.' Gilbert Colville, one of the old-time settler establishment, hired the most expensive lawyer who ran rings round the inexperienced police prosecutor and secured an acquittal for his foreman, a notorious oath administrator. Two Moral Rearmament brothers lied like Ananias to cover their labour. An Irish anglophobe, although one of his people had confessed in his presence, in the DC's office, to administering oaths, complained to the Attorney General, the Governor and the Secretary of State of the DC's 'harassment' and 'abuse of power'. Christie-Miller had to dissuade his neighbours from lynching him. Most farmers, told of Mau Mau on their farms, took it philosophically, realizing by now that the DC was doing his best. Saddest were the old settlers, heartbroken that Kikuyu they had known thirty years were implicated in Mau Mau. One such was Lilian Graham, who lived alone near the forest on a farm full with Kikuyu squatters. Christie-Miller took it upon himself to break the news that her cook was to be arrested as the local Mau Mau treasurer. She burst into tears. 'David,' she sobbed, 'how *can* you do this to me, when I knew your father?'

There were some abuses by screening teams. In any civil war feelings run so high that such things seem inevitable. Never by a nod or a wink did the administration connive at them.

General Hinde told me to see what was going on in a screening camp run by two missionaries in KPR uniform. I found that, by third degree methods, they had uncovered a conspiracy to end all conspiracies, summarized in a 30-page typewritten report. The Mau Mau, they revealed, was the joint creation of Stalin, Chairman Mao and the Emperor Haile Selassie of Ethiopia. It secretly ruled every Kenya tribe. On the *dies irae*, which they named, Russian and Chinese paratroops would drop by the thousand on Nairobi; Haile Selassie's armies would swarm across the NFD; and every houseboy and cook would cut his master's throat and put arsenic in his mistress's coffee. I took this to the General, and within hours the camp was disbanded and the sleuths returned to their spiritual duties. It was a revelation to me what rubbish some people will believe.

In Central Province an occasional blind eye was turned. Baring wrote in 1964,

> No doubt there were abuses. I do not believe they were very bad. The chief screening officer in Kiambu is now a permanent secretary in charge of an important department in the independent government. This could not have happened if he had been a really dishonest villain.

There were other examples of prominent screeners rising to high rank after independence.

The emergency committees were much concerned with efforts to deny food to the forest gangs. Farm labour was concentrated in villages so that terrorists could not get food from isolated huts; cattle were *boma*-ed at night under armed guard. But while fields of maize could be stripped at harvest, the combine was bound to leave gleanings of barley and wheat; and no matter how carefully potatoes were dug, some were bound to be left to sprout and grow again. The problem was never solved and a farm guard with a shotgun could not be expected to resist a determined, hungry gang.

In the settled area there was virtually no fighting, but the steady squeeze worked. Farmers lived in great danger; they suffered from stock-theft, and crop-theft, and arson; their labour was oathed and terrorized. There seemed no end to it. But after the Ruck murders in January 1952 there were no serious attacks on farms. By the end of the year the worst was over throughout the settled areas.

Those who took a romantic view of the Masai imagined that if only the moran were unleashed, the Mau Mau would flee, gibbering with terror. This was a fallacy. Early in the emergency

State of Emergency, II

Fionn Holford-Walker, who held the glamorous post of DO Moran in Narok and Kajiado districts, took a war-party of a hundred into the Aberdares to scout for the KAR. They complained incessantly of the cold, the rain, the cloud, the dripping bamboo-forest. It was not their scene, and they returned thankfully to their sunbaked plains. Thereafter the Masai were, as in two world wars, neutral. They might, if they could be bothered, report the presence of a Mau Mau gang down from the escarpment forest; but unless these went for their cattle, they let well alone, far from eager to pit spears against guns. Among the Il Purko, the clan most intermarried with Kikuyu, there was even some oathing; but they were as lukewarm in support for the Mau Mau as they had been in opposing it.

Early in the emergency the two Kamba districts, Machakos and Kitui, were grouped with the two Masai districts, Kajiado and Narok, in the new Southern Province, to leave the PC Central Province free to concentrate on the Mau Mau. But there was always some apprehension that the Mau Mau might get a grip on the Kamba, close to the Kikuyu racially, linguistically and geographically. A considerable number of Kamba in Nairobi were oathed; so the trouble there was scotched by a Kamba screening team, led by Noel Hardy, DO Machakos and a Kamba-speaking farmer. Sundry small incursions into Ukambani from Kikuyu districts were all annihilated by the Kamba themselves – chiefs, headmen, TPs, home guards and Kamba ex-soldiers enlisted in the Kenya Police Reserve. It caused hardly a hiccup in the development programme. Indeed in 1954 Douglas Penwill, the DC, asked for *fewer* Kenya police in his district because there was nothing for them to do, law and order being maintained by the administration and tribal police. There was a need for an armed mobile reserve to deal with a big incursion from outside, but not for eight inspectors and 200 men.

As for the army, the only soldiers to enter the district were the Pipes and Drums of the Black Watch, much appreciated by the Kamba who found their music just the job for dancing.

In March 1954 a new cabinet was formed including three elected Europeans, two elected Asians, and one elected Arab, joined shortly afterwards by one nominated African. These held ministerial portfolios and were known hereafter as 'Ministers' instead of 'Members'. Certain ministries, notably African Affairs and Defence, remained in official hands. The Attorney General was relieved, not before time, of his responsibility for law and order and could thereafter give his undivided attention to the prosecution of members of the security forces. For many of the older officials it was distasteful to serve a minister who was an elected settler politician. Baring, a former Indian civil servant, wrote:

> It is a fair comment that members of the Colonial Administrative Service were not generally as intelligent as those of the Indian Civil Service, and consequently found adjustment to a ministerial system more difficult.

In the following month the high command was reorganized by the setting up of a war council. Composed only of the Governor, the newly arrived Deputy Governor (Sir Frederick Crawford), the Commander-in-Chief and Blundell, it was small enough, and high-powered enough, to reach decisions quickly. This council, with Tom Colchester as Secretary, arranged very efficiently the final defeat of the Mau Mau, of which there were already encouraging portents.

In August 1953 the forest gangs had been urged by various means to come in bearing green branches in token of surrender. Some people thought this premature, some thought it too lenient; but by the end of the year 815 terrorists had surrendered. In Fort Hall 1953 ended with the killing by the KG of 'General' Matenjagua, a prize of some worth, since he was noted for pitiless cruelty. Candler had formed mobile battle-groups of picked TPs charged with the task of hunting down the enemy wherever he could be found, which they did with marked success. In February 'General' Kago's forces rashly moved against the divisional headquarters and school at Kangema. There ensued a two-day running fight until the gang was surrounded. While the Inniskilling Fusiliers held the ring, Chief Ignatio's TPs and KG killed 97 terrorists. There is no record of prisoners.

On 4 March Candler wrote of this hotbed of Mau Mau, 'The situation has improved. The people are more confident, more cheerful and better behaved.' Next day, having borne the brunt

State of Emergency, II

during the terrible year 1953, he was killed. Paul Kelly and his wife, on ALDEV business, were staying with the Pinneys when John Pinney was called out to make formal identification of Jimmy Candler's headless corpse, the 'worst thing for any DC to experience. He took it with complete stoicism.' A month later another of his DOs, Wood-White, was killed. But Wood-White's Kikuyu Guard bagged General Kago during that month.

In January 1954, 'General' China, leader of the terrorists on Mount Kenya and second in prestige only to Dedan Kimathi, was wounded and captured. Under sentence of death, he gave his interrogator, Ian Henderson of the Special Branch, details of all the Mount Kenya gangs and offered, in exchange for his life, to arrange their surrender. Dick Wilson was in on subsequent events.

He was smuggled out of the death-cell in Nairobi prison, and flown to Nyeri disguised as a police constable and manacled to a weighted brief-case to impede any attempt to escape. A ten-day cease-fire was arranged, but did not last as long owing to differences between the Mau Mau leaders. However, this opened the door to subsequent surrenders.

Early in 1954 Nyeri KG combat units operated successfully in the Aberdares forest. From September 1953 to June 1954 in Nyeri alone 1,052 Mau Mau were killed and 887 captured, for a loyalist loss of 276. Nearly five times as much bench terracing was done in 1954 as in 1953, a good measure of government control.

It had been urged for some time by those who did not have to do the job that the Kikuyu should be concentrated in defended villages rather than live in scattered homesteads where terrorists could always get food from them. But the administration had enough on its plate without forcing on *loyalists* an unpopular change in their lifestyle. In Kiambu Tony Swann, who knew his own mind and seldom hesitated to speak it, flatly refused to play. Since the Lari massacre there had been little terrorism in Kiambu where the typical Mau Mau was a politician, not a freedom-fighter. Eventually he had to villagize only a two-mile strip along the forest edge, a reasonable compromise.

But in Nyeri George Hampson saw a change.

As KG posts were made almost impregnable, there was a spontaneous move of people to seek safety close to them. Towards the end of 1953 this gained momentum, with the women demanding protection, often vociferously. Thus there was built up a degree of support for what was to become a deliberate policy of villagisation.

After his return from leave in July 1954, 'Ozzie' Hughes conceded, 'The villages have gone further than many of us thought in removing the burden of fear from the people. The Mau Mau do not like these villages at all.'

During the first half of 1954 Hughes reported six spontaneous 'uprisings' against Mau Mau, with hundreds of men and women beating through high crops and bush to flush out lurking terrorists and drive them towards the waiting police, TPs and KG. When any were spotted, the women set up a great screaming and ullulating to warn the 'guns' to be ready.

Such was the improvement during the first six months of 1954 that in Fort Hall district it was decided in August to stand down 3,450 KGs to go back to their *shambas* and businesses, retaining only 1,850 on active duty.

In January 1954 Michael Blundell, seeking to increase the influence on events of European elected members, had warned Lyttleton's Parliamentary Secretary, 'My own view is that things are deteriorating so rapidly that we have no further than June before we lose the whole country.' But even as he rang the desperate tocsin, the tide had turned in the forests, the reserves and the settled areas – everywhere but in Nairobi.

The Mau Mau had an active and a passive wing. The active wing were the armed gangs; the passive wing comprised those who in fear or sympathy provided them with food, money, clothing, recruits, blankets, shelter; prostitutes who charged cartridges instead of money for their services; and the Nairobi criminal gangs. The passive wing was ubiquitous in Nairobi; and not merely the passive wing, for there were Mau Mau murders almost every night, including those of two African members of the city council.

State of Emergency, II

Men were shot in broad daylight, the guns passed from hand to hand as the killers disappeared in the crowd.

Early in 1954 it was decided to lay on a vast operation to clean up Nairobi. In charge of it – this was before the war council – was Turnbull, then Minister for Internal Security and Defence. His assistant was Wilson.

After weeks of secret planning for Operation ANVIL, in the morning of 24 April people in the African locations awoke to find every exit blocked. Police and TPs then moved in and checked every male KEM to see if he had a valid reason to be in Nairobi. Those who had not, some 30,000, were sent to holding camps for screening and sorting into three categories – 'Whites', innocent or with minor Mau Mau involvement who would be returned to their reserves; 'Blacks', deeply involved and perhaps irreconcileable, who would be sent to remote work-camps in Coast Province; and 'Greys', who could work their way to freedom through work-camps serving large ALDEV irrigation projects. ANVIL was an enormous vacuum cleaner, sucking out of Nairobi most of the guilty and a good many innocent. The fighting was not all over, but after this it could end only in one way. There remained the battle for Kikuyu hearts and minds.

Dick Wilson, coming to Embu after doing much of the planning for ANVIL, took over from Roger Wilkinson a rapidly improving situation, felt the turn of the tide and pressed on with villagization.

Sites were chosen to meet the requirements of security and water-supply. Officers' wives kept an eye on the sick and destitute, and Red [Cross] workers did a wonderful job of training village women in practical hygiene. In Embu itself the DO built a special village for TB cases, under the eye of the medical officer.

Gradually the great migration took place, to villages each with living huts, food storage areas, churches, schools, cattle-bomas; each ditched and wired and guarded by a KEM Guard post. Curfews were imposed on villages found to be still feeding gangs.

The key figures were the divisional DOs. They had to balance from day to day the need for a swift tightening of controls here, a welcome relaxation there. It was their job to maintain the morale of chiefs, KEM guards and other loyalists who were the eyes and ears of the security forces. They often had to show great courage and initiative, living among a frightened population who could react overnight to the presence of an oath administrator or a terrorist gang.

In March 1954 Jon Wainwright joined the regular administration and was posted as divisional DO to Kerugoya. The Mau Mau there was stronger than elsewhere in the district, but the atmosphere was far more relaxed than in Fort Hall three months earlier. He wrote:

> I brought horses from my farm and moved round on horseback, much to the surprise of the population. I had much more contact with the people than by travelling by car, like other DOs. Among the district staff morale was high, and there was a great spirit of friendship and co-operation.
> Concentrating the Kikuyu into villages was the most decisive action leading to the defeat of the terrorists. Once everyone was in a village, guarded by TP-led Kikuyu guard recruited from the villagers themselves, the people felt secure enough to report infiltrators. When a gang approached a village, the women set up a great ullulation which would be taken up from village to village until security forces arrived.
> At the same time the whole population was turned out to dig a ditch along the district-forest boundary. It was deep enough and wide enough, filled with panjis, to deter not only terrorists but disgruntled elephants which, driven from the forest by bombing, devastated the crops.

The great ditch was 20-30 feet wide at the top and 16 feet deep. At every crossing place there was a guard post. Terrorists could cross elsewhere, but not without leaving clear signs where patrols could pick up their tracks in the morning.

The work was done with much goodwill. To encourage everyone, 45-gallon drums of maize-beer were provided, and

State of Emergency, II

competitions organised with prizes for the villages which did the best job; and there was much singing and dancing.

During 1954 and 1955 the forest gangs were worn down by well-trained troops, police and KGs. Nevertheless, when G. J. W. Pedraza (Sandhurst, ex-regular army, MC) took over Nyeri in January 1955 there were still gangs of two and three hundred at large. He was a thruster with a greater capacity for command than for consultation. He speeded up villagization, even sending TPs to burn the huts of those who were tardy in moving. Communal work was stepped up as a wholesome discipline. KGs escorted women in long crocodiles to work in the fields. J. R. Greyburn, who succeeded Hampson as DO Othaya, specialized in KG ambushes on routes used by forest terrorists to collect food; he made authority felt all day and half the night. The administration was very much in control. Greyburn at one time had a brigadier on his emergency committee: 'No way would I give way to him, I didn't care how senior he was.'

In February 1955 a letter from a Mau Mau 'general' was found in a tree, offering to surrender all the gangs in the Aberdares and Mount Kenya forests. After protracted negotiations with terrorist leaders, conducted perilously by Windley, Henderson and Erskine's Chief of Staff, it transpired that the 'general' who had made the offer could not deliver. But by July the Mau Mau was on the run, streaming from the forests to surrender. Thereafter the surviving terrorists were reduced to the status of homicidal bandits, dangerous if encountered but bent only on survival. These were eliminated by the celebrated and fantastically brave 'pseudo-gangs'; and at last Dedan Kimathi himself was shot by a TP. Military operations formally ended in November 1956.

In these final events the administration took little part. It was busier than it had ever been, conducting the agrarian revolution which was the biggest and best thing it had done since the original pacification of the tribes.

21

Agrarian Revolution

From the beginning of the emergency Baring felt that 'a great effort must be made to balance the inevitably repressive measures by a striking step forward in the country's economy'. He persuaded the British government to make a further grant of £5 million for African agriculture. Under the aegis of a reconstruction committee, chaired by the Deputy Governor, Sir Frederick Crawford, with Richard Hennings, Chairman of ALDEV, as its secretary, a master plan was compiled – mainly from district plans which had been shelved for lack of funds – by Roger Swynnerton, Deputy Director of Agriculture.

The essence of the Swynnerton Plan, published in February 1954, was to concentrate effort where it would make most impact, in the Central Province where the soil was the most fertile in Kenya and the rainfall reliable. The Kikuyu were intelligent, hardworking and eager to better themselves if only the politicians would let them. With most opposition leaders behind wire, from 1954 onwards the authority of the government was unchallenged. In KEM districts there were DOs, district assistants and agricolas galore, and scores of DOs KG who when the fighting was over were glad to lend a hand wherever required. Moreover there was a need to employ usefully thousands of detainees and ex-squatters.

Baring identified five main needs in Central Province:
1. Soil conservation.
2. Land consolidation. That is, the gathering of fragmented holdings into viable farms and the grant of freehold tenure to the owners.
3. The development of cash-crops.

Agrarian Revolution

4. The introduction of grade dairy cattle.
5. Irrigation. There was a tremendous increase in bench-terracing. In Nyeri the mileage completed was

1951	1952	1953	1954
33	123	107	508

The *sine qua non* of cash crops and grade cattle was land consolidation. Nothing much could be done for the man with a dozen scattered holdings, some only a few yards square; and he could obtain no credit until he was the legal owner of a viable farm.

A start was made on a modest scale in Nyeri in 1953 and in Fort Hall in 1954, but with terrorists still on the rampage, there was not much progress. It really got going in Kiambu when John Golds, a Lessos farmer who had come into the administration via the KG, became convinced that a clear majority in his South Githunguri division wanted to consolidate, and urged that 'we strike while the iron is hot.' He was supported by Chief Charles Koinange on the grounds that 'if we wait till the detainees return, we will find ourselves in big arguments.' Swann's successor as DC, Frank Loyd, told him to go ahead. In March 1956, a new DC, Douglas Penwill, pulled out all the stops and made Golds Land Consolidation supremo for the whole district. His task was made easier by Loyd villagizing it all.

John Golds was a human dynamo, and needed to be. The 280,000 acres of the Kiambu reserve were divided into over half a million fragments, some hardly bigger than a bathroom. All had to be re-assembled into viable farms or smallholdings. From every farmer's acreage about 7 per cent had to be deducted to provide land for 110 villages, 1,860 miles of new access roads, 285 schools, 225 churches, cemeteries, sports-grounds, markets, cattle-dips, tea and coffee nurseries. The final figures, when consolidation was complete, were:

Smallholdings less than 4 acres, around villages	17,316
Farms 4 to 7 acres	10,359
Farms 7 to 20 acres	7,975
Farms over 20 acres	1,484
	37,134

The average holding was of 5.3 acres, made up of eight gathered fragments.

Consolidation was the administration's job, with other departments in support. No one was compelled to consolidate. At innumerable *barazas* DOs, chiefs and Kikuyu Land Consolidation (LC) staff explained what it meant, its advantages and the procedure by which it would be introduced. A powerful incentive was that only by consolidating could one obtain a title to land, and without a title it was impossible to obtain credit for a share in a tractor, a grade milch-cow, a dip or anything else. Each area, smaller than a location, larger than a *mbari* (a small area consisting of one or more ridges, inhabited mainly by one clan), was given a free choice for or against consolidation. In the end all accepted – after a certain amount of mind-changing.

The LC staff had to be trained. Golds took on 14 senior LC assistants, at first mainly DOs KG, replaced as they were demobilized by Kikuyu. 600 survey assistants were taught to measure small plots by chain. Base-maps were prepared from air-photos. Then came the trickiest part of the whole process, piecing together the jigsaw puzzle.

> Each location had a LC committee of 20–30 elected members, plus the LC assistant. These included representatives of all the *mbaris*. They worked out, from the survey assistants' plans, each owner's total holding, subtracted 7 per cent for community purposes, and decided where his new farm should be. If he had any permanent buildings, or one fragment much larger than the rest, his consolidated holding would be based on that. The survey assistant then measured and demarcated the new farm in the owner's presence. To share out fairly the good and the poor land, where possible every farm stretched from the top of the ridge to the stream at the bottom.

The land of a few terrorist leaders, about 0.02 per cent of the total, was compulsorily purchased for community purposes. Otherwise it was accepted that Mau Mau were as much entitled to their land as anyone else. Golds visited all the detention camps to ascertain their claims and wishes as to who should represent them: some were released on parole to see for themselves that they got a fair deal.

Of course mistakes were made. Measurement by hastily-trained survey assistants were proved by air-photos to be faulty. Some got less than their fair share of good land, others more. There were disputes about land ownership going back three generations, settled in a few hours by adjudication committees (with no lawyers present). The job had to be completed before the opposition got back from detention. Before the emergency it had been reckoned that land consolidation, if attempted, would take twenty years. Golds in Kiambu did it in two. Without computers, it was done by the LC staff and the 2,750 (unpaid) members of locational LC committees, all Kikuyu. DOs provided little more than the drive, the ginger and an occasional *decision* on a case which baffled the adjudication committee. To the landless *ahoi*, land consolidation offered nothing but the chance of a job on the farm of a more fortunate cousin: it was not a panacea for all the ills of Kikuyu society.

His farm having been demarcated, a boundary fence planted (some delays arose here) and the fee of shs 10 per acre having been paid, the proud owner was handed a Certificate of Title under the Land Tenure Rules. Once issued, this was not subject to litigation: it was the last word. He could then borrow for development from ALDEV, or from the bank. Contrary to many predictions, the repayment rate was good.

But he could not mortgage or sub-divide his holding without permission, and permission was seldom given to sub-divide below four acres: fragmentation must not start again. On his death his farm at a government valuation went to one son, who must within five years pay each of his brothers an equal share. There was scepticism about how this would work. In general it has worked not perfectly, but pretty well. A lot of farms nominally owned by one man are in fact family farms, but there has been little re-fragmentation. Kikuyuland is still composed of prosperous peasant farms, the recipe for political stability, as it was when the British handed it over in 1963.

In Nyeri land consolidation was completed in 1959. It started during Pedraza's iron rule, of which a visitor from the Colonial Office gave his impression.

> Tremendous enthusiasm and faith in the land revolution. Intensive, close administration employs immense European staffs and large sums of money. African population under strictest discipline. Official attitude to the Kikuyu, perhaps naturally, strongly dictatorial, somewhat aloof and without cordiality ... From the results to be seen on the ground one would think that almost any of the major problems of Africa could be solved by simply concentrating enough European staff and money in the area, and the elimination of political activity.

In Kiambu, under Frank Loyd and his senior DOs Peter Derrick and Dick Symes-Thompson, the style was more relaxed and relations with Kikuyu almost cordial. One DO KG, a gifted musician, used to stimulate adjudication committees' endeavours by a trumpet solo at the end of every case; and Jon Wainwright rewarded working-parties from a 45-gallon drum of beer, and arranged for the Kenya Show-Jumping Association to hold a competition at the uproarious, enthusiastic Agricultural Show which celebrated the end of the emergency.

In Fort Hall the story was less happy. There were many inaccurate measurements and some dishonesty by adjudication committees. The work, supposedly complete in 1960, had to be scrapped and done again. In Embu and Meru there was less fragmentation and less urgency in land consolidation. In Embu it was completed in 1962, in Meru it was started in that year.

After the holdings had been fenced, farmers were provided with cheap and simple 'farm layouts' produced by an agricultural instructor and showing where to site the house, stores, cattle-sheds and paddocks – some for food crops, some for cash crops, and half under grass on a simple 7-year cycle. A farmer need not take this advice, but might find credit hard to obtain if he didn't.

The most important cash crops were coffee, pyrethrum and tea. The emergency was a setback. Most of the owners of viable

Agrarian Revolution

farms in 1952 were loyalists. During 1953 the men were too busy fighting and the women too frightened to look after their farms; and along the forest edge 'scorched earth' was enforced, to deny food to the gangs. When people moved into villages, they could not bring their cattle which were left on the farms, *boma*-ed and guarded. This produced by 1955–6 an unexpected bonus: immense quantities of manure just when it was most needed. Coffee production increased sixfold between 1955 and 1960 when there were 10,000 growers. Pyrethrum came a bit later, but by 1961 it was being grown by 2,000 high altitude farmers.

It had been thought that tea was a plantation crop, too difficult for peasants. But pressure on land made it necessary to find something that suited the high, acid-soil bracken areas. The cultivation of tea, starting in 1951, ended abruptly in 1953, but was resumed in 1955 in all Central Province districts. Tea is an exacting crop. The stumps are expensive, and the grower will get no return for four years. Plucking and pruning goes on most of the year; and proper plucking – only two leaves and a bud from each twig – requires self-discipline by the grower. It must be taken promptly and fresh to the factory. But it is very profitable, and transformed the economy of the high-altitude areas whence many of the forest terrorists came. In 1959 Ragati Tea, grown by Nyeri Kikuyu, fetched the top prices for East Africa.

The grade dairy cattle were at first humped tropical breeds, Sahiwal and Boran crosses. Later, to much head-shaking and lip-pursing by the vets, Guernseys were introduced. They did well provided they were properly looked after: regularly dipped and sprayed against tick-borne diseases, surplus bulls castrated, grazing supplemented by fodder crops.

At the Embu Agricultural Institute men and women were given short courses in the management of half- and pure-bred Guernseys. Much of the district being fairly flat, the ADC bought tractors for contract-ploughing the larger farms of which by 1959 there were over forty near Embu, each making about £750 a year besides feeding the farmer's family, wealth beyond his dreams ten years earlier. The Embu Coffee Co-operative Union exported £250,000 worth in 1959, and exports were shooting up every year. Its chairman said:

Our members were complaining that European coffee made the best prices, but I have been to many auctions and have told them that this is untrue. African coffee is fetching higher prices than European.

Meru had empty, fertile land with good rainfall, which facilitated settlement schemes at a fraction of the cost of Makueni. After the Njuri Ncheke had endorsed the agricolas' rules, this was opened to settlement and proved ideal for dairy cattle, potatoes, lucerne and pyrethrum. Chief Stanley's 9-acre farm gave Elspeth Huxley

> a wonderful impression of bursting fertility, of work and care, of happiness. The Guernsey calves in their little paddocks came prancing up to suck my fingers, their mothers quietly chewing the satisfying cud; and piglets lay stretched out voluptuously in the sunshine. The chief's four workmen hoed potatoes gently on the terrace.

By 1959, a total of 250 settlers were established in this scheme on farms from 8 to 20 acres; by 1962 there were 1,500. They needed no capital, only a willingness to follow the basic rules of good farming.

The largest irrigation project in the Swynnerton Plan was the Mwea-Tebere scheme in lower Embu. Before the emergency it was a modest one, a furrow from two mountain streams watering an area of controlled grazing. As the emergency began to run down in 1954 and the detention camps to fill up after ANVIL, Hennings planned a more ambitious scheme served by two Mau Mau work camps. By June five miles of canal had been dug. In 1955 five more work camps were added to the labour force, and Hennings got much bigger ideas. By 1960 nearly 5,000 acres were under irrigation, mainly soil suitable for rice which was leased in 4-acre plots to landless Kikuyu, including many who as detainees had sweated under the sun to dig the furrows and build the embankments. A man who followed advice could make £150 a year on rice, besides feeding his family on other crops.

Much of the credit for all this belongs to Michael Blundell who was Minister for Agriculture 1955–59. 'With old C. B.,' said

Agrarian Revolution

Hennings, 'the difficulty was to get him to do anything. With Michael, it is to stop him doing things.' Peter Gordon found working for him 'a joyous and exhilarating experience', even when he was told, 'Now, Peter, you'll have to get cracking on this. But first I want to hear *your* views.'

'Well, sir, I think . . .'

'Hang on just a moment. May I tell you what *I* think? I believe – but you say if you don't agree – that we should . . .' There followed a crisp analysis, followed by a decision already made.

Let the last word on this be with Turnbull who in 1945 asked Coutts, 'What would *you* do, if you could, to save the Kikuyu country?'

'Well,' replied Coutts, 'What I should do . . .' and he enlarged on all the things which should be done.

> Do you know, when we had the political leaders locked up for a couple of years, we got it all done. We saved that land. Land is hardly ever saved in the history of the world, but we did it.

The rice irrigation schemes would have been prohibitively expensive without Mau Mau labour. The conditions were strictly regulated. As Permanent Secretary for Community Development Askwith was made responsible for 'Rehabilitation of Detainees' and selected a staff of devout Christians who shared his liberal views. He laid down that discipline in camps must not be imposed by force. Nor must detainees be compelled to work since forced labour by men who had been convicted of no crime was in breach of the rules of the International Labour Organisation. Adult education, lectures, sports and games and a Christian approach by the staff were expected to achieve the desired end of returning the detainees, reformed characters, to their districts.

So they did, to a considerable degree, with 'Greys' in the main rehabilitation camps. Many were in a work camp serving the Perkerra Irrigation Scheme in Baringo district where security was hardly necessary, no one tried to escape, and the detainees seemed cheerful, friendly and interested in the work by which they would qualify for a passage home.

'Blacks' were a different proposition, a hard core of irreconcileables. Operation ANVIL had poured 60,000 Kikuyu into holding camps, notably Manyani near the Nairobi-Mombasa railway, which three years later still held some 20,000, closely incarcerated but virtually unapproachable. The responsible Minister, C. M. Johnston, holding the portfolios of Community Development, Rehabilitation and African Affairs, decided that the dilution of this indigestible mass by separating 'Greys' from 'Blacks' and their movement through rehabilitation camps to work camps in their own districts must be speeded up to keep pace with political advance, even if discipline were imposed by force. Askwith made a formal protest, and expressed no surprise at being replaced 'by a more amenable officer' appointed with the knowledge of the Governor and Secretary of State. This was Terry Gavaghan, in connection with whom the adjective 'amenable' does not spring readily to mind. Johnston gave him verbal orders to reduce the hard core residue to 6,000, but did not specify how this should be done.

Gavaghan, with Community Development and Prison Department colleagues, supplemented the regular warders, mostly of tribes hostile to the Kikuyu, with a corps of young, educated Kikuyu trained in unarmed combat and armed only with short belt-slung truncheons. The camp compounds were sub-divided into manageable units to reduce the fear of the oath administrators and camp executioners. Mau Mau oaths were purged by public declarations before traditional elders. Detainees who co-operated were offered early release to their consolidated farms, and a part in the progress towards independence. But obedience to reasonable and lawful orders was firmly enforced. The use of necessary and compelling, as opposed to punitive, force was witnessed and authorized by the responsible ministers and departmental heads. By these methods the number of those deemed irreconcileable was reduced by mid-1958 to under a thousand. These, it was announced, would never be released, and they were held in remote, secure camps as uncongenial to staff as to inmates. The Governor referred to rehabilitation as a 'crusade'.

One of the camps for the hard core was at Hola, in the northern part of Coast Province. There, in March 1959, a working party

Agrarian Revolution

of some 200 detainees, heavily escorted by unsupervised prison warders, mainly non-Kikuyu, concertedly refused to work and started a frenzied mass demonstration. The warders lost their nerve and laid into the detainees with batons, killing eleven and injuring eighty-one. The 'Hola Massacre' became an international *cause célèbre*, attended by confusion, evasion and a futile attempt at a cover-up. Official enquiries resulted only in the punishment of some of the warders and the retirement of some of the camp officers. The Commissioner of Prisons, a former DC, honourably taking responsibility for an event outside his control, resigned. No minister resigned and Swann, who had become Minister for Defence a few days *after* the 'massacre' was understandably furious at having to answer questions in Legco about it.

After this there could be no question of holding unconvicted detainees. They must be shovelled back home, come what may. Nothing very awful came of their return: some dropped into the criminal world of Nairobi; most settled down on their farms, consolidated in their absence, and realized that the party was over.

There was surprisingly little trouble between ex-Mau Mau and ex-loyalists. For this credit goes to Jomo Kenyatta on his release (see p. 291) and to those who ensured that detainees got a fair deal in land consolidation. But some ex-detainees made a dead set at headmen, KGs and DOs who had made themselves vulnerable to charges, true or false, of assault, theft, malicious damage. The most distressing case was that of the valiant DO, Sam Githu, charged with the murder of a detainee who died after being beaten up at a camp of which he was in charge. This caused hot disputes in the administration, some agreeing with Gavaghan that, rather than let him go on trial without any supporting evidence on his services during the emergency or the circumstances of detention, every DC and DO who suspected that violence was sometimes used against prisoners should resign. Most agreed with Swann's dictum, in another context, that the proper line to take was:

If you are in the right, I'll stand by you to the last. But if you are in the wrong, I'm sorry, chum, but there is nothing I can do but let justice take its course.

It was Tom Askwith who passed the hat round for the defence, but the best lawyer could only get the charge reduced to manslaughter, for which Sam Githu was sentenced to three years' imprisonment. After a few months he was released under an amnesty for offences on both sides, announced as a measure of reconciliation. He retired to his shop with his George Medal and, no doubt, mixed feelings about the government he had served so faithfully. To the Kikuyu his prosecution was quite incomprehensible.

Mau Mau has been the subject of endless debate, research and comment among academics, journalists and politicians. It was a complex and bloody episode. This account has been written as the administration saw the difficult and painful experience at the time. It was a major military operation by any reckoning: by the end of 1956 there were over 11,000 Africans connected with Mau Mau killed, over 5,000 were captured or surrendered, and over 26,000 were arrested and many thousands detained under administrative Detention Orders; there were 166 members of the security forces killed and nearly 1,600 wounded, the majority being Africans; there were nearly 1,900 loyal civilians killed and almost 1,000 wounded, again the vast majority being Africans. The emergency operation cost the British and Kenyan governments over £55 million up to mid-1959.

The emergency was formally declared at an end in February 1960. So ended Mau Mau – a phenomenon which cast such a shadow over the latter years of the administration. These are, of course, bare statistics and do little to conceal the brutality and cruelty – and atrocities – involved, some of which have been described in these chapters.

22

The Pastoral Revolution

The pastoral districts, inhabited by semi-nomadic tribes, were inimicable to progress, but had it thrust on them in the 1950s. For forty years they had been slowly destroyed by erosion caused by overstocking.

In the later 1940s John Carson, DC Samburu, accompanied a KAR recruiting safari. To impress the simple tribesmen with the marvels of modern science, the soldiers laid on a cross-country demonstration by a Bren-gun carrier. Their officer said to a strapping, ochre-smeared moran, 'That would get you about nicely, wouldn't it?' The moran grunted sceptically and felt the carrier's tracks. 'Much too loose. You'd never have got away with that in the Fourteenth Army.'

He was a sergeant on leave, one of hundreds of Samburu soldiers and ex-soldiers. The moran who went to the war came back much better men than their fathers and elder brothers who had been the scourge of Laikipia. Of course their younger brothers still regarded stock-theft as essential to their life-style, but spear-blooding was no longer necessary. Some were almost ready to admit that their traditional way of life, based on huge herds of poor quality cattle was not, perhaps, the ultimate perfection.

In 1951 there arrived Terry Gavaghan, forceful, energetic and articulate. At that time Metro-Goldwyn-Mayer was looking for a suitable location for a mega-safari film, *Mogambo*, starring Clark Gable and Ava Gardner. Gavaghan gatecrashed a M-G-M party in Nanyuki where he switched on the blarney full-strength. 'A thousand pig-tailed, ochre-smeared, spear-toting moran as extras?' 'As many as you want.' 'Shots of charging elephant and rhino?'

'No problem.' So the stars descended on Maralal, shot their scenes, lashed out lavish pay to their extras and on departure handed on to Gavaghan, for the ADC, refrigerators and electrical equipment for the district's hospitals and, a princely gift, a near-new, 4-wheel drive, Willys station-wagon ambulance.

The Samburu were delighted with manna from Hollywood – until Gavaghan set out his terms for accepting it: regular cattle-sales with each section producing its quota. It required a good deal of administrative pressure before this was achieved, and financial inducements to the headmen. Before Gavaghan left they were selling to the African Livestock Marketing Organisation (ALMO) 9,000 cattle a year which, together with a possible local consumption of 21,000 a year, took off the estimated annual increase. Despite the hovering tax-collectors, stock-sales became popular social occasions with dancing, singing and flirtation as the tribesmen pocketed their cash. It still remained to reduce the total of cattle to the carrying capacity of the land, but Gavaghan's achievement was a breakthrough. So also was the acceptance on Leroghi of a simple scheme of grazing control in which each family kept to its own small area and alternated between dry and wet weather grazing, a great change from the traditional free range. The scheme was supervised by 'Bwana Leroghi', a livestock officer, Fritz Brauer, lately of the German artillery, who ran it on German army lines, '*Zu Befehl!*'

Gavaghan also induced the ADC to set aside 40,000 acres of Leroghi for the Samburu Ranch on which, for the ADC's profit, 2,000 of the best cattle from the sales were fattened for the up-country market. The poorest of the cattle were turned into blood- and bone-meal, hides and biltong at a field abattoir set up at Archer's Post.

No administrative pressure was required for the moran to turn out in hundreds for anti-Mau Mau sweeps through Laikipia. The bag was disappointing; but when the police, without informing the DC, sent a 'pseudo-gang', disguised as Mau Mau, to investigate rumours of outlying gangs in the forests of the Matthews Range, Chief Lepuyapuyi and his moran rounded them up and delivered them, trussed with rawhide thongs, to the DO at Wamba: 'Look what we've got!'

The Pastoral Revolution

Across the Rift Valley was the district of West Suk, with headquarters at Kapenguria and a population of about 40,000. The Suk were sullen and suspicious, and had not had their vision broadened by KAR service. Their district was as overstocked and eroded as Samburu, but better watered, by streams flowing down from the highlands.

The system of grazing control selected there was known as the Texas system, applied to communal grazing schemes. Each scheme was divided into equal quarters, each grazed for four months and rested for a year, so that its grazed period came at different months each time round. Charles Wilks in the early 1950s got going an experimental scheme in the Rewa location. The grass-regeneration was remarkable, thick star-grass on previously sheet-eroded land.

He was followed as DC by David Shirreff who first had to deal with a very nasty outbreak of witch-murder. A man attributed the deaths of his two children to sorcery by a headman. He and four relatives took the headman into the bush and slowly beat him to death with light rods, burying the body in an ant-bear hole. On being arrested they freely, indeed proudly, confessed to the killing, and were committed for trial by the Supreme Court for murder. But the state entered a plea of *nolle prosequi*, because of some technical flaw in the recording of the confessions, and the accused were free to go home. Swiftly the news spread from hilltop to hilltop, 'The Government says it's OK to kill witches.' In the next three months seven suspected sorcerers were beaten to death, over several hours, in the presence of full *barazas*. Shirreff was reluctant to hazard another case in the Supreme Court, so he tried the killers himself, for inflicting grievous bodily harm, and sentenced them to three years and a flogging, which convinced the Suk that the government did *not* approve the killing of witches.

For safari, grazing control and general purposes Shirreff bought from the KAR a dozen horses and taught his TPs to ride. 'General purposes' included a great sweep to drive off the Trans-Nzoia farms a herd of the rare Rothchild's giraffe which were doing great damage to crops and fences. It took a lot of hard galloping to move the giraffe where they did not want to go, down the escarpment into the Suk low country where they could do no harm. The horsemen returned home, nursing sundry bruises and contusions but conscious of a good job well done. Next day the giraffe were all back on the farms.

When it came to persuading the Suk to do what they did not want to do, Shirreff had two advantages: he liked them, and he was with them for five years. To run the grazing schemes he set up a committee consisting of himself; Hugh Yorke, an agricultural officer who had been there eight years and spoke Suk; Ian Bond, an efficient livestock officer; James Tolon, a lively-minded Suk schoolteacher; and three public spirited Trans-Nzoia farmers. They planned the extension of the Texas system over much of the district.

To be effective, the cattle in each scheme had to be limited to what the grazing would carry. The big question was, 'What happens to the cattle squeezed out?' The surplus must be sold, said the DC and his committee, but the Suk would not hear of it. Nor was the impasse resolved by a Governor's *baraza* which Sir Evelyn Baring chose to address in his rudimentary Swahili. What he meant to say was, 'You must sell some of your cattle.' What he said was, 'You must sell all your cattle.' There was a terrific uproar, and it was all Shirreff could do to persuade the people that His Excellency did not mean what he said.

After months of pressure and propaganda Shirreff managed to cajole the ADC into passing a by-law under which the owner of cattle in a scheme could be ordered to sell up to 10 per cent. No wonder, thought the Suk, that a chief who had voted for this iniquitous by-law should die suddenly on his way home from doing so. But there it was, a by-law properly passed by the duly constituted authority.

After this remarkable achievement Shirreff departed on four months' home leave and his relief (the author) temporarily replaced him. On my way through Nakuru the PC, Robin Wainwright, said to me, 'God knows how David got that through the ADC, but he did. Your first job is to get it going on the ground. Nothing is more important'.

We devised a lawyer-proof method of ordering stock-owners to sell by a written chit, delivered in full *baraza*, receipt acknowledged by a thumb-print. Remembering the incident at Kolloa, I arranged for a Kenya Police General Service Unit to be training in the

The Pastoral Revolution

vicinity, out of sight but not out of mind. I then handed the first sales order to the most recalcitrant chief who accepted it with manifest distaste, as did all the others.

Two days before the sale I received a telegram from Windley, the Chief Native Commissioner, saying that no compulsion was to be used; and that if there was any possibility of trouble, the sale must be cancelled. It was then too late to cancel: the cattle, we hoped, were on their way. We decided that we must go ahead, knowing that we were for the chop if things went wrong. In the event they went right. The full quota of cattle were sold. Windley came down to Kapenguria and was extremely displeased.

When David Shirreff returned from leave he continued the sales, resorting to the by-law when necessary. Grazing schemes on the Texas system spread over much of the low country which resulted in spectacular grass regeneration. One result was an influx of zebra, kongoni, oryx and eland, accompanied by lions which had not been seen in the district for years. Oddly enough there were no reports of them killing cattle; they seemed to prefer their natural prey.

From West Suk I was posted to Samburu, in 1956, the finest job I ever had. I immediately bought horses from the Laikipia ranchers at £5 for any we could catch, and with the help of one who had served in the KPR Mounted Section, taught about twenty TPs to ride. The PC agreed to a Mounted Man's allowance of shs 5 per month, shs 15 for instructors, and shs 50 for every horse trained. It was remarkable how the Samburu TPs took to it, men who a few months ago had never seen a horse were training horses which had scarcely seen a man.

Nothing would wean the moran from stock-theft, from Laikipia ranches to the south or Boran to the north-east. But the law allowed the levying of compensation from the family/section/tribe responsible. When a theft from Laikipia was reported Kenya Police trackers followed the spoor into Samburu where they were joined by mounted TPs, who could both track and move faster than the rustlers. Eventually the spoor was lost, and the local elders were informed that unless they could follow it out of their area, they would have to pay up. This produced great activity and intensive tracking. Eventually the spoor could be followed no further, and compensation was duly levied. So skilled were the trackers that their verdict was seldom disputed. So the Laikipia ranchers got some compensation for their losses, but they would much rather have kept their cattle.

On the Samburu-Boran border stock-theft had a different pattern, often tit-for-tat accompanied by spearings and general mayhem, for the two tribes were ancient enemies. Every few months a joint *baraza* was held by the DCs Samburu and Isiolo at which each side gave a totally different account of the same incident, neither giving way one inch. After a day of this the two DCs, probably the only people present who did not know exactly what had happened, had to assess blame and compensation.

I arrived full of zeal to introduce the Texas system to the Samburu low country. The DO most involved was Robert Chambers, a young man of incredible energy and enthusiasm who in a few months learned quite good Samburu.

It was more difficult than in Suk because of the shortage of permanent water. Each block had to have enough for all the cattle in the scheme. With ALDEV grants, an ADC tractor unit for small dams and heavy machinery from the colony's Soil Conservation Service for big dams, a terrific effort was made. Sinking a borehole could be unbearably exciting. None of the experts, whether they dowsed or used more orthodox scientific methods, were reliable prophets. Water might be predicted at 1,000 feet. You get down to 1,000. No water. But it might be only a couple of feet further down – or 500 feet down. So do you cut your losses or risk wasting more money?

Almost as hazardous was the selection of dam-sites by ALDEV experts. I took Expert A on a long ride across the El Barta plains to look at a site I fancied. He was enthusiastic: 'Catchment – twenty million gallons – spillway – good clay for dam wall. Perfect!' Three weeks later I took Expert B to the same place. Moodily he viewed the scene. 'A dam? *Here?*' he said. Without another word he turned his horse towards home.

Permanent water was the bait with which to gain the Samburu and Turkana consent to grazing schemes. We started at Baragoi, centre of the El Barta plain grazed by both tribes. From the first we made clear that cattle within a scheme would have to

The Pastoral Revolution

be limited in number and branded, so that interlopers could be detected; and that their owners would have to pay a small grazing fee to help cover the cost of grazing guards and the running expenses of boreholes. The vital question was, what happens to cattle excluded from the scheme? We said that many must be sold, so that there would be grass for the remainder. They said, 'No way!' At *baraza* after *baraza* we heard the same speech, until we could have repeated it verbatim. 'You have your government pay, you have farms in England. We have nothing but our cattle. If you sell half of them, how shall we live?' It was utterly useless to explain that fifty fat cattle produced more milk and ate less grass that a hundred bags of skin and bones. 'If I have a hundred cattle and fifty die, I still have fifty left. But if I have only fifty cattle and fifty die, I have none left.' We hoped that those who had paid grazing fees to keep their cattle in a scheme would help to keep trespassers out. But to the Samburu that would be grossly anti-social: one *must* help a neighbour who has no grass. Said Robert Chambers, 'I'm afraid we're teaching them to be selfish shits.'

Endless argument and the sight of dams actually being built and boreholes sunk eventually secured a reluctant agreement to three lowland communal grazing schemes, all on the Texas system, each block having its permanent water: Seya-Barsalinga, of 130,000 acres holding 10,000 cattle; Ngarone, of 180,000 acres holding 8,000 cattle; and El Barta of 280,000 acres holding 12,000 cattle. It was a triumph for Chambers and for David Adams, the Samburu-speaking Kikuyu district clerk at Baragoi. All were supervised by Terry Smyth, a livestock officer with a talent for constructing sub-surface dams and rock-catchment water-holes. Mounted TPs and grazing guards patrolled the schemes, examining herds for unbranded animals which were impounded until the owners paid 10 per cent as a trespass fine.

In 1958 everything was going swimmingly; the three big lowland schemes were not popular, but they were working, and the grass was coming back splendidly. In that year over 10,000 cattle were sold, and 6,000 in the first six months of 1959. Then the district was sorely stricken by an outbreak of a peculiarly virulent type of foot and mouth disease. All stock sales were cancelled. It was hard enough to collect poll tax and ADC rates, quite impossible to collect fines for trespass, grazing fees and compensation for stolen stock. Then the short rains, November-December, failed, as did the long and short rains for 1960. Interlopers swarmed into the grazing schemes; only there could grass and water be found. Somehow we kept things ticking over until the first African general election on universal adult franchise in February 1961, just after I left the district. Candidates of all parties vied with each other in denouncing anything the government did which was unpopular. The Samburu had got what they wanted, more permanent water, and were more than willing to renege on their side of the bargain. Finally the ADC refused to vote any more money for grazing control, and there was nothing my successor could do but let them have their way. One must admit that the long drought did more to remove surplus stock than any of our efforts could have achieved. For the rest of the colony independence came at the end of 1963; for the Samburu it came in 1961, when grazing control ended. Nor did the Suk grazing schemes survive independence.

Years later Robert Chambers, contemplating the ruin of our hopes, asked sadly, 'What *should* we have done? Less, I suppose.'

No one bothered the inhabitants of the coast about such matters. John Carson found Lamu in 1951 unchanged since the 1930s, with the same Somerset Maugham bachelors presiding over the scene. Calling on the legendary 'Coconut Charlie', Carson was surprised to find no beachcomber but a dignified, rather portly, white-haired old man, immaculately turned out, sipping his John Collins as he contemplated the Indian Ocean. 'Nice to see you. This is like old times when Jack Clive used to drop in for a chat. Now what can I do for you? Any information about Lamu required?' – or, for that matter, about English railway timetables.

As proprietor of the only garage on the island, he still punctiliously took out an annual driving licence, though there were no cars. He showed Carson his remarkable collection of Lamu antiques – Chinese porcelain vases, Arab daggers, ornate chests, and a small wine-flask with a bearded head embossed on it. 'Do you recognise the head? It is of King Stephen of Hungary, twelfth-century, a strange find in Lamu. I imagine some Crusading

The Pastoral Revolution

knight must have given it to an Arab friend. It must have a story to tell.'

Percy Petley and Robert Milne still ran the shabby, hospitable Lamu Hotel where Arabs, Goans, Africans and Europeans drank at the bar, and Carson's daughters were regaled with Coca-Cola. But Lamu was no place for a DC with three young children. It was incredibly difficult to get the eldest to school in Nairobi and back three times a year, and very tiresome to carry the baby up and down the long flights of stairs in the DC's huge, shadowy, bat- and cockroach-ridden house. His wife condemned the furniture at first glance, riddled by woodworm and reduced to powder by white ants. They burnt the lot, and were then baffled by the refusal of the storekeeper in Mombasa to replace it unless they first produced the unserviceable articles for condemnation.

He was followed by Peter Lloyd, a young bachelor thrilled at his first posting as DC. He loved everything about Lamu, forty years later it still 'tugs at the heartstrings'. He approved of the leisurely progress of the bearded Liwali through the streets, stopping to chat as though he had the whole day at his disposal, for any sign of haste would be unmannerly. He enjoyed the safaris to the islands, his Bajun crew capping his tale of the Loch Ness monster by showing him the *exact* beach where a python had swallowed an elephant, and had then taken to the sea to be the first sea-serpent. The mainland Bajuns' greatest problem was *shamba*-raiding by elephants and baboons. Lloyd got the Game Department to deal with the elephants, shooting or scaring them off with Verey lights and thunder-flashes; but flatly refused to involve the government in the battle of wits against baboons.

Sometimes a dhow-captain, rolling into harbour before the monsoon, would ask for a private talk with the DC on a confidential matter. There was, he would explain, a grave shortage of slaves in Arabia. He understood that the British government kept several hundred Kikuyu slaves at a place called Hola. Would it be possible . . . ?

The position of Provincial Commissioner, Coast, was generally considered to be one of *otium cum dignitate*. Denis Hall in 1959 found ample *dignitas* but little *otium*. As Queen's representative, his relations with visiting naval captains were governed by strict protocol. An officer of the rank of captain or below paid the first call on the PC, each wearing white undress uniform, was met at the PC's front door and spent precisely a quarter-hour sipping coffee and making conversation before returning to his ship. The PC then paid a call on him, inspected a guard of honour, spent a quarter-hour and departed to a 5-gun salute. After this relations could be less formal. If the visiting officer were an admiral, the order of calling was reversed. Hall was interested in the differences between navies. Naturally he thought the Royal Navy by far the smartest and best. The Indian and Pakistan navies were very smart and more British than the British. The American ships varied greatly in quality, and relations with their officers was inhibited by the ships being 'dry' and the officers anti-colonial in their prejudices.

In 1960 there was a total failure of the short rains, and a consequent food-shortage. There was no crisis. Maize was bought from the colony Maize Control Board, brought in by rail and lorry and distributed to chiefs' centres where it was rationed out to all who did a modest day's public work – improving roads, clearing and maintaining dams, repairing schools. There was no serious hunger.

But the drought was broken by terrific rain in April 1961. The desiccated soil could not absorb it, and it ran down in torrents to the sea, sweeping away the bridge over the Sabaki river by which alone lorries could reach the northern part of the province. To Hall, flying over it, the whole country seemed to be a lake, dotted with islands which were the hillocks on which villages were built. This *was* a crisis: it would obviously be weeks before the bridge could be replaced or a ferry improvised. The navy provided a commando carrier which was ideal for landing bags of maize on open beaches or in small harbours. The RAF laid on transport planes, and when parachutes ran out, devised methods of packing 200-lb maize bags so that they did not burst when dropped from a low altitude. There was no appeal for international aid, no pop-concerts for starving Kenyans. The administration, the navy and the RAF coped.

The media of course were soon onto it and one tabloid's headlines screamed, 'Famine. 1,000 dead.' Hall called a press

The Pastoral Revolution

conference. The newshounds, eager to disclose official ineptitude, asked for his comments on the appalling death-toll. Hall, who knew from DCs and chiefs' daily reports the true figures, replied, 'Not a thousand – three. One – two – three.' But the media had the last word: next day the headlines proclaimed, 'Famine. Official denies 1,000 dead.'

23

Wind of Change

At the end of the 1950s Kenya seemed bursting with confidence. The Mau Mau had been smashed. Relations between the victors – loyal Kikuyu, settlers, other tribes, officials and Asians – were better and closer than they had ever been. Surely Kenya would now show the world what a colony could be. But the 'wind of change' took them by surprise.

In 1959 two main African political parties were formed; the Kenya African National Union (KANU) representing the biggest and most sophisticated tribes, Kikuyu, Luo and Kamba; and the Kenya African Democratic Union (KADU) representing the coastal and pastoral tribes. Jomo Kenyatta on his release from prison would obviously lead KANU.

In the first election on virtually universal adult franchise in February 1961, KANU got most of the votes but refused to join the government until Kenyatta was released. KADU then joined the government, and proceeded to negotiate with the British government an absurd federal constitution in which Kenya would be divided into eight regions each with its own administrative and other services. It was devised to break up the KANU vote and help KADU in future elections, and it was complete nonsense. But it landed the administration in a vast amount of work in devising new boundaries, dividing powers between central and regional governments, re-distributing staff and organizing new elections. At the same time many DCs were up to their eyes in work settling Africans (mainly Kikuyu) on a willing-seller-willing-buyer basis, with loans to the buyers, on European farms. 7,500 families had been settled by the end of 1962.

Wind of Change

The security situation was unsatisfactory, with KANU politicians making inflammatory speeches and a sort of neo-Mau Mau which was suppressed by sixty detention orders before it could do any harm. DCs were downgraded to the amorphous status of 'Regional Government Agent', stripped of the responsibility for law and order (a belated triumph for the Kenya Police) and even of their status as *primus inter pares* among other departments. (Almost the first act of President Kenyatta after independence was to restore to DCs their proper title and former powers.)

In 1961 Kenyatta was released, and following the KANU victory in a general election in May, became Prime Minister. Promptly he scrapped the absurd KADU federal constitution, and DCs had to unscramble the eggs.

The fact that Kenya since independence has done so much better than any other ex-colony is due mainly to Jomo Kenyatta's magnanimity and change of heart after becoming Prime Minister. At a packed settlers' meeting at Nakuru, he brought the house down with an emotional appeal to forgive and forget and to work together for a new Kenya. He made the same sort of appeal to Kikuyu loyalists and it is noteworthy that none of the chiefs, headmen and Kikuyu Guard who had beaten the Mau Mau were penalized by his government. He was known everywhere as Mzee, the old man, a term of respect.

It was widely surmised that Kenyatta's surprising change of heart was due largely to Leslie Whitehouse, who was DC Turkana all the time Kenyatta was in prison in Lokitaung. Whitehouse in his unpublished memoirs does not confirm this. Nor does he quite deny it, writing, 'For political reasons and since times have changed so much since Mzee's death, I am obliged to inhibit some part of our acquaintanceship.' What he did on his monthly visits to Lokitaung was to talk to Kenyatta, lend him books, ensure that he was treated with scrupulous fairness within the prison rules and maintained in as good health as possible in the circumstances. He also prevented the other Mau Mau prisoners, who blamed Kenyatta for their plight, from persecuting him (one had even attacked him with a knife). A rapport approaching friendship grew up between the DC and his important prisoner, which lasted until Mzee's death. After independence Whitehouse was employed for many years as Resident Magistrate for Turkana and Kitale, appointed to boundary commissions and awarded a high Kenya decoration.

The second stabilizing factor in Kenya since independence was the agricultural revolution in most of the agricultural tribes (but not the Luo) brought about by the administration, Agricultural and Veterinary Departments, and approved by Kenyatta's government. The heart of Kenya remains a country of prosperous yeoman farmers, a recipe for stability.

The third factor is the wonderful productive farms built up by the settlers. Nearly all were bought out by Africans, with British government grants. Many reverted to patchwork *shambas* growing wretched crops of maize among stumps of felled trees. But an increasing number were bought by well-off Africans (conspicuously by some government ministers) and farmed well, some by European managers. Although it has no oil or mineral resources, nothing but its agriculture, and despite a fearful population explosion, Kenya has never had to appeal for international aid in feeding its people.

To the Somalis of the north-east independence meant independence from Kenya, be it ruled by whites or blacks, and union with Somalia. Outraged by the prospect of being handed over to the government of men of tribes which from the bottoms of their haughty hearts they despised, they responded unanimously to SYL propaganda, carrying with them most of the semi-Somali tribes and many Muslim Boran. Whatever the sympathies of many individual frontier officers, in no way could the British government countenance this. Allowing north-east Kenya to secede would give the worst possible start to British relations with independent Kenya. It would be almost as unpopular with Ethiopia, and good relations with Ethiopia were considered more important than with Somalia. Finally, it would greatly facilitate the southward and westward pressure of Somalis into Kenya.

The storm centre of SYL agitation was Wajir, where John Golds was posted as DC in 1961. He found it quite a change from Kiambu, and the most fascinating job he ever had. New to the frontier, he raised some old timers' eyebrows by reviving the African District Council (ADC) which had lapsed through sheer

Wind of Change

lack of Somali interest, and providing it with a reliable source of income: instead of vainly trying to prevent the import and sale of that fairly harmless drug, *miraa,* he allowed and taxed it. With this income, and a cess on all exported livestock, the ADC became very rich, and spent most of its money on water supplies, notably the capping and straightening of the Wajir wells so that water could be drawn out more quickly.

And in other respects Golds was a model frontier DC. He revived the Dubas *rakub* (camel-riding) section, which had waxed and waned with the interest of other DCs, and did a lot of camel-riding safaris which had all the advantages of horse safaris except for extra speed when it was needed. He did what he could (very little) to counter SYL propaganda. He was assiduous in his duties as Commodore of the Royal Wajir Yacht Club, wearing on ceremonial occasions a Royal Navy cocked hat and piping 'aboard' John Profumo, British Minister of War on a visit to Kenya. During the great floods of 1961 when intending visitors to Wajir were advised to consult a shipping firm before setting out, he constructed a boat in which he navigated round the *boma.*

In 1963, shortly before independence, Golds went on leave, handing over his district to Neville Judge, a New Zealander. During his absence all the Somali chiefs resigned, and SYL agitation flared up into full-scale rebellion. Golds was summoned from Stockholm to the Colonial Office in London to be told that Judge had been murdered; as had H. C. Wright, a District Officer in Mandera; David Dumbasso Waweru, the DC Isiolo (one of the first African DCs); and Haji Galma Dida, the stout-hearted Boran chief. In each case they had ignored *Dubas* advice and been ambushed. Golds was officially advised not to return, as the murder of British DCs after independence was very embarrassing. But he had given his word to Kenyatta to serve him at Wajir for a year, and insisted on doing so.

The chiefs' resignation he simply ignored, treating them as though it had never happened, and one by one they formed up for their pay and resumed their duties as well, or as badly, as before. The *Dubas,* he found, had been disarmed by the police and confined to barracks. Golds went straight to the Commissioner of Police, Catling, and persuaded him not only to countermand the local order, but to release for the Wajir *Dubas* bren-guns, sub-machine guns and radio sets from police stocks. With these he conducted a vigorous and not unsuccessful campaign during which only two of his *Dubas* deserted to the enemy. In a desperate year, this was the last manifestation of *Dubas* loyalty – not, of course, to the Kenya government but to their DC.

Eventually the Kenya Army entered the district in force and suppressed the rebellion with far more severity than the British had ever used. But when the last British DCs had left, their African successors regarded such places as Wajir, Mandera and Moyale not as administrative centres but as punishment stations, beleaguered fortresses whence the garrisons emerged from time to time to shoot a few Somalis and perhaps collect a little tax.

The last has not been heard of the Kenya Somalis' determination to unite with Somalia, however chaotic Somalia may be. Somali *shiftas*, armed with automatic rifles roam far into Meru and Kitui districts shooting rhino, elephant, and anyone who interferes with them.

By far the most important task of the DCs and DOs in the run-up to independence was training (not before time) Africans to replace them. It was not very enjoyable. However they might intellectually agree that it was time to go, they were being thrown on the job market while still quite young and with no skills or experience which would be of much use in the Britain of the 1960s. Gavaghan was appointed 'Localization and Training Officer'. His target was to 'Africanize' one-third of the top 10,000 jobs, in all departments, by independence, whenever that might be. To train DCs and DOs, The Kenya Institute of Administration was set up in the Jeanes School, Kabete, in July 1961, and followed a syllabus similar to the Oxford and Cambridge Colonial Cadets' courses. Problems which worried Robin Wainwright, Minister for African Affairs and departmental head of the service, included the morale of European officers who must receive fair compensation for the loss of their careers. There was strong pressure from African politicians to accelerate the Africanization process. But in September 1962, the first four African DCs took up their posts, and by independence one-third of the senior administration posts

Wind of Change

were held by Africans. Nearly all the remaining European officers left within the next two years.

They could look back with regret at half-completed work and vanished ambitions, but with some pride at the country they had helped to make. Kenya has not sustained a democratic system of government; it is nowhere near solving Africa's insoluble problem, the population explosion; or the conflict of interest between tourism which requires an abundance of wild animals, and farming which requires the opposite. At least Kenya passes the acid test of being able to feed itself and help feed its hungry neighbours, thanks to the agricultural reforms of the 1950s which governments since independence have preserved and protected. In pushing these through against the clock, caring and conscientious DCs, agricultural officers and vets made an impact on East Africa at least as great, and perhaps more permanent, than that made by the more colourful, rough and tough characters who had imposed law and order seventy years earlier.

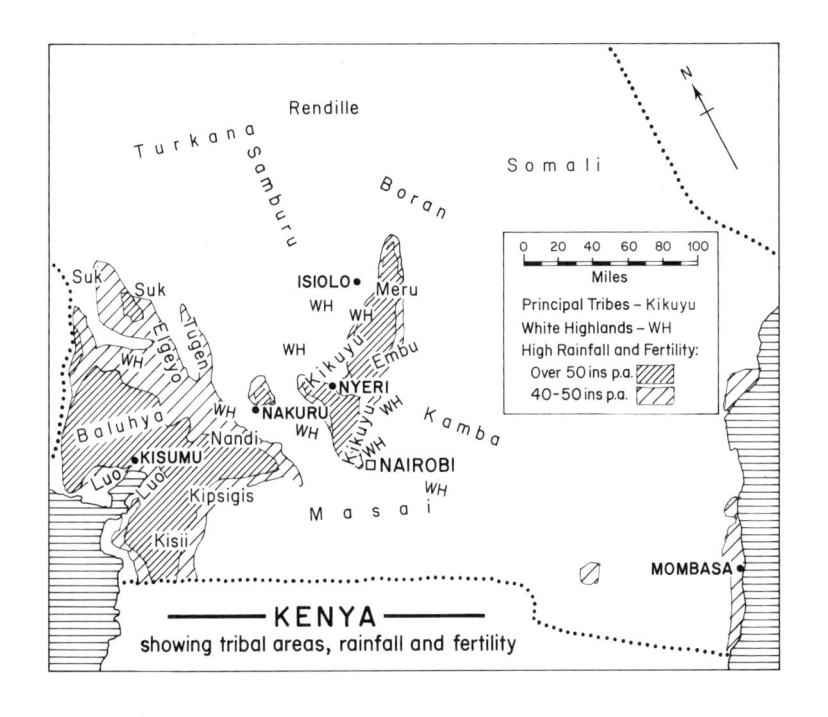

KENYA
showing tribal areas, rainfall and fertility

Principal Tribes – Kikuyu
White Highlands – WH
High Rainfall and Fertility:
Over 50 ins p.a.
40–50 ins p.a.

KENYA
1925

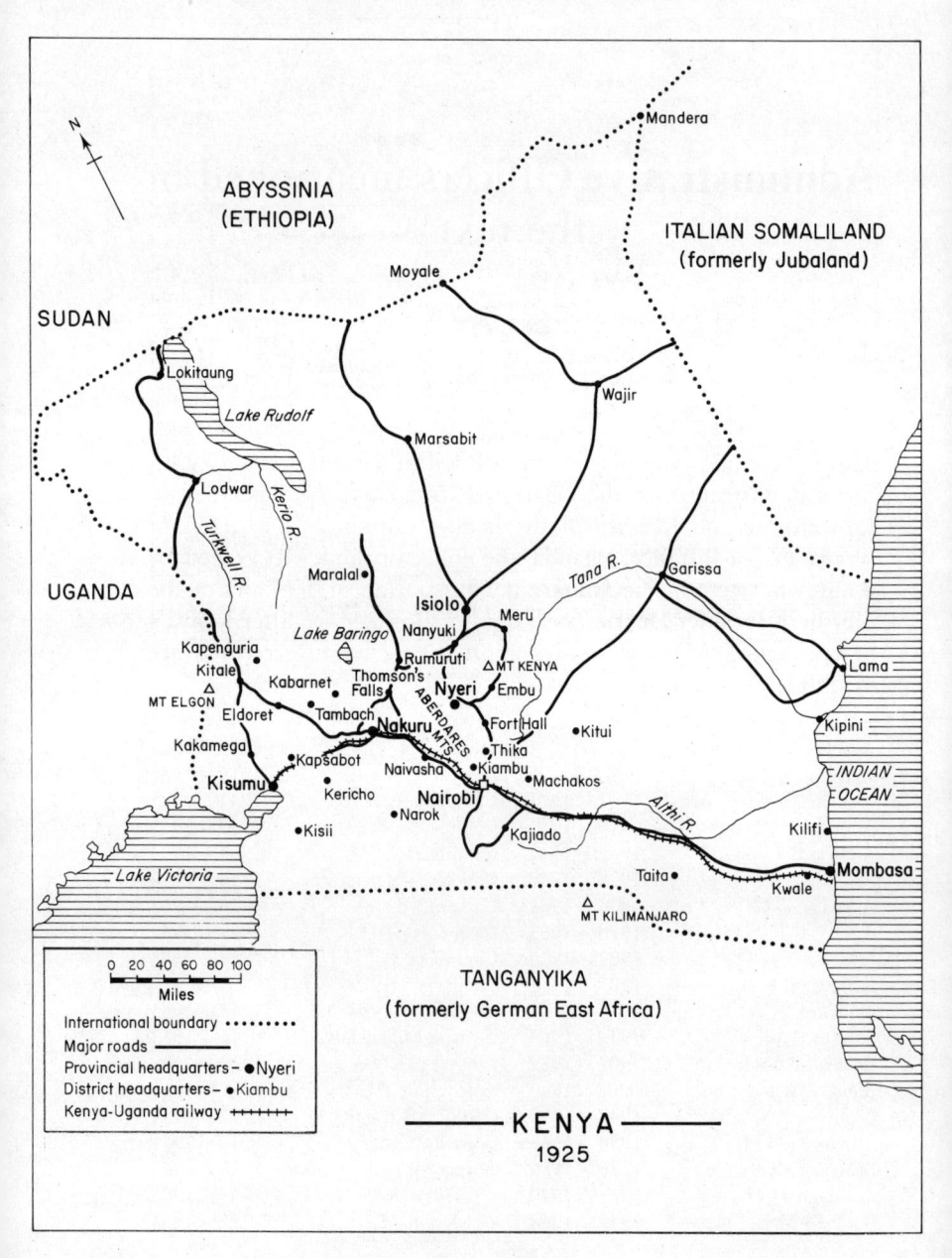

Administrative Officers mentioned in the text

This list includes all those mentioned with their dates of service in the Administration of the Chartered Company, the East African Protectorate and Kenya Colony. It does not show their dates of service in, for instance, Uganda, the police or the KAR, except for a few who were in the military administration of Turkana or the Northern Frontier District. Nor does it show service after Kenya's independence. Many dates are approximate because records are incomplete.

Ainsworth, J (John)	1887 – 1922	Butter, J H	1947 – 1963
Ainsworth, J B (James)	1901 – 1911	Buxton, C E V	1919 – 1938
		Campbell, C	1941 – 1963
Anderson, E L B	1919 – 1951	Campbell, J D	1953 – 1960
Archer, G F	1902 – 1912	Campbell, W F G	1907 – 1934
Armitage, R	1929 – 1947	Candler, J H	1946 – 1954
Askwith, T G	1936 – 1961	Carson, J B	1936 – 1963
Atkins, C F	1930 – 1963	Cashmore, T H R	1953 – 1963
Bagge, S S	1902 – 1910	Chambers, R J H	1958 – 1963
Barrett, W E H	1907 – 1916	Chenevix Trench, C P	1948 – 1963
Bailward, A N	1920 – c1939		
Balfour, J W	1946 – 1963	Christie-Miller, D G	1945 – 1963
Beech, M W H	1907 – 1922	Clive, J H	1920 – 1948
Bond, B W	1920 – c1940	Colchester, T C	1931 – 1961
Brothers, P M	1947 – 1950	Cooke, S V	1917 – 1931
Brown, G H H	1950 – 1963	Cornell, C H	1921 – c1954
Brown, G R B	1926 – 1950	Coutts, W F	1936 – 1949
Brumage, D O	1919 – c1940		1957 – 1963
Butler, J M B	1949 – 1963	Cowley, K M	1935 – 1963

Men Who Ruled Kenya

Cumber, J A	1947 – 1963	Jackson, F J	1902 – 1907
Cusack, J W	1930 – 1959	Jenner, A C W	c1893 – 1900
Davies, E R StA	1928 – 1954	Jennings, F G	1919 – 1947
Deck, S F	1907 – c1920	Johnston, C M	1933 – 1963
Derrick, F P B	1944 – 1949	Judge, H N A	1954 – 1963
	1953 – 1963	Keir, W	1935 – 1941
Dobbs, C M	1906 – c1937	Kelly, W P F	1936 – 1963
Dowson, G C M	1936 – 1963	Kennaway, N F	1931 – 1959
Dumbasso, D	1958 – 1963	Kihori, J	1952 – 1953
Dundas, C C F	1908 – 1920	Kittermaster, H B	1908 – 1921
Ellerton, G J	1945 – 1963	La Fontaine, S H	1910 – 1934
Elliott, F	c1914 – 1916	Lambert, H E	1919 – c1956
Fazan, S H	1911 – 1936	Lambert, J D	1955 – 1963
Galton-Fenzi, A D	1945 – 1963	Lambert, R T	1925 – 1948
Gavaghan, T J F	1943 – 1963	Lane, C R W	1894 – 1923
Gilkison, T C	c1890 – c1911	Lewis, J H	1931 – 1954
Githu, S	1954 – 1957	Llewellin, J L B	1914 – 1924
Glenday, V	1913 – 1938		1940 – 1945
Golds, J M	1955 – 1963	Lloyd, G P	1951 – 1963
Gordon, P M	1946 – 1963	Loudon, W N B	1941 – 1963
Grayburn, J R	1953 – 1963	Loyd, F A	1939 – 1963
Grant, H M	1930 – 1946	McDougall, K	1899 – 1917
Gregory-Smith, H G	1929 – 1946	McKean, J D	1917 – 1948
Hale, W H	1930 – 1949	McLellan, J W T	1895 – 1922
Hall, F G	1893 – 1901	Mahony, M F J R	c1920 – c1936
Hall, D W	1936 – 1963	Martin, J (alias	
Hampson, G N	1948 – 1963	Antonio Martini)	c1890 – c1900
Hardy, N G	1946 – 1963	Maxwell, G V	1921 – c1923
Hemsted, G S	1900 – 1919	Mayes, W	c1895 – c1905
Hemsted, R W	1899 – 1933	Montgomery, H R	1908 – c1936
Hennings, R O	1945 – 1963	Morgan, D L	1926 – 1951
Hinde, S L	1895 – 1915	Mullins, A C M	1926 – 1953
Hobley, C W	1902 – 1923	Mure, G A S	1909 – 1917
Holford-Walker,		Napier-Bax, S E	1950 – 1963
A F	1944 – 1963	Norman, C B	1925 – 1936
Hope, J O W	1899 – 1928	North, M	1934 – 1963
Hopkins, J G H	1917 – 1938	Northcote, G A S	1904 – 1927
Horne, E B	1904 – 1934	Okwirri, I	1947 – c1960
Horne, H H	1903 – 1927	Partington, H B	1902 – 1913
Hosking, E B	1913 – 1938	Pedraza, J G W	1949 – 1963
Howard, J W	1939 – 1940	Pedraza, R	1914 – 1946
	1943 – 1963	Peet, F A	1945 – 1963
Howes, R J C	1929 – 1953	Penwill, D G	1947 – c1960
Hughes, O E B	1947 – 1963	Pinney, J	1941 – 1963
Hunter, K L	1919 – 1954	Potter, H S	1926 – 1954

Administrative Officers mentioned in the text

Rankine, J D	1947 – 1952	Trafford, H H	1913 – c1936
Reece, G	1925 – 1948	Turnbull, R G	1931 – 1958
Reddie, C S	1895 – 1914	Wainwright, J M E	1953 – 1961
Rimington, G B	1920 – c1940	Wainwright, R E	1935 – 1963
Shackleton, E R	1927 – c1934	Watts, T A	1941 – 1963
Sharpe, H B	1919 – c1936	Whitehouse, L E	1940 – 1960
Shirreff, A D	1945 – 1963	Wightman, J W E	
Silvester, J M	1913 – c1932	(name changed	
Simpson, A B	1947 – 1963	from Gegg by	
Stevens, A J	1944 – 1949	deed-poll)	c1914 – c1924
Stone, R G	1911 – 1933	Wilkinson, R A	1935 – 1963
Storrs-Fox, D	1920 – c1934	Wilks, H C F	1946 – 1963
Swann, A D	1936 – 1940	Wilson, F R	1947 – 1963
	1945 – 1963	Windley, E H	1931 – c1957
Symes-Thompson,		Wood-White, R	1953 – 1954
R H	1946 – 1963	Wright, H C	1956 – 1963
Thorp, R J C	1935 – 1953	Wynn-Harris, P	1926 – 1949
Todd, ?	c1893	Zaphiro, P	1905 – 1908

Principal Sources

Published	Cited as
G. H. Mungeam, *British Rule in Kenya 1895–1912* (Oxford, 1966)	Mungeam
F. H. Goldsmith, *John Ainsworth* (London, 1955)	Goldsmith
R. Meinertzhagen, *Kenya Diary, 1902–1906* (Edinburgh, 1956)	Meinertzhagen
C. C. F. Dundas, *African Crossroads* (London, 1955)	Dundas
C. W. Hobley, *Kenya, from Chartered Company to Crown Colony* (London, 1929)	Hobley
E. Huxley, *White Man's Country* (London, 1935)	Huxley
E. Huxley and M. Perham, *Race and Politics in Kenya* (London, 1944)	Huxley & Perham
Ed. V. Harlow & E. M. Chilver, *History of East Africa* (Oxford, 1965)	History of East Africa
G. Archer, *Personal and Historical Memoirs* (Edinburgh, 1963)	Archer
F. J. Jackson, *Early Days in East Africa* (London, 1930)	Jackson
N. Leys, *Kenya* (London, 1924)	Leys
*H. Seaton, *Lion in the Morning* (London, 1963)	Seaton
C. W. L. Bulpett, *John Boyes, King of the Wakikuyu* (London, 1911)	
A. C. Hollis, *The Masai* (Oxford, 1905)	
A. C. Hollis, *The Nandi* (Oxford, 1909)	

*The author's real name was J. Gegg, which he changed by deed-poll to Wightman

Jubaland and the Northern Frontier District
(East Africa Govt Publications, 1916) — *Jubaland & NFD*
R. O. Hennings, *African Morning* (London, 1951) — *Hennings*
J. B. Carson, *Sun, Sand and Safari* (London, n.d.) — *Carson*
W. MacGregor Ross, *Kenya from within* (London, 1927) — *Ross*
Harry Thuku — *Thuku*
African Land Development in Kenya 1946–1962 (Ministry of Agriculture, Kenya) — *ALDEV*
Alys Reece, *To my wife, 50 Camels* — *Reece*
E. A. T. Dutton, *Lilliburlero or the Golden Road* (Zanzibar, 1944) — *Dutton*
Sir Michael Blundell, *So Rough a Wind* (London, 1964) — *Blundell*
D. W. Throup, *Economic and Social Origins of Mau Mau* (East African Studies, 1987) — *Throup*
L. S. B. Leakey, *Mau Mau and the Kikuyu* (London, 1955) — *Leakey*

Unpublished

Most of these are in Rhodes House. References are to Rhodes House Library. Unless otherwise specified, cited simply by writers' or interviewees' names.

S 1034 — T. H. R. Cashmore, *Your Obedient Servants 1894–1918*, PhD Thesis (Typescript, 1964)
S 509 — Sir P. Girouard, *Memorandum for the Guidance of PCs and DCs*   Cited as *Girouard Memo*
G. 131 — *The Masai Move, 1911–1913*
S 678 — J. H. Clive, *A Cure for Insomnia* (autobiography)
S 1675 — F. D. Corfield, *A Busy Man's Guide to the Historical Survey of the Origin and Growth of Mau Mau*
J. Pinney, *A History of the Kikuyu Guard in Fort Hall*
Oxford Development Records Project, Report 6
  Anne Thurston, *The Intensification of Smallholder Agriculture in Kenya, Swynnerton Plan*
Private Possession
  Sir Evelyn Baring, unpublished memorandum on Mau Mau and agricultural development   Cited as *Baring Memo*
  Interviews: Anthony Kirk-Greene with R. G. Turnbull, A. D. Swann, R. E. Wainwright, F. A. Loyd, F. R. Wilson

Principal Sources

Letters, diaries, miscellaneous papers etc

S 56–62	F. G. Hall
S 567	J. L. G. Llewellin
S r/147	C. W. Hobley
S 665, 504	C. M. and Mrs Dobbs
S 583	Copies of official papers relating to the NFD made by the author in Nairobi Records in 1963 and lent to Rhodes House Cited as *NFD Misc.*
S 1579	Loyalist versus Mau Mau
S 1397, 1388	R. H. Lambert and Mrs Lambert
S 1153	S. H. Fazan
S 742	T. C. Colchester
S 1676	D. G. Christie-Miller
S 1750	K. M. Cowley
S 1580	W. R. Hinde
S 1717	J. M. Golds
S 1792/5/10	K. L. Hunter
S 760	A. C. M. Mullins
S 377, 378	J. Ainsworth
S 1624	F. R. Jackson
S 390	C. E. V. Buxton
S 742	T. G. Askwith
S 1469	J. W. Balfour
S 1248	A. D. Galton-Fenzi
S 787	J. W. Howard
S 1630	O. E. B. Hughes
S 998	E. B. Hosking
Restricted	Ian Henderson R. G. Turnbull
	P. M. Demster R. E. Wainwright
	R. Armitage

Letters, diaries, memoirs etc in private possession

H. H. Horne
H. G. Grant
G. B. Rimington
R. A. Wilkinson
H. E. Lambert
D. G. Penwill

R. Tatton-Brown
D. Storrs-Fox
G. Reece
Mrs P. Schofield (stepdaughter of
H. G. Gregory-Smith)
J. M. Silvester

Personal correspondence

G. Hampson
W. H. Hale
J. Cumber
J. D. Lambert
G. J. Ellerton
G. P. Lloyd
A. D. Shirreff
F. A. Peet
W. F. Coutts
P. M. Gordon

C. F. Atkins
G. C. M. Dowson
A. F. Holford-Walker
T. J. F. Gavaghan
J. M. E. Wainwright
C. Campbell
P. M. Brothers
W. P. F. Kelly
W. N. B. Loudon
J. M. Golds

Chapter Sources

1 The Conquistadors
Published   Mungeam   Goldsmith   Huxley   *History of East Africa*
Unpublished   F. G. Hall   Ainsworth   Cashmore

2 Which Man's Country?
Published   Mungeam   Goldsmith   Huxley   *History of East Africa*   Meinertzhagen   Hobley   Jackson   Dundas   Archer
Unpublished   Cashmore   Dobbs   Horne

3 The Smack of Firm Government
Published   Mungeam   Goldsmith   Huxley   *History of East Africa*   Ross   Dundas
Unpublished   Cashmore   Girouard Memo   The Masai Move 1911–1913

4 The North
Published   Jubaland and NFD   Mungeam   Seaton
Unpublished   NFD Misc.   Llewellin

5 Kenya Colony
Published   Huxley   *History of East Africa*   Ross

6 The Sophisticates
Published   Huxley and Perham   *History of East Africa*
Unpublished   Buxton   Clive   H. E. Lambert   Colchester   Nyeri, Fort Hall, Kiambu, Embu, Meru District Annual Reports

Men Who Ruled Kenya

7 *The Unsophisticates*
Published   Seaton   Hennings   Carson
Unpublished Hosking   R. H. Lambert   Silvester   Hunter   Hale
Reece   Buxton   Mullins   Rimington   Atkins
Cowley   H. E. Lambert   Sundry papers on the Powys murder assembled by the author in 1963

8 *Gold-diggers, Rustlers and Wizards*
Unpublished Atkins   Cowley   Hosking   Hunter   Buxton   Fazan
Clive   Armitage   Kelly   Colchester

9 *Sloth-belt*
Unpublished Atkins   Mrs Schofield   Clive   Swann
R. E. Wainwright

10 *Half-term*
Unpublished R. E. Wainwright   Coutts   R. A. Wilkinson

11 *The Silent North*
Published   Dutton   Thuku
Unpublished Storrs Fox   Reece   Grant   Clive   Armitage
R. H. Lambert   Hale   Turnbull   Wajir, Mandera, Moyale, District Annual and Handing-over Reports

12 *Ities, Bandas and Shiftas*
Published   Reece
Unpublished Grant   Armitage   Turnbull   Swann
R. A. Wilkinson   Hunter   Dowson   Kelly   Moyale, Mandera and Turkana District Annual Reports

13 *Breakthrough*
Published   ALDEV
Unpublished Swann   Howes   Howard   Askwith   Christie-Miller
Balfour   D. N. Hall   Kelly   Penwill   Kericho, Machakos, Kitui District and Handing-over Reports

14 *No Breakthrough*
Unpublished R. E. Wainwright   R. A. Wilkinson   Atkins   Gordon
Official Report on the incident at Koloa

308

Chapter Sources

15 Northern Province
Published   ALDEV
Unpublished Reece   Gavaghan   Turnbull   Gordon   Peet

16 Nairobi's Fair City
Unpublished Ellerton   Askwith   Atkins

17 The Heart of the Matter
Published   Throup   Leakey
Unpublished Corfield   Thurston   Hughes   Hennings   Swann   Loyd   Coutts   Cumber   Wilson   Central and Rift Valley Provinces; Nyeri, Fort Hall, Kiambu, Embu, Meru District Annual and Handing-over Reports

18 Mau Mau
Published   Throup   Leakey   Blundell   Thuku
Unpublished Corfield   Thurston   Hughes   Swann   Loyd   Coutts   Wilson   Hampson   Pinney   Napier-Bax   Wilson   Baring Memorandum

19 State of Emergency, I
Published   Blundell
Unpublished Corfield   Thurston   Hughes   Swann   Loyd   Wilson   Hampson   Pinney   Hinde   R. E. Wainwright   J. M. E. Wainwright   Loyalist versus Mau Mau   Pinney, *History of the Kikuyu Guard*   Baring Memorandum

20 State of Emergency II
Published   Blundell
Unpublished Thurston   Hughes   Swann   Loyd   Wilson   Hampson   Pinney   R. E. Wainwright   J. M. E. Wainwright   Christie-Miller   Loudon   D. J. Lambert   Holford-Walker   Penwill   Loyalist versus Mau Mau   Pinney, *History of the Kikuyu Guard*

21 Agrarian Revolution
Published   ALDEV
Unpublished Baring Memorandum   Thurston   Hennings   Golds   Kelly   Askwith   Gavaghan

22 *The Pastoral Revolution*
Published   ALDEV
Unpublished Carson   Gavaghan   Shirreff   Lloyd   D. N. Hall

23 *Wind of Change*
Published   Blundell
Unpublished Information on White House and Jomo Kenyatta
               from Mrs June Knowles   Golds   Gavaghan
               R. E. Wainwright

Index

Abdurrahman Mursaal, 63–5
Administration, general, 15, 33–7, 42, 58–9, 68–72, 73–6, 204–5, 226, 294–5
Abyssinia, 49–52
Abyssinian boundary, 52, 53, 55, 134, 159–60
Abyssinians, 53, 125–6, 134–5, 137–8, 142, 145–6
African District Councils (ADC), 166, 168, 195, 286, 292–3; *see also* Local Native Councils
African Land Development Board (ALDEV), 165, 168, 173, 178, 215, 265, 268, 284–6
Agricultural development, 165–79, 206–8, 215–6, 268–75
Ainsworth, J. B. (James), 13, 14, 37, 46
Ainsworth, J. (John), 2–4, 6, 9, 12, 14–7, 20–1, 31–3, 38–9
Ajuran tribe, 56, 196
Amhara tribe *see* Abyssinians
Anderson, E. L. B., 99–100, 165
ANVIL, operation, 265, 276
Archer, G. F., 55–6
Armitage, R., 105, 143–6
Askwith, T. G., 169–70, 275–6, 278
Atkins, C. F., 96–7, 99, 109–10, 183–4, 200
Aulihan tribe, 57, 63–5, 139

Bagge, S. S., 22–3, 33–4, 43
Bailward, A. N., 117–8, 126, 181
Baluhya tribe, 23, 99–100
Baring, Sir Evelyn, 226, 227, 231–2, 236, 262, 268
Barrett, W. E. H., 56
Beech, M. W. H., 38, 45
Bevan, A. D., Lieutenant-Colonel, 239–40
Blundell, M., 225–6, 228, 230, 241–2, 254, 262, 264, 274–5
Bond, B. W., 119–20
Boran tribe, 49, 53–7, 283–4
Boyes, J., 14, 55
British Army
    39th Infantry Brigade, 243
    Lancashire Fusiliers, 243
    Black Watch, 261
Brothers, P. M., 215
Brown, G. R. B., 95–6
Brumage, D. O., 105–6
Butler, J. M. B., 251
Butter, J. H., 108
Buxton, C. E. V., 87–9, 102–4

Campbell, C., 131
Campbell, W. F. G., 87
Candler, J. H., 189, 247, 262–3
Carson, J. B., 118, 279, 286–7
Catling, R., 246, 293
Central Province, 204–16, 218–23
Chambers, R. J. H., 284–6

311

Cheese, J. A., 112, 149–50
Chenevix Trench, C. P., 192–7, 225, 228, 233, 239, 257–60, 282–6
Churchill, Winston, 28–9, 32, 37
Clive, J. H., 74, 79, 106–7, 111–4, 137–9
Coast Province, 109–16, 287–9
Coffee cultivation, 40, 215–6, 272–4
Colchester, T. C., 82–4, 107, 201, 262
Colville, G., 94–5, 259
Cooke, S. V., 111
Corfield, F. D., 219, 221, 223, 225
Cornell, C. H., 94, 95, 110
Cowley, K. M., 97–8, 100
Coutts, W. F., 118–9, 209, 211–3, 225, 275
Crawford, Sir Frederick, 262, 268
Cumber, J. A., 211–2
Cusack, J. W., 153, 155–6, 198–9, 219, 223, 225, 227–8, 233

Davies, E. R. St A., 184, 216, 224–5, 228
Deck, S. F., 57, 59, 65
Degodia tribe, 56, 61, 66, 133, 138–9, 196–7
Delamere, Lord, 11–12, 20, 33–4, 38–9
Derrick, F. P. B., 176, 272
De-stocking *see* Stock limitation
Devonshire Declaration, 72
Dini ya Msambwa (DYM), 185–7
Dobbs, C. M., 31, 102
Dowson, G. C. M., 157–9
Dubas *see* Police, Tribal, Frontier
Dundas, C. C. F., 37–8, 44

Eliot, Sir Charles, 19, 21–3, 51
Ellerton, G. J., 198–9, 221, 241
Elliott, F., 62–5

Emergency Committee, Colony, 228, 232
Emergency Committees, District and Provincial, 239–40, 244, 254, 255, 267
Embu, 28, 213–5, 273–4
Erskine, Lieutenant-General Sir George, 244–5, 262

Famine, 16–7, 288–9
Fazan, S. H., 86, 102–3
Female circumcision, 80–2
Fort Hall, 18–19, 77–9, 209, 228, 238, 246
Fort Smith, 2–3, 10
Furse, R., 68

Gabbra tribe, 125, 159–60
Galton-Fenzi, A. D., 190
Garissa, 139–40, 193–5
Gavaghan, T. J. F., 190–1, 276, 277, 279–80, 294
Gelubba tribe, 125–6, 140–1
Gilkison, T. G., 10, 27–8
Girouard, Sir Percy, 33–7, 38, 43–4
Githu, Sam, 248, 249, 277–8
Glenday, V., 62, 66, 90, 122, 125–8, 136, 140
Goat Bag, 74–5, 107, 116, 143, 181, 191
Gold rush, 99–101
Golds, J., 269–72, 292–4
Gordon, Mrs Marianne, 184–5, 192–3
Gordon, P. M., 184–5, 192–3, 275
Grant, H. M., 130–4, 142–3, 154–5, 181–2
Grazing control, 190–1, 280, 281–6
Gregory-Smith, H. G., 110–12, 157–8, 160–2
Greyburn, J. R., 267
Gurreh tribe, 58, 61, 62, 133

Index

Habash *see* Abyssinians
Hale, W. H., 92, 140–1
Hall, Mrs 'Bee', 13–14, 18
Hall, D. W., 175, 287–9
Hall, F. G., 2–10
Hampson, G. N., 219–20, 249–50, 264
Havelock, W., 225, 228
Hemsted, R. W., 19, 44, 125, 129
Henderson, I., 221–2, 263, 267
Hennings, R. O., 215–6, 250, 268, 274–5
Hinde, S. L., 21, 28
Hinde, Major-General Sir Robert, 238, 239, 240, 243–5, 247, 254, 257, 259–60
Hobley, C. W., 22–4, 33, 41–2
Hola, 276–7, 287
Holford-Walker, A. F., 261
Home Guard, 229, 238, 243; *see also* Kikuyu Guard
Hopkins, J. G., 83–4
Horne, E. B., 28–9
Horne, H. H., 26–8, 29–30
Hosking, E. B., 101, 146, 163–4
Howard, J. W., 169, 171
Howes, R. J. C., 168–9
Hughes, O. E. B., 204–5, 219, 229, 250, 264
Hunter, K. L., 87–9, 101–2, 150–1
Huxley, Elspeth, 96–7, 170, 274

Imperial East Africa Company, 2, 9
Intelligence and Security, Director of, 218–24, 227; *see also* Police, Kenya, Special Branch
Irrigation, 176, 191–2, 274, 275–6
Italians, 134, 142–3, 150–1, 153–5, 157–8, 192–3

Jackson, F. J., 22–3, 43
Jenkins, T., 227
Jenner, A. C. W., 49–50
Jennings, F. G., 120, 121, 137, 138
Jock Scott, operation, 232
Jubaland, 48–9, 58–9, 123
Judge, H. N. A., 293
Judiciary, Judicial Department, 15, 36, 42, 95, 138, 221, 235–6, 246

Kabarnet, 209
Kajiado, 104, 180–1
Kakamega, 99–101
Kamba tribe, 2, 3, 12–13, 37, 86–7, 117–9, 168–79, 261
Kavirondo tribe *see* Luo
Kelly, W. P. F., 153–5, 160–3, 263
Keir, W., 159–60
Kennaway, N. F., 100, 215
Kenya African Union (KAU), 202, 210–11, 217–8, 222–3
Kenya Regiment, 231
Kenyatta, Jomo, 80, 173–4, 202–3, 209, 211–2, 217, 229, 230, 234–7, 253, 277, 290–2
Kiambu, 210, 242, 272, 263, 269–71, 272
Kihori, J., 238, 249
Kikuyu Central Association (KCA), 80–2, 202
Kikuyu Guard, 243, 244, 247–51, 262–4, 266, 267; *see also* Home Guard
Kikuyu Independent Schools Association (KISA), 82, 217, 222, 228
Kikuyu tribe, 4–8, 45, 47, 76, 77–82, 207–11, 217–8, 219–20, 228–30, 242–3, 247–50, 253–4, 262–7, 269–73, 277
King's African Rifles (KAR), 24, 45, 150, 154–8, 165

7th Infantry Brigade (KAR), 243
Kipini, 109–10, 113–4
Kipsigis tribe, 101, 105–7, 165–8
Kisii, 32, 45
Kisumu, 19, 23–4, 31–2, 183–4
Kitui, 12–13, 37, 117–9, 177–9

La Fontaine, S. H., 79
Laibons, 5, 8, 24–5, 93–4, 101
Laikipia, 27–8, 43–4, 92–5
Lambert, H. E., 81–3, 97, 114, 207
Lambert, J. D., 256–7
Lambert, R. T., 86, 90, 139–40
Lamu, 29, 110–14, 286–7
Land consolidation, 269–72
Lane, C. R. W., 33, 41, 43
Lari, 242–3
Lekopen, 93–5, 97
Leroghi, 92, 95, 98, 280
Legislative Council (LegCo), 39, 72, 199
Lenana, 5, 8–9, 43
Llewellin, J. L. B., 59–62, 122
Lloyd, G. P., 287
Local Native Councils (LNCs), 69, 73; see also African District Councils
Locust Officers, 196
Lodwar, 90, 92, 158–9, 160–1, 192
Loudon, W. N. B., 160, 253–4, 257
Loyd, F. A., 205, 207–8, 220, 269, 272
Luo tribe (Jaluo), 23–4, 31–2, 183–4

McClennan, J. W., 33
Macdonald, M., 236
McDougall, K., 29–30, 51
Macharia, Rawson, 234–6
Mandera, 128, 130–4, 144, 153–4, 189, 190, 191, 192–3

Maralal, 96
Marehan tribe, 51, 54, 57, 62–4, 66, 133
Marsabit, 55–6, 125–6, 140–1
Martin, J. (alias Antonio Martini), 2, 9–11, 13
Masai tribe, 3–9, 22–3, 25, 27, 42–4, 102–4, 180–3, 260–1
Mau Mau, 176, 217–267, 275–6
Maxwell, G. V., 77–9
Mayes, W., 16, 25
Meiklejohn, Commander and Mrs, 254–5
Meinertzhagen, R., 1, 21-2, 23–5, 101
Merille tribe, 91, 150–1, 161
Meru, 29, 63, 81–4, 124, 215, 274
Miles, A. T., 134–6, 138
Mitchell, Sir Philip, 106, 171, 179, 206, 211, 223, 225, 227, 231
Mohamad Zubair tribe, 60–2, 122–4
Mombasa, 2, 3, 114, 287–8
Montgomery, H. R., 111
Moyale, 53–5, 134–6, 142–3, 152–3, 155–6, 196–7
Mullins, A. C., 91, 211
Mure, G. A. S., 57, 59
Mwichuki Land Case, 77–9

Nairobi, 14–15, 17, 20–1, 198–203, 264–5
Naivasha, 2, 13, 255
Naivasha raid, 243
Nakuru, 254
Nandi tribe, 24–6, 101–2
Napier-Bax S. E., 221, 246
Narok, 102–4, 181–3
North, M., 148–9, 171–2
Northcote, G. A. S., 32, 78
Northern Frontier District (NFD), Northern Province, 48–67, 97, 122–41, 188–97

Index

Nubian tribe, 13, 27, 58
Nyeri, 120–1, 204–5, 219–20, 238, 250

Ogaden tribe, 49–51, 56–7
O'Rorke, M. S., 224–5, 228, 245
Outlying Districts Ordinance, 14, 124

Partington, H. B., 26
Pastoral development, 279–86
Pedraza, J. G. W., 267, 271–2
Pedraza, R., 91, 118–9
Peet, F. A., 193
Peet, Mrs June, 193
Pinney, J., 228, 246, 250, 263
Police, Kenya, 37, 69–70, 90, 92, 130, 131–2, 163, 186–7, 189, 243, 245–6
 Special Branch, 218; see also Intelligence and Security, Director of
 Reserve (KPR) 255, 259, 261
Police, Tribal, 69–70, 151, 246–7, 248–9, 262–4
Police, Tribal, Frontier (Dubas), 129, 132, 190, 196–7, 293
Potter, H. S., 224, 227, 228, 230–31
Powis, T., 93–7
Pritt, D. N., 235
Protectorate, East African, 9, 22, 68

Railway, Kenya and Uganda, 9, 13–14, 19, 24
Reece, G., 89, 90, 128–30, 134–6, 147–9, 159–60, 188–90
Reece, Mrs Alys, 195–6
Rimmington, G. B., 91–2, 145
Ruck, R. and Mrs, 254, 255
Rudd, B., 236
Rumuruti, 27, 93, 95, 96

Samburu tribe, 92–8, 279–80, 283–6
Screeing, 238, 258–60
Secretariat, 22, 158, 198–9, 204, 224
Serenli, 62–5
Settlers, settlement, European, 19–21, 30–1, 37–42, 71–3, 225, 237, 255–9, 292
Shackleton, E. R., 70, 91
Sharpe, H. B., 71, 96–7, 113, 122–4, 126, 127, 140
Shirreff, A. D., 281–3
Silvester, J. M., 86–7
Simpson, A. B., 185–7
Slade, H., 225, 228
Soil conservation, 169–71, 206, 208–9
Somali tribe, 48–52, 58, 292–4
 Somalis, 'alien', 124, 135
Special Districts Ordinance, 124
Stevens, A. J., 185–7
Stewart, Sir Donald, 23, 27, 30
Stock limitation, 97–8, 181–2, 280–1, 282–3, 284–6
Stock theft, 40–1, 92–3, 180, 182, 283–4
Stone, R. G., 77–9, 129, 137–9
Storrs-Fox, D., 124–5
Suk tribe (Pokot), 92, 185–7, 281–4
Suk, West, 88, 89, 91, 92, 281–4
Swahili language, 3, 70–1
Swahili tribe, 3, 5
Swann, A. D., 114–5, 150, 165–8, 207, 208, 221, 222, 226, 227, 231, 242–3, 263, 277
Swynnerton Plan, 268, 269, 274

Taxation, 19–20, 58, 69, 74–6, 136, 151–2, 286
Tea cultivation, 216, 273
Thacker, R. S., 236–7
Thomson's Falls, 253–4, 257

Thuku, Harry, 76, 126–7, 207, 230
Trafford, H. H., 94
Tugen tribe, 85
Turkana tribe, 89–91, 92, 139–52, 157–8, 161–4
Turnbull, R. G., 108, 124, 130, 144, 146–50, 152–3, 190, 193–6, 229, 265, 275

Villagization, 263–4, 265–6

Wainwright, J. M. E., 240–1, 266–7, 272
Wainwright, R. E., 71, 115–6, 117, 121–2, 180–1, 213–4, 244, 282
Wajir, 56–7, 59–62, 65–7, 122–5, 137, 143–4, 292–3

Water supplies, 166, 171, 176, 177–8, 191–2, 274, 284–5
Waweru, David Dumbasso, 293
Whitehouse, L. E., 192, 291–2
Whyatt, J., 224, 228, 230, 234, 237
Wilkinson, R. A., 120–1, 146–7, 156–8, 160, 181–3, 200, 208, 265
Wilks, H. C. F., 281
Wilson, F. R., 210, 235–6, 237, 240, 263, 265
Windley, E. H., 104, 210, 220, 222, 223, 267, 283
Wynn-Harris, P., 120–1, 207, 216
Wright, H. C., 293

Zaphiro, P., 52–5